Rethinking appraisal and assessment

EDITED BY
Helen Simons and
John Elliott

OPEN UNIVERSITY PRESS
Milton Keynes • Philadelphia

Open University Press
Celtic Court
22 Ballmoor
Buckingham MK18 1XW

and
1900 Frost Road, Suite 101
Bristol, PA 19007, USA

First Published 1989
Reprinted 1990
Copyright © The Editors and Contributors 1989

British Library Cataloguing in Publication Data

Rethinking appraisal and assessment.
  1. Great Britain. Teachers. Performance.
  Assessment.
  I. Simons, Helen II. Elliot, John, *1938 June 20 –*
371.1'44' 0941

ISBN 0–335–09518–6
ISBN 0–335–09517–8 (paper)

Library of Congress Catalog number available

Typeset by Inforum Typesetting, Portsmouth
Printed in Great Britain by St Edmundsbury Press,
Bury St Edmunds, Suffolk

Contents

Notes on contributors   v
Acknowledgements   ix
Abbreviations   x

Introduction   The volume: its contents and contexts   1
               Helen Simons

1   The evaluation of teaching   13
               Robert E. Stake

2   Teacher appraisal and/or teacher development: friends
               or foes?   20
               Michael Eraut

3   A problem in search of a method or a method in search
               of a problem? A critique of teacher appraisal   24
               Robert G. Burgess

4   Teacher appraisal, collaborative research and teacher
               consortia   36
               Clem Adelman

5   Problems in teacher appraisal: an action-research
               solution   44
               Richard Winter

6   Teacher appraisal   55
               Ernest R. House and Stephen D. Lapan

7   Criterion-referenced assessment of teaching   64
        Donald McIntyre

8   Evaluation of competences of teaching practice
        supervisors within the naturalistic paradigm   72
        Franz Kroath

9   Appraisal of performance or appraisal of persons   80
        John Elliott

10   Perspectives on teacher appraisal and professional
        development   100
        Mary Louise Holly

11   Pupil assessment from the perspective of naturalistic
        research   119
        David Bridges

12   Assessing the whole child   131
        Louis M. Smith and Carol S. Klass

13   Psychometric test theory and educational assessment   140
        Harvey Goldstein

14   Negotiation and dialogue in student assessment and
        teacher appraisal   149
        Mary James

15   A critique of the 'new assessment': from currency to
        carnival?   161
        Ian Stronach

16   Conclusion: rethinking appraisal   180
        John Elliott

Name index   194

Subject index   197

Notes on contributors

Clem Adelman is Reader in Educational Research at Bulmershe College of Higher Education, Reading, England. Among his current funded research are studies of accreditation in the USA and UK, assessment in the creative arts and in oral English. He has conducted numerous evaluation studies including an evaluation of new agreements on CNNA validation completed in 1986, and written widely in the fields of evaluation, qualitative research and curriculum change. His publications include *The Self-Evaluating Institution* (Methuen, 1982), with R.J. Alexander.

David Bridges is Professor of Education, School of Education, University of East Anglia, Norwich, England. He has recently completed the local evaluation of the Suffolk Records of Pupil Achievement Scheme and is extensively involved in evaluation work including In-Service Education in several local education authorities and the Sainsbury/Suffolk Schools and Industry Project. His publications include *Education Democracy and Discussion* (originally published by NFER/ Nelson, shortly to be re-issued by University Press of America), *School Accountability* with J. Elliott *et al.* (Grant MacIntyre, 1981) and *Mixed Ability Grouping* with C.H. Bailey (Allen and Unwin, 1983).

Robert G.Burgess is Director of CEDAR (Centre for Educational Development, Appraisal and Research) and Professor of Sociology at the University of Warwick. His main teaching and research interests are in social research methodology, especially qualitative methods and the sociology of education – in particular, the study of schools, classrooms and curricula. He is currently writing an ethnographic restudy of a comprehensive school on which he has already published several papers. His main publications include *Experiencing Comprehensive Education* (Methuen 1983), *In the Field: An Introduction to Field*

Research (Allen and Unwin 1984), *Education, Schools and Schooling* (Macmillan, 1985) and *Sociology, Education and Schools* (Batsford, 1986), together with 11 edited volumes on qualitative methods and education.

John Elliott is Professor of Education and a founder member of the Centre for Applied Research in Education, University of East Anglia. He has directed numerous research projects in curriculum and teacher development including the Ford Teaching Project, the Cambridge Accountability Project (Elliott, J. *et al.*, Grant MacIntyre, 1981), and a project sponsored by the Schools Council on Teacher–Pupil Interaction and the Quality of Learning (1981–3). Currently, he is directing the curriculum development phase of the Home Office Review of Police Probationer Training and the ESRC project Teachers' Jobs and Lives. Over the past 14 years he has conducted numerous action-research workshops both in the UK and overseas, and published extensively on such topics as educational action research, teacher and curriculum development and accountability.

Michael Eraut is Professor of Education and Chairman of the Continuing and Professional Education Area at the University of Sussex. His main research interests are in mid-career professional education, evaluation, curriculum development and educational technology. His recent publications include *Policies for Educational Accountability* (with T. Becher and J. Knight, Heinemann Educational, 1981), *Local Evaluation of INSET: A Metaevaluation of TRIST* (with D. Pennycuick and H. Radnor, University of Sussex), contributions to the *International Encyclopedia of Education* (Pergamon, 1985) for which he edited two sections, and several articles on teacher learning and management learning.

Harvey Goldstein, an educational statistician with an interest in quantitative methods, is Professor of Education at the Institute of Education, University of London. His interest in educational assessment centres on problems of statistical modelling and its relation to substantive concerns. Most recently, he has been developing 'multilevel' models for analysing data, especially on educational attainment, and relating these to studies of school effectiveness.

Mary Louise Holly is Associate Professor in the College of Education at Kent State University. Her graduate work was in Curriculum Development and Teaching at Michigan State University where she received her doctorate in 1977. First as a 'travelling' art consultant and then as a classroom teacher she became curious about teacher professional development. Her research focusses on teacher life histories and the social and cultural contexts of teaching and schooling. Her recent publications include *Reflective Writing and Teacher Inquiry: Keeping a Personal-Professional Journal* (Heinemann Educational, 1989), and *Perspectives on Teacher Professional Development* (with C. McLoughlin (eds), Falmer Press, 1989).

Ernest R. House is Professor and Director of the Lab for Policy Studies in the School of Education at the University of Colorado at Boulder. He has published numerous articles and books on the topics of educational evaluation, change and policy. His latest book is *Jesse Jackson and the Politics of Charisma* (Boulder, Colorado, Westview Press, 1988).

Mary James is Senior Research Fellow in the School of Education at the Open University, Milton Keynes, England. She is also Deputy Director of the DES-funded national evaluation of Pilot Records of Achievement Schemes (PRAISE). Her research interests include student–centred approaches to assessment and profiling, school self-evaluation and case-study methodology. Recent publications include PRAISE reports and the second edition of *Curriculum Evaluation in Schools* (Croom Helm, 1983), which she co-authored with Robert McCormick.

Carol S. Klass is Coordinator of Research and Evaluation for the Parents as Teachers National Center at the University of Missouri–St. Louis. Parents as Teachers, sponsored by the Missouri Department of Education, is an early prevention family support programme for families with children, from birth to 3 years of age. Previously, Klass was Director of the Therapeutic Family Day Care Project, an early intervention programme for abused and neglected infants, toddlers and preschoolers, sponsored by the Illinois Department of Children and Family Services. Klass is author of *The Autonomous Child: Day Care and the Transmission of Values* (Falmer Press, 1986).

Franz Kroath is Senior Lecturer at the Department of Education, University of Innsbruck and Director of the teaching practice centre within the initial teacher training programme of the University. He has also had several years of teaching practice in secondary schools. His research studies include evaluation of initial in-service teacher training courses based on action-research, development and evaluation of a training model for teaching practice supervisors, and case studies on the reconstruction and modification of teachers' practical theories.

Stephen D. Lapan is Associate Professor of Gifted Education, Center for Excellence in Education, Northern Arizona University, USA, and editor of the journal *Excellence in Teaching*. His research interests include career education for minority gifted youth, teacher thinking and evaluation and improvement of college instruction. His recent publications include 'The driver of the classroom: the teacher and school improvement' in *Policies for America's Schools: Teachers, Equity and Indicators* (R. Haskins and D. Macrae, eds, Abplex Publishing, 1988), with E.R. House.

Donald McIntyre is Reader in Educational Studies at Oxford University. His main research interests are in teaching and teacher education. He has published books and papers on a wide range of educational topics including the development of teachers' attitudes, teachers' perceptions of differences among their pupils, the use of microteaching in teacher education, criterion-referenced assessment, bilingual teaching, teacher accountability and, most recently, the nature and accessibility of teachers' professional craft knowledge. Most of his research has been conducted in the context of Scottish education.

Helen Simons is Reader in Education and Head of the Centre for Educational Evaluation in the Department of Curriculum Studies at the Institute of Education, University of London. For the past 20 years she has specialized in curriculum and educational evaluation, and has published widely in the fields of school, policy and programme evaluation and the politics of curriculum change. Her current research interests include the impact of government policies on the curriculum and the professionalism of teachers, and local education authorities' response to the management of evaluation and change. Her latest book, *Getting to Know Schools in a Democracy*, was published in 1987 by Falmer Press.

Louis M. Smith has been Professor of Education in the Department of Education, Washington University in St Louis, since 1955. He also spent 2 years (1953–5) as a school psychologist for the St Paul, Minnesota Public Schools, and 10 years part-time (1966–76) at Cemrel Inc., one of the Regional Laboratories carrying out curriculum evaluation and research. He has published numerous articles and books on educational innovation and change and qualitative research. Most recently, he has completed a trilogy of books with colleagues David Dwyer, Paul Kleine and John Prunty published by Falmer Press: *Educational Innovators: Then and Now* (1986), *The Fate of an Innovative School* (1987) and *Innovation and Change in Schooling: History, Politics and Agency* (1988).

Robert E. Stake is Professor of Education and Director of the Center for Instructional Research and Curriculum Evaluation (CIRCE) at the University of Illinois at Urbana-Champaign. He is a leading authority on the evaluation of educational programmes, an author and researcher. His students have become prominent in assessment and curriculum analysis specializations on campuses, in government agencies, and in schools around the world. Stake is the author of *Quieting Reform* (University of Illinois Press, 1985), a metaevaluation study of an urban youth programme called Cities-in-Schools and *Evaluating the Arts in Education* (Charles E. Merrill Publishing Company, 1975). With Jack Easley he co-authored *Case Studies in Science Education* (University of Illinois, 1978), sponsored by the National Science Foundation.

Ian Stronach is a Lecturer at the Centre for Applied Research in Education, School of Education, University of East Anglia. His research interests centre on pre-vocational education, Technical and Vocational Education Initiatives (TVEI), assessment, and the general field of programme evaluation. He is involved in a number of research and evaluation projects including the ERSC-sponsored project Teachers' Jobs and Lives, TVEI evaluation and evaluation of teacher development.

Richard Winter is Senior Lecturer in Education at the Essex Institute of Higher Education, and Course Tutor for the M.Ed. in Educational Research and Evaluation. He has published numerous articles on the methodology of action-research, arising out of a research project on teaching practice. In 1987, a longer theoretical study – *Action-Research and the Nature of Social Enquiry* – was published by Gower Press. His current concerns are accreditation of work-based learning, and the use of fictional writing in courses of professional development.

Acknowledgements

The editors wish to thank all contributors for helping to further the debate on the contentious issues of appraisal and assessment, and The Nuffield Foundation for sponsoring the conference which provided the springboard for this book.

Abbreviations

ACAS	Advisory Conciliation and Arbitration Service
CGLI	City and Guilds of London Institute
CNAA	Council for the Accreditation of National Academic Awards
CPVE	Certificate of Pre-Vocational Education
CSE	Certificate of Secondary Education
DES	Department of Education and Science
GCSE	General Certificate of Secondary Education
HMI	Her Majesty's Inspectorate
INSET	In-Service Education and Training
LEA	Local Education Authority
NUT	National Union of Teachers
OED	*Oxford English Dictionary*
RSA	Royal Society of Arts
SOED	*Scottish Oxford Education Dictionary*
MSC	Manpower Services Commission
TRIST	TVEI Related In-Service Training
TVEI	Technical and Vocational Education Initiative

INTRODUCTION

The volume: its contents and contexts

Helen Simons

A knowledge of history does not enable us to predict with any confidence what will happen next, but it can help to make sense of current events. This collection of papers, written mainly by academics with a predominant interest in the evaluation of schooling, has one history, and the focus of their attention, the concepts and practices associated with teacher appraisal and pupil assessment, has another. The purpose of this introductory chapter, in addition to that of providing the reader with a map of the contents of the book is to locate its appearance within an appropriate context and background. Most of the contributors are British, and the introduction will reflect this bias, but some are from the United States where, in particular, political and public concern to obtain evidence of teacher competence already offers a corpus of experience to reflect upon, and where the testing of pupil achievement is an established and, in principle, non-controversial element of educational assessment. We also have a contribution from the European continent, so that the collection as a whole has a strong international flavour. Since a great deal of academic comment in this country has of late been offered in the form of a reaction to specific government initiatives and proposals, and many of the domestic contributions in this book do not escape this characterization, the presence of contributors from other countries provides a useful check on the generalizability of our own preoccupations as well as being of value in their own right. It would be difficult, I believe, for anyone to read this book and not conclude that teacher appraisal and pupil assessment are valuable concepts in any plan for the professional development of schooling, but are problematic bulwarks of any plan for its public accountability.

The politics of school development

The improvement of what goes on in classrooms – in terms of input (content),

process (teaching) and outcomes (learning) – has been a political and professional objective of increasing importance in this country, as well as elsewhere,
during the past 25 years. Initially, with the setting up of the Schools Council for
Curriculum and Examinations, political anxiety was eased by investment in and
reliance upon an established tradition of power-sharing collaboration between
central government, local government and teacher associations. The Council,
based in London, but with teacher majorities on all its interlocking committees,
was the negotiated mechanism, and a better quality curriculum across the
board, particularly to meet the needs of expanded secondary school provision,
was the priority. It was to be met mainly by funding national curriculum
development projects that would offer teachers new, well conceived and well
produced materials for use in classrooms, and some guidance on appropriate
pedagogies. At this first stage in centre/periphery interventionism teacher
autonomy was not, at least publicly, questioned. The approach to the classroom
door was cast in terms of support for enhanced teacher choice and no more than
gentle, respectful persuasion.

Such an indulgent view did not survive the economic downturn that began to
loom in the early 1970s for long. With little evidence to show for the transforma-
tional potential of the Council's approach, and with evaluators particularly
drawing attention to the resilience of established practice, the stage was set for
new kinds of initiatives. Successive governments, increasingly convinced of the
need to harness schooling directly to economic regeneration and to limit its
social, political and financial costs, began to favour more targeted and selective
forms of intervention and more assertive modes of interaction with teachers to
bring the curriculum and its practitioners into line. As categorical funding
increased, and teacher autonomy gave way to the rhetoric of customer–contract
relationships, the Schools Council rapidly diminished in importance, its image
tarnished by open attacks from Whitehall, its funding reduced. It was mar-
ginalized, and eventually disbanded as schools and teachers began to reel from
the persistent blame ascribed to them for the economic and social ills of the
nation. The design and management of the curriculum moved inexorably out of
the control of the education professions and into the hands of government
agencies, as politicians, for the most part aided and abetted by their civil
servants, consolidated their public case for greater influence.

The advent of a radical right government in 1979 brought more bad news for
those, including most education professionals, who continued to favour a
supportive rather than a coercive framework for curriculum development. The
attack on school performance was intensified as an inflation-obsessed government sought to contain welfare spending by a combination of fiscal control,
deregulation and a populist appeal to consumer sovereignty. Legislation came
thick and fast in the 1980s in a bewildering mixture of free market and State
control metaphors. The central thrust, however, was clear enough. The 'providers' (central government) and the 'consumers' (parents) would join forces to
hold the 'producers' (teachers and their professional allies) to account.

That is where we are now. At the time of going to press, a complex set of proposals concerned with schooling – its governance, its content and its assessment – is in the process of legislative enactment in Parliament. Opposition may modify some proposals, and it is difficult to predict how some significant but discretionary powers may be exercised, but the broad shape of the future of schooling is readily discernible. The curriculum will be centrally specified and standardized to a much greater degree than hitherto. The specified content will be in terms of traditional subjects and skills, readily familiar to the parents of pupils now at school and even more so to their grandparents, especially if they attended grammar schools. The curriculum will be so specified as to enable national achievement tests to be applied to the performance of every child in school at the ages of 7, 11, 14 and 16. These measures are designed to facilitate comparative public judgement of how well or badly individual schools, teachers and pupils are doing in relation to each other and in relation to normative benchmarks of how well they should be doing.

It is these proposals, in the light of the government's power and determination to legislate and implement them, that constitute the immediate context in which the domestic contributors to this book consider teacher appraisal and pupil assessment. That similar political trends are taking place elsewhere will be evident from the contributions of commentators from overseas. In case there may be readers who think either that the proposals constitute a welcome injection of assessment where none existed, or that they simply extend and reinforce existing practice, I should draw attention to some key words in the foregoing description of government intentions. They are 'comparative', 'public' and 'individual'. I should also emphasize the direct links that are implied between pupil performance and judgements on teachers and schools.

Judgements on performance have always been part of the self-evaluative framework of the schools – judgements by Her Majesty's Inspectorate at the national level (involving both case studies and surveys), by advisers and inspectors employed by Local Education Authorities, by head teachers, school governors, heads of departments, classroom teachers, by teacher unions and subject associations, by teacher educators, by Local Education Committees and their officers, by Royal Commissions and other public enquiries, and so on. And there is, of course, a system of public examinations in the later years of schooling that plays a crucial role in the determination of pupil futures. Other than in public examinations, however, comparative judgements have been difficult to make because of both the known and unknown diversity of contexts and provision within which performance is embedded, and public judgements have been frustrated by the reluctance of professionals to share either their data or their judgements with those to whom they are democratically accountable. This has given rise to various suspicions on the part of those excluded from professional discourse and exchange – that too little is done to identify inadequate performance, that even less is done to remedy deficiency, or even to ensure that teachers, particularly, are not exploiting their insulation from scrutiny to subvert or assert majority values in the classroom. When we talk, therefore, of new measures being introduced, we are talking of measures specifically designed to penetrate the professional insulation of schooling, and to render teachers accountable for what children learn.

Teacher 'appraisal' is the in-vogue term for new ways of determining the quality of teaching in our schools. As we shall see, there are many ways in which the concept of appraisal can be construed and many paths that could, and have been, followed in prosecuting this goal, but we should not forget as we read about these that we shall soon be working in a situation where the performance of pupils on national tests of achievement related to a prescribed curriculum is intended to constitute evidence of teacher effectiveness. Thus teacher appraisal and pupil performance will be directly linked in a way that has not been contemplated since the 'payment by results' of the nineteenth century was abandoned. And that is why it was thought necessary in this book to review both ends of this proposed link.

The professional context of the book

I have already mentioned that this collection of papers represents mainly evaluative perspectives upon its topic. This requires explanation. The book is the product of a conference which all the contributors attended by personal invitation. The conference was the fourth in a series of international invitational conferences on educational evaluation held in Cambridge, England, over the past 16 years and sponsored by the Nuffield Foundation. Since 1972, when the first conference was convened in order to bring together a disparate group of project and programme evaluators on both sides of the Atlantic in order to share new ideas about how the task of evaluation should be conceived and practised, a professional network of like-minded evaluators has developed and kept in touch, reconvening formally every 3 or 4 years in Cambridge to review progress and ideas in the light of experience and changing circumstances. Individually and collectively these evaluators have made significant contributions to what has come to be known as the naturalistic school of evaluation, 'naturalistic' being a term which in its connotations suggests opposition to positivist traditions of social science and mechanistic models of evaluation.

The first conference explored shared reservations about the objectives model of curriculum development and the overwhelming emphasis in evaluation of testing for student learning gains. It yielded a well-known manifesto (MacDonald and Parlett, 1973) and a widely read book, appropriately titled *Beyond the Numbers Game* (Hamilton *et al.*, 1977). This helped to launch the 'new evaluation', a movement which exerted some general influence on both broadening the agenda of evaluators and changing their methodology to give more emphasis to the study of context and process in innovation as well as continuing attention to its outcomes. The second conference in 1975 reflected a growing consensus that the accommodation of an expanded agenda and more flexible methods called for a case-study approach, and 'case study' was its methodological focus. This led to the publication of *Towards a Science of the Singular* (Simons,

1980), concerned with the justification for, and explication of, a concept which offered greater potential both for integrating diverse kinds of data and communicating more effectively with lay audiences. At this point, in the mid-1970s, it was widely recognized that those who would intervene in schooling needed a better understanding of what they were intervening in if their interventions were to be successful and beneficial. But even then, as I indicated in the first part of this introduction, the political tide was turning unfavourably, so that when the conference reconvened for the third time in 1979, it was to critically review the implications for naturalistic inquiry of the changing political and administrative framework of support of educational evaluation and research.[1]* The general view was that, whereas a great deal of progress had been made in the interim in terms of influencing the growing community of specialist evaluators, the encouragement and confidence we had to some extent won from policy makers was now under threat of erosion by the rise of a form of managerialism in education that wanted simple answers. 'Power and Policy' was the theme, and we found no simple answers, but renewed determination.

That brings us to the fourth and latest conference, from which this book derives. There was no difficulty in deciding a focus for the conference. Both here and in the USA the escalation of political demand for school accountability and the particular forms which this demand has taken have forced pupil assessment and teacher appraisal to the forefront of professional concerns. In setting the agenda for the conference, we were acutely aware of the extent to which such narrowly focussed concerns were already undermining the gains we had made in bringing to the attention of policy makers the relevant complexity and idiosyncrasy of the contexts of educational action and performance, and the consequent difficulty of making judgements of merit on the basis of limited and singularistic sources of data. On the other hand, it is true to say that some features of newly emerging forms of performance assessment, and some aspects of their attendant rationales, are highly congruent with the broader focus, as well as the concern for participant rights, that are associated with the methods and values of naturalistic evaluation. We saw an opportunity, as well as an obligation, to bring our perspective to bear upon the issues now in contention, and to contribute to features of emergent plans such as the following:

- The opening up of educational processes to public scrutiny.
- The use of performance assessment to support personal development rather that simply to locate individuals in categories, whether norm or criterion referenced.
- The appraisal of events and situations from multiple perspectives.
- The development of holistic judgements based on a range of evidence.
- The validation of external appraisal against self-appraisal.
- The negotiation of appraisals with the appraised as a safeguard against harmful consequences of release.

* Superscript numerals refer to numbered notes at the end of each chapter.

The overall question set for the conference was 'How far and in what ways can naturalistic approaches to educational inquiry facilitate *educational* forms of performance appraisal of teachers and pupils?'

In keeping with previous conferences, invitations were extended to some individuals, not associated with naturalistic evaluation, but who had a particular expertise in the topic under scrutiny.[2] The papers reflect this diversity of membership. They were not written for the conference, but subsequent to it, and therefore can be taken to incorporate the influence of the 4 days of discussion which took place in Cambridge.

The structure and contents of the book

The book is in two parts. The first set of papers explores fundamental issues in teacher appraisal. The second part examines new approaches to pupil assessment. The final chapter discusses the interrelationship between the two and, from a review of the papers, formulates general principles for performance appraisal utilizing naturalistic methodology. Throughout, the emphasis is clearly on educational forms of appraisal, whether this be appraisal of teachers or of pupils.

Though administrative interests are not neglected (and the use of appraisal and assessment for probation, promotion, selection and even dismissal are discussed), the main thrust of the first set of papers is towards elucidating forms of appraisal that genuinely enhance the professional development of teachers. This is a very complex issue requiring analysis rather than the rhetoric frequently invoked to make appraisal palatable to teachers. Similarly, the main emphasis in the assessment papers is on how to develop and provide the underlying rationale for forms of assessment that are connected to the processes of teaching and learning.

In Chapter 1, Robert Stake argues that the several purposes of appraisal need to be kept separate, and that we should proceed cautiously, introducing appraisal schemes 'only when it can be demonstrated that the capacity for promoting education will be helped more than hurt by formal processes of teacher evaluation should it occur'. Eschewing the notion of the 'ideal teacher' and hence the search for absolute criteria, he draws our attention to the need to appraise an individual in context, to the fact that teachers often act in concert and hence the need to evaluate teams of teachers and to adopt multiple criteria or different criteria for different teaching situations. Finally, he argues for a system of appraisal in a context of institutional support that leaves improvement of teaching firmly in the hands of the teacher and enhances rather than diminishes his/her autonomy.

In Chapter 2, Michael Eraut also focusses upon purposes, and the consideration of appraisal within a broader context of curriculum and institutional development. The distinction he draws between the annual staff development interview and a staff appraisal interview once every 5 years (or more often for probationers) parallels the wider distinction he notes between *monitoring*, the ongoing informal process by which those responsible for education satisfy themselves that teaching is of quality, and *reviewing*, an occasional, semi-formal process that asks more challenging questions about practice. Eraut also draws our attention to the very important issue of opportunity costs of appraisal. Recognition of the fact that the 'collection of evidence on which to base an appraisal is a delicate, costly and highly professional task' leads him to cast severe doubt on the utility of the annual staff appraisal interview as a mechanism for improving teaching. There is a danger, he argues, of drawing too close an analogy with industrial and commercial practice, which is rarely evaluated, in any case, for its effect on improving performance.

Robert Burgess (Chapter 3) looks at what he sees to be a methodological vacuum at the heart of current advocacies. Reviewing recent government documents and the Suffolk appraisal study, he argues that the process of collecting and adjudicating appraisal data is at best represented as technical procedures within a managerial model of conduct. The ideological assumptions about the social world and about the appraiser, issues intrinsic to methodological determination, are not discussed. Hierarchy is the taken for granted fact and value of current schemes, and their implications for power, authority and gender relations are not examined. Burgess advocates an alternative approach aspiring to research-based professional collaboration. Teachers will, however, need adequate levels of methodological knowledge to conduct this research and Burgess concludes by pointing to the training implications of his proposal.

Clem Adelman (Chapter 4), continues this line, drawing evidence from both the US and the UK to point out that no national or local appraisal scheme initiated by administrators has been based upon criteria from teachers' systematic research into their own pedagogic practice. Citing two US examples, he explores the limitations, validity and reliability of schemes devised primarily in the interests of administrative control. He then suggests an alternative that is built upon collaborative peer research of pedagogic and management practice, and that is moderated by a Teachers' Professional Council.

In Chapter 5, Richard Winter examines three different models of teacher appraisal – 'The Target-Output Model', 'the Performance Criteria Model' and 'the Diagnostic Model'. While these are conceptually distinguishable, he argues that in the various schemes on offer, they are proposed as part of a single set of procedures which can be described as the 'Product Model of Appraisal'. This ignores a wide range of evidence indicating that 'a plurality of aims renders appraisal schemes ineffective'. His explanation is that the product model enables administrators to justify decisions about how they spend public money. This bureaucratic principle he contrasts with the professional principles underlying the process model of appraisal he advocates. Educational action-research is the process he favours as a basis for developmental appraisal.

Ernest House and Stephen Lapan (Chapter 6) analyse the underlying concepts of the teacher implicit in different appraisal schemes and the criteria necessary for a teacher appraisal scheme that concentrates on quality performance not minimum competency. Minimum competency is the prime focus of appraisal schemes in the US, they point out, because their major purpose is for account-ability rather than for recognizing good teaching or improving teaching. House and Lapan's view of teacher appraisal, directed towards the professional/art dimension of Wise's (1984) categories, is based upon two assumptions; first, that evaluation should focus on dimensions that can logically be equated with teaching success; and, secondly, that teacher appraisal schemes should consider teaching at its highest levels, not as a minimum pass/fail standard. The concluding part of their chapter notes what would be central components of an appraisal scheme within the professional/art view of teaching and suggests several ways in which features of 'good' teaching within this category may be brought to the surface and utilized in such a scheme (see also Holly, Chapter 10).

Donald McIntyre (Chapter 7) brings us to the heart of the problem of appraising teacher performance. Focussing upon criterion-referenced assess-ment as offering the only real possibility of devising valid assessment schemes, he suggests three types of inter-related justification for choosing criteria against which to evaluate teaching before taking a standpoint and delineating a set of criteria by which teaching should be assessed. He then outlines some of the problems that can occur when clarifying the criteria, by taking an example from each of the three categories. What McIntyre makes absolutely clear is that appraisal is no easy task. Selecting criteria is a complex activity, and establishing a valid and reliable basis for their application equally so. He also makes clear that presenting summary accounts of teachers' performance is extremely difficult (as it has to be related to the criteria of an individual's aspiration for teaching). No general theories of teaching competence can serve to underpin such a scheme.

In Chapter 8, Franz Kroath has a very specific focus. In the context of a new programme for initial teacher training in Austria that has as its core curriculum a 3-month teaching practice period for student teachers guided by a supervisor, Kroath examines the basic qualifications and competences of supervisors. These fall into three broad categories: personality traits and properties; competences in the art of teaching and in special didactics; and academic knowledge and expertise in one's field. He then outlines an INSET course for experienced secondary teachers interested in becoming a supervisor in which classroom observation and analysis and self-evaluation, both individually and collectively, form an important part. Finally, Kroath examines the characteristics of natu-ralistic evaluation in the training model he outlines, and discusses how to resolve the dilemmas inherent in using such a model within a hierarchically structured, selection-orientated school system.

John Elliott (Chapter 9) offers a detailed analysis of perhaps the best known and most widely discussed document in the field – *Those Having Torches . . . Teacher Appraisal: A Study*. His analysis points out the inconsistencies in the espoused purposes of appraisal for professional development focussing par-ticularly on the renunciation of judgements about personal qualities. Contrary to most of the general principles advocated for teacher appraisal Elliott argues a strong case for the appraisal of personal qualities as a source of teaching competence at the highest level: 'Professional development in short, implies personal development'. He articulates a process of professional development that takes account of public and private criteria and that involves a transition from the self to the social domain.

Mary Lou Holly (Chapter 10) examines the interrelationship of teacher appraisal and the personal and social development of teachers. She locates the scope for improvement of teaching and learning clearly in an understanding of the teacher as a person in the context of his/her social life history; and in the growing recognition of the teacher's capacity to theorize about practice: 'Knowing is *in* action.' The two are interactive. Attempts to appraise teachers, she argues, will only be useful to the extent that they enable deeper and ongoing reflection on practice and engage the person psychologically in the process. Crucial to their development as professional educators is an understanding of how and why they came to be teachers and what it means for them in the future – their professional autobiography if you like. Equally necessary is creating the conditions for collegial interpretation of practice, for it is in the social and educational world that life histories unfold. The paper outlines five essential principles of professional development that build upon naturalistic assumptions and that are consistent with a form of appraisal that can facilitate the quality of teaching and learning. Some practical suggestions are given for how to begin to engage in the collective reflective practice she sees as crucial for the professional development of teachers.

David Bridges (Chapter 11) begins by noting how many of the new developments in pupil assessment both in the US and UK encapsulate some characteristics of naturalistic inquiry, such as more holistic assessment of a range of dimensions of the human personality, multi-faceted judgements of worth, negotiation of agreed statements by teacher and pupil, the use of assessment as a developmental tool over time, and the integration of assessment as part of the curriculum. This chapter, first written as a report for the assessment section of the Conference, is structured around 10 key concepts, features of naturalistic inquiry that serve as a focus for debate on these issues. The issues are discussed with reference either to a critique of more traditional assessment or in regard to new assessment forms. Bridges examines both the difficulties and the potential of the 10 concepts for assessment processes.

Louis Smith and Carol Klass (Chapter 12) take up the theme of holistic assessment raised by Bridges and explore how this is perceived and understood. Rather than attempt to delineate the construct from the various conceptual analyses on offer, they approach the problem situationally and pragmatically through a case example, a research project with which they were involved. The problem they discuss through this project is, how is it possible and whether it is desirable to translate rich graphic illustrations and sets of images obtained through close observations of individuals into theoretical language and measurable dimensions and formats. The major question they address is do we lose more than we gain by such efforts at translation and objectivity? The paper examines four major issues in naturalistic inquiry relevant to the development of a 'measure' for the whole child and concludes by suggesting that one way

forward is a blending of contextualized descriptions with quantitatively measured profiles of dimensions.

In Chapter 13, Harvey Goldstein, writing from the perspective of a statistician, focusses upon clarifying a distinction that he makes between 'separated'
and 'connected' assessment measures. The distinction is an important one, not
least because it reinforces the case made repeatedly by other contributors to this
volume – the case for connected assessment and appraisal – connected to
learning and teaching, to contexts of performance. Goldstein argues that
historically the development of mathematical theory in support of assumed
context-free traits has mistakenly been taken to validate their existence and that,
moreover, this tradition has misleadingly conditioned approaches to connected
assessment. 'If we are to have theoretical bases for educational measurement', he
concludes, 'alternatives to existing psychometric theory are needed.'

Taking as a focus 'new forms' of descriptive assessment (such as profiling and
records of achievement) Mary James (Chapter 14) examines a distinction
between 'negotiation' and 'dialogue', two procedures characteristic of both
naturalistic inquiry and descriptive assessment. In profiling, she points out,
these words are often used interchangeably, masking quite different assumptions about intent and control. Negotiation in particular, she argues, where
students are in a relatively powerless situation compared with their teachers, is a
form of social control, especially where profiles are assumed to be both
formative and summative in function. Negotiation and dialogue, James argues,
are two 'logically distinct processes which assume different contexts, have
different purposes and need to be governed by different sets of principles and
procedures'. The central question she addresses is whether it is possible to
accommodate both these processes in a single appraisal or profiling scheme.
Through the analysis of an example she draws attention to disparities of power
and authority in the negotiating process and to the central issue of what
constitutes a valid assessment. She outlines three ways in which the balance of
power could be shifted in the student's favour, but concludes that these mostly
rest upon a conflict model and that a better description of a process that is
educational in intent is 'dialogue'.

Finally, Ian Stronach (Chapter 15) examines critically the educational and
political values of pupil profiling in the historical context of vocational prepara-
tional programmes. He notes that in the content and constructs of profiles there
seems to have been a shift from individualized 'self-concept' theories to personalized 'work ethic' formulations – 'a retreat from self to workplace conducted
under the rubric of student-centredness'. The learner is invited to match him/
herself against these constructs and negotiate his/her assessments. What
emerges, argues Stronach, is a *social* assessment, not an educational dialogue:
'The profile is channelled towards a particular version of the self, not towards
the learning process. What such statements imply is a pupil-focussed confession
rather than a learner-centred dialogue'. Profiling and reviewing, he concludes,
are anti-educational, alienating and anti-vocational. The promise of power
redolent in the rhetoric is confined to the training bubble. Outside of that

training the world looks very different. Hence to Stronach's conclusion and new metaphor for understanding the paradoxes in profiling 'What is such a "fantasy of structural superiority", if it is not a carnival?'

It will be clear from the resumé of the chapters which comprise this volume, that no easy answers to matters of legitimate concern are on offer. At the same time, one of the lessons we have learned from the post-war history of innovation in education is that interventions in schooling, no matter how single-minded and limited in intent, have multiple effects, many of them unintended and unexpected. Partially as a result of the work of people such as the contributors to this volume, we are now in a better position than before to conduct a risk analysis of emerging aspirations and proposals for further intervention. If there is a consensus among our contributors on the issues of teacher appraisal and pupil assessment, it surely consists of a fear that pressures for easily manageable indicators of performance put at risk the conditions of better teaching and learning, conditions we are slowly coming to understand. Understandings we must put to work for both educational accountability and educational growth.

Notes

1 A report on each of these three conferences was published in the *Cambridge Journal of Education* (see MacDonald and Parlett, 1973; Adelman *et al.*, 1976; Jenkins *et al.*, 1981).
2 The conference sponsored by the Nuffield Foundation was held at Hughes Hall, Cambridge, 10–13 December 1985, and was attended by the following:

John Elliott (Convenor), *Centre for Applied Research in Education (CARE), University of East Anglia, Norwich, England.*
Helen Simons (Convenor), *University of London Institute of Education, London, England.*
Clem Adelman, *Bulmershe College, Reading, England.*
David Bridges, *Homerton College, Cambridge, England.*
Robert Burgess, *University of Warwick, Warwick, England.*
Michael Eraut, *University of Sussex, Brighton England.*
Harvey Goldstein, *University of London Institute of Education, London, England.*
Mary Louise Holly, *Kent State University, USA.*
Ernest House, *University of Colorado at Boulder, Colorado, USA.*
Mary James, *Open University, Milton Keynes, England.*
Franz Kroath, *University of Innsbruck, Innsbruck, Austria.*
Carol Klass, *Department of Children and Family Service Program, Illinois, USA.*
Barry MacDonald, *University of East Anglia, Norwich, England.*
Donald McIntyre, *University of Oxford, Oxford, England.*
Roger Murphy, *University of Southampton, Southampton, England.*
Desmond Nuttall, *Open University, Milton Keynes, England.*
Louis Smith, *University of Washington, St Louis, USA.*
Robert Stake, *University of Illinois, Illinois, USA.*
Ian Stronach, *University of East Anglia, Norwich, England.*
Harry Torrance, *University of Southampton, Southampton, England.*

References

Adelman, C., Jenkins, D. and Kemmis, S. (1976). Rethinking case study: notes from the second Cambridge conference. *Cambridge Journal of Education,* **6**(3).

Hamilton, D., Jenkins, D., King, C., MacDonald, B. and Parlett, M. (eds) (1977). *Beyond the Numbers Game.* London: Macmillan.

Jenkins, D., Simons, H. and Walker, R. (1981). 'Thou nature art my goddess': naturalistic inquiry in educational evaluation. *Cambridge Journal of Education,* **11**(3).

Macdonald, B. and Parlett, M. (1973). Rethinking evaluation: Notes from the Cambridge conference. *Cambridge Journal of Education,* **3**(2), 74–82.

Simons, H. (ed.) (1980). *Towards a Science of the Singular: Essays about Case Study in Educational Research and Evaluation.* Occasional Publication No. 10. University of East Anglia: CARE.

1
The evaluation of teaching

Robert E. Stake

Teacher evaluation – the appraisal of qualifications and performance of the individual teacher – has at least four purposes:

1 To provide data for the reward of merit and the correction of shortcomings.
2 To aid selection of the best qualified teachers in new positions and retention of the most needed in old.
3 To assist in continuing professional education for teachers.
4 To contribute to the understanding of the operation of the school as a whole.

Although these purposes regularly coexist, they get in each other's way. Data for one purpose may unethically be used for another purpose, e.g. data volunteered for staff improvement should not be used for accountability.

The evaluation of teaching is an inseparable part of the evaluation of the school itself. An effective evaluation of teaching requires concurrent study of institutional goals, classroom environments, administrative organization and operations, curricular content, student achievement, and the impact of school programmes on the community. Teaching can be judged properly only in the context of these other factors, and if no effort is made to study them, the evaluation of teaching will probably be invalid.

Teachers (and all persons) consider evaluation a threat. And with reason. Whether the evaluation is valid or invalid, they may get hurt. The evaluation will inevitably be less sensitive to their aims and talents than anyone would like. It will be more attuned to institution-wide aims and structures (Meyer *et al.*, 1981, p. 167), but even to those quite imperfectly. Benefits to individuals should prevail over benefits to institutions. And only when it can be domonstrated that the capacity for promoting education will be helped more than hurt by formal processes of teacher evaluation should it occur. The burden of those demonstrations rests with school administrators. It should be a stern obligation. The harmony and respect of the staff, and thus the classroom learning environment, should not be put at risk just because teacher evaluation might make some things better.

Evaluation is a process of judgement based on information, formal and informal. Various kinds of data gathering procedures, observers and situations can and should be used. Both quantitative and naturalistic research methods can help discipline the appraisal.

In the real world, what is done with the evaluation information gathered is more a social than analytic process. Good data seldom leads directly to problem solving – in fact it often leads to political manipulation. Until we have the know-how and political facility for improving teaching based on evaluative information, we should proceed cautiously. This is not to conclude that we should not evaluate teachers; they must be evaluated, we should get better at doing it. But doing it should be based on the realities of school and community, not only on idealizations of teaching.

Placement and selection

One of the most valuable books for personnel evaluation is *Psychological Tests and Personnel Decisions* (Cronbach and Gleser, 1965). The authors made an important distinction between placement and selection processes. If we are evaluating a teacher already on the faculty with the expectation that this teacher is likely to remain on the faculty, it is usually a placement situation. From the evaluation we hope to get a better idea of talents and shortcomings. Noting both, we want to place the teacher in a situation that will result in an improved working condition and better performance – possibly a minor adjustment, possibly major.

In most of the following, the discussion will be on the placement circumstance. For placement evaluation one concentrates on the immediate work context. When selection is to result in hiring people who will stay a long time, the immediate circumstances are not so important.

Comparability and contextuality

One of the greatest mistakes in evaluation procedures is to emphasize comparisons with teachers in general. One cannot help but make such comparisons, but these are often of little value. Usually, more needed within the school is recognition (based on actual observation) of the range between the best and the worst this teacher could be – given the conditions of work here, especially the conditions that can be little altered by teachers. We should study the alterable conditions and decide how the greatest good may occur. Teachers should be rewarded for being better now than they have been and helped towards being better still. The range of worst possible to best possible (within their contexts) cannot be stated precisely, but even roughly conceived is needed for teacher appraisal.

There is no one ideal teacher. Even in the narrowest training programme, students have many things to learn. However standardized the pedagogical plan, different teachers teach different things. For example, a teacher who emphasizes critical thinking seldom models mobilization for action. The need for diverse talents is not because good teachers do not teach broadly, but because teachers are consistent in the kinds of learning situations they create. Dissimilar teachers are needed to create other situations.

To know the quality of teachers' work requires a knowledge of that work. Records of what a teacher actually does are seldom kept. An effort to keep such records can be burdensome, even oppressive, but brief descriptions and vignettes are common to the best efforts.

Most teachers are afforded considerable autonomy in the classroom, yet teachers often act in concert. It should be obvious then that evaluating a teacher well depends on recognizing what talents are already available on the faculty. In other words, one needs not only to evaluate individual teachers but teams of teachers as well. Effective teaching requires an understanding of what else is being taught right now as well as what has been taught and what is still to come. It requires understanding of the topics and a good order of presentation. The effective teacher comprehends how the student's mind is perceived by others to be developing. The effective teacher helps other teachers. An evaluation of individual teachers is not complete without taking into account how the teacher works with other teachers, and other people, and the strengths and weaknesses of those people. Every teacher is a member of one or several groups, and each group has its own uniqueness and context.

Criteria

Evaluation is usually thought of as based on criteria, certain descriptive characteristics indicating more or less something and drawing forth a judgement of goodness or badness. Whether the judgement follows or precedes the recognition of the criterion is not always clear, but the association is regularly to be found when anything is evaluated. The criteria by which teachers and teaching are evaluated are numerous (e.g. see Dunkin and Biddle, 1974).

Exhaustive as the list may be, one set of criteria cannot be found that adequately fits all teaching situations. Furthermore, high marks on all criteria do not indicate the most valuable teacher for all situations, and an excess of any good quality can be too much of a good thing (Land, 1985).[1] The ways to wrong are many. For something beyond a superficial indication of the quality of teaching we at least need information of diverse types, relating to diverse situations, and drawn from diverse sources. To evaluate on the basis of any single instrument, or to rely on only a single authority (e.g. Madeline Hunter, 1984), is mindless.[2]

Common to many formal appraisals of teachers are checklists featuring criteria such as knowledge of subject matter, effectiveness in disciplining and quality of lesson plans. Such characteristics are often not highly correlated with effective teaching, but they serve to announce what school patrons and others admire in teachers. Such checklists are tolerated by most teachers, particularly when more objective procedures have been needed in their school. They can be useful if used with other evidence of merit.

There are rules for the sensible use of checklists. For example, sums or averages (across items or across teachers) are not necessarily more meaningful than individual descriptions, and they have often not been validated empirically. Even when used properly evaluative checklists usually produce nothing more refined than impressions. Most are deliberately context free, and that often leads to unwarranted generalizations. Understanding the qualifications of teachers requires a review of what they have done in specially sensitive situations. Gathering good data on those situations is difficult, but should not be avoided. Just because it happened only once is not a proper basis for ignoring a critical act. Evaluation checklists do help to remind us of criteria to pay attention to.

The goal context

Evaluation of teaching, as with the evaluation of other aspects of the educational system, needs evaluators who can analyse goals. Every school has patrons and clients to whom it has commitments. It is the responsibility of administrators[3] to interpret the wishes of patrons and the needs of clients and thus to shape a formal curricular plan.

Administrators have the responsibility to formalize institutional goals, particularly long-range curricular goals. In words or in action, attendant to ideology and institutional mission, teachers set intermediate and tactical goals. Within constraints of custom and taste teachers choose instructional strategies and tactics. The integrity of a curriculum is maintained only when faculty members perceive themselves – within limits and a certain division of labour – to be free to pursue institutional goals as each sees fit (Peters and Waterman, 1984). Supervisors or committees charged with evaluative responsibility should assess the discharge of such responsibility but should not presume that there is but one proper way of teaching or that there is but one set of educational objectives, even for a single lesson. They may make known to the teacher certain perceptions and valuations of past contributions and certain hopes for the future, but – based on what we know about teaching – the final choice of intermediate goals and means of instruction should largely be left to the teacher.

Still, maintaining meritorious teaching is one of the primary responsibilities of the administrative staff. The administrators should collect evidence of merit – and lack of it – from various sources. They should avail themselves of results of achievement testing and should at least informally follow up former students. Throughout the year, and across the years, they should encourage each teacher formally and informally to submit evidence of merit. Together they should submit plans and artifacts of teaching to the scrutiny of experts in subject matter and pedagogy.

Each teacher is responsible for contributing to the evidence of the effectiveness of teaching. The evidence may be 'process' or 'product' data, preferably both. Process data (e.g. lesson plans, counselling, self-evaluation) are useful because we believe that certain teaching activities promote student accomplishment. For example, it is expected that a conspicuous concern for ethical behaviour in the classroom will encourage ethical behaviour in youth. Product data provide actual observation of accomplishment or correlates of accomplishment (e.g. achievement tests indirectly indicate students do understand certain important relationships). Product data at first appear preferable, but the need for assessing the quality of working conditions and the difficulty of attributing student achievement to what the teacher does makes the inclusion of process data a necessity.

Leaving teachers in charge

Because autonomy is not only a fact of life but a demonstrated contribution to good work,[4] the means available to administrators for redirecting instructional programmes are and should be limited. In many places merit adjustments in pay are not provided and modification of asssignment is greatly constrained. Still, administrators can modify the direction of teaching through persuasion, by reallocation of incidental resources and classload, by reassignment of responsibility, and sometimes by employment of aides or even additional faculty members.

Teachers themselves are mainly responsible for the continuing improvement of instruction. Administrators are responsible for encouragement and facilitation of that improvement. The following should be provided by the school for voluntary, sometimes confidential, use:

- checklists of classroom, laboratory and field conditions which have been demonstrated to promote learning;
- course content reviews (selection of topics, texts, resource works, etc.) conducted outside the classroom by experienced and specially trained colleagues;
- observational and remediation services by specialists in instruction and testing.

Feedback from these three sources will work best in the long term if it is seen – as should be – the property of the individual instructor, not to be evaluated by others without his/her release.

The worth of an educational programme is not entirely, but at least partly, attributable to its impact on students. Impact is difficult to measure. Part of the evaluation of teaching should be an attempt to assess student learning. Some indication of a gain in skills, understanding and attitude can be obtained informally, but also formally through observation and performance tests, and to a lesser extent with conventional achievement tests and interest and personality inventories. These measures should be seen as merely sampling the full set of achievements.

In this chapter teacher evaluation has been discussed with an emphasis placed on the context of work, the multidimensionality of competence, and the uniqueness of individual teachers. These qualities – plus emphases of personal intentionality and empathic understanding – have been common aspects of naturalistic, phenomenological and ethnographic studies of teaching.[5] Inquiry methods used in such studies have a potential for enhancing the quality of appraisal efforts.

Of the four purposes of evaluation of teaching, none is more important than long-term support of a teacher's continuing education. Self-study and career development need to be undertaken with a commitment to institutional goals, awareness of existing instructional conditions, and a certain expectation of the results of alternative pedagogies. The school should provide a supportive environment for professional growth, partly by making periodic reviews of purposes, attending to the findings of research on instructional processes, and ensuring fair (though often subjective) judgements of teaching quality. It is an institutional obligation usually best discharged by evaluation so cleverly devised that the teacher is left better informed and even more in charge of instruction than before.

Notes

1 Take the criterial item 'always explains things thoroughly'. It sounds good, but inventor Edwin Land (1985) reminds us that some teachers explain too much, needing occasionally to just show wonder.
2 As revealed in such statements as 'Knowing, Teaching and Supervising', Hunter (1984) has a broad and complex view of teaching. Yet, as pointed out in a rejoinder by Costa (1984), Hunter's views draw people to thinking of the technological side of teaching.
3 To identify evaluation responsibilities here it is desirable to call some members 'administrators' and others 'teachers'. Obviously, all teachers have administrative responsibility and many administrators are members of the instructional staff. It is not implied that administrative and instructional responsibilities should be assigned to separate people. For convenience here we oversimplify the two roles of administration and teaching.
4 The autonomy of the teacher is documented by Meyer *et al.* (1981) in a survey of elementary schools in the San Francisco Bay Area. These researchers tended to treat autonomy as a barrier to school improvement, but its merit is well argued and illustrated by Schon (1982).
5 For example, see Denny (1978) and Smith and Geoffrey (1968).

References

Costa, A. (1984). A reaction to Hunter's 'Knowing, Teaching and Supervising'. In Philip L. Hosford (ed.), *Using What We Know About Teaching,* pp. 196–203. Alexandria, Va: Association for Supervision and Curriculum Development.

Cronbach, L.J. and Gleser, G.C. (1965). *Psychological Tests and Personnel Decisions.* Champaign, Ill.: University of Illinois Press.

Denny, T. (1978). *Some Still Do.* Evaluation Series Report No. 3. Kalamazoo, Mich.: Western Michigan University.

Dunkin, M.J. and Biddle B.J. (1974). *The Study of Teaching.* New York: Holt, Rinehart and Winston.

Hunter, M. (1984). Knowing, teaching and supervising. In Philip L. Hosford (ed.) *Using What We Know About Teaching*, pp. 169–92. Alexandria, Va: Association for Supervision and Curriculum Development.

Land, E. (1985). *Beckman Lecture*, 21 November 1985. University of Illinois.

Meyer, J.W., Scott, R.S. and Deal, T.E. (1981). Institutional and technical sources of organizational structure: Explaining the structure of educational organizations. In H.D. Stein (ed.), *Organization and the Human Services,* pp. 151–79. Philadelphia: Temple University Press.

Peters, T.J. and Waterman, R.H.Jr (1984). *In Search of Excellence.* New York: Warner Books.

Schon, D. (1982). *The Reflective Practitioner.* New York: Basic Books.

Smith, L.M. and Geoffrey K.L. (1968). *The Complexities of an Urban Classroom: An Analysis Toward a General Theory of Teaching.* New York: Holt, Rinehart and Winston.

2
Teacher appraisal and/or teacher development: friends or foes?

Michael Eraut

My interest in school-based INSET has led me to favour the idea of an annual staff development interview between a teacher and head (or head of department or senior teacher). This interview would cover:

1 The teacher's own view of his or her strengths and weaknesses.
2 The teacher's own priorities for developing his or her professional knowledge and skills.
3 School priorities for staff development arising from proposed curriculum change, school review, developing class teachers' all-round capabilities, etc.

The product would be an action plan for the teacher's professional development over the following year to which both teacher and school were committed. In many cases this might include one area of teacher priority and one area of school priority, thus expressing their mutal obligations and protecting the teacher from an unrealistic level of school expectation.

In a number of cases, and almost certainly not every year, one of the planned development activities would be some form of teacher self-evaluation assisted by an external observer. This could be achieved without assigning the observer role to the interviewer, either by forming mutual observer groups of two to four teachers, or by seeking the help of an experienced teacher of the evaluand's own choosing. Work of this kind is becoming increasingly common in primary schools.'

Another interest of mine, accountability, has led me to realize that the main plank in a school's accountability platform is the quality of its teaching (they are all trained and competent professionals, etc.). But how should this aspect of accountability be properly exercised if the mere fact of qualified teacher status is considered an insufficient guarantee of 40 years good teaching? Although it spent relatively little time on teacher appraisal *per se*, the Sussex Accountability Research Project (Becher *et al.*, 1979, 1981) did produce two relevant concepts – monitoring and reviewing.

Monitoring is the ongoing, largely informal, process by which those responsible satisfy themselves that teaching is of an acceptable quality. The assumption is that suspicions of any class receiving teaching that is of unacceptable standard will be checked, and, if confirmed, lead to some kind of remedial action. The justification is that pupils should not be allowed to suffer. Only when remedial action is repeatedly unsuccessful (in improving teacher performance) does the question arise of initiating formal procedures of inspections, warnings and, in extreme cases, dismissal. Thus, monitoring is normally an informal, private, trouble-shooting process, which is quite distinct from appraisal. No doubt people can learn to do it better, but it is not logically dependent on having a formal appraisal of every teacher. Some would argue that an annual appraisal system would make monitoring more effective, whereas others would argue that serious problems have to be tackled as and when they occur without waiting for appraisal time to come round again. One important difference is that monitoring concentrates resources on those who are perceived to have the greatest problems. The most common criticism of monitoring is not that it fails to detect problems, but that the monitors fail to deal adequately with the problems. That can only be remedied by training senior staff how to be more effective in helping weaker teachers, not in formalizing the detection process.

Review is an occasional, semi-formal process. Unlike monitoring, it should not take existing norms for granted but should rather ask more challenging questions about existing practice. Thus, a review of somebody's teaching will be concerned with aims and strategy as well as effectiveness. However, questions of aims and strategy cannot be separated from the process of curriculum evaluation. Hence, reviews of teaching and curriculum have to be considered within the same framework.

One of the recommendations of the Taylor Committee (see Taylor, 1977), endorsed by the Sussex Accountability Project, was the notion of a 3- to 5-year cycle of reviews, taking each area of the work of the school in turn. A similar period would seem sensible for reviews of individual teachers, perhaps 5 years for longer-serving and 2–3 years for those who are newly appointed. In secondary schools, at least, this could be carefully coordinated with curriculum reviews. Such a review cycle would be entirely compatible with annual staff development interviews of the kind described above.

The quinquennial review would provide:

1 An agreed appraisal of performance for the file, which would note the achievements of the previous 5 years.
2 An explicit demonstration of the teacher's and the school's commitment to teaching quality, and their continuing desire to improve it.

But it should also be a time to take serious stock of one's teaching. So there should also be some release time for reflective self-evaluation and additional staff development opportunities. Though the teaching review would be individual, taking two to four colleagues together would enhance reflection and development. Lighter loads could be planned for a term or even a year; and there could also be links to relevant external INSET at the same time. Could this be a reconceptualization of the James Committee's (DES, 1972) suggestion of teacher sabbaticals?

Now where do recent proposals for teacher appraisal fit into this picture? Most of them seem to claim that an annual teacher appraisal would fulfil all three of the functions I have carefully distinguished – staff development, monitoring and review – and several others besides. My own view is that it is the product which will decide the real purpose of appraisal. If the product is an action plan for development, then the appraisal interview will become a staff development interview under another name (a sheep in wolf's clothing?). But if the product is an agreed appraisal of a teacher's performance for insertion into their file, the appraisal foreground will put staff development purposes very much into the background.

More worrying still is the question of opportunity costs. In so far as an appraisal interview is leading to an agreed statement about performance, great care must be taken to collect sufficient evidence. We can probably assume that classroom observations will be undertaken *before* the interview by one or more senior teachers. In contrast, where a development interview system operates, any classroom observation will be undertaken *after* the interview, with a developmental rather than evidential purpose; and it will probably be carried out by a less senior, and therefore less expensive, person. In the former case, the resources go into improving the record in the file, in the latter they go into teacher development. Since it is unlikely that there will be sufficient resources for both, we have to ask which will yield the best return in terms of improved quality of teaching. By the time we have paid for the MOT, there will be no money left for the servicing.

Finally, there are dangers in drawing too close an analogy with industrial and commercial practice. This is rarely evaluated for its effect on improving performance and is usually based on two major assumptions: first, that evidence about performance is readily available and, secondly, that the appraiser's judgement of that performance is accepted. In teaching, however, performance is mostly behind closed doors; and student learning is not a reliable indicator of teaching quality (because individual students' capabilities vary, and the number and diversity of learning outcomes makes it difficult to assess them all and impossible to rank them). Thus, the collection of evidence on which to base an appraisal is a delicate, costly and highly professional task. The validity of an appraiser's judgement is also likely to be questioned, either because he or she does not know the subject, or because promotion to higher office is perceived to be based on qualities other than good teaching. For all these reasons, the real cost of appraisal is higher for teaching than for most other occupations. So we must examine the benefits and opportunity costs of appraisal schemes with considerable care.

My tentative conclusions on the basis of these argumnents are as follows. The annual appraisal interview:

- is too infrequent for monitoring;
- is unnecessary for identifying low performing teachers;
- is so frequent that it is likely to lapse into an expensive piece of bureaucratic tokenism after the first couple of years;
- is unlikely to address the fundamental issues that ought to be faced in a quinquennial review;
- is likely to be divorced from curriculum evaluation;
- will divert resources away from staff development.

References

Becher, T., Eraut, M., Barton, J., Canning, T. and Knight, J. (1979). *An Analysis of Policy Options*. Final Report of the East Sussex LEA/University of Sussex Research Project, Brighton.

Becher, T., Eraut, M. and Knight, J. (1981). *Policies for Educational Accountability*. London: Heinemann Educational.

Department of Education and Science (1972). *Teacher Education and Training*. The James Report. London: HMSO.

Taylor, T. (1977). *A New Partnership for Our Schools*. Report by a Committee of Inquiry appointed by the Secretary of State for Education and Science and the Secretary of State for Wales. London: HMSO.

3
A problem in search of a method or a method in search of a problem? A critique of teacher appraisal

Robert G. Burgess

The social and political context of English education in the 1980s has provided the conditions under which teacher appraisal can be brought on to the agenda by the Department of Education and Science (DES) and in turn by Local Education Authorities (LEA's). Two questions are addressed in much of the 'official' literature from the DES. First, why appraise? Secondly, how can appraisal be conducted? In addressing the first question, educationalists have fallen back on managerial accounts, while the second results in a series of statements about interviews and in some cases observation. At this point the languages of 'management' and 'methodology' have been mixed together with relatively little thought being given to the appropriateness of these approaches to the appraisal of teachers. This chapter therefore is intended to provide a brief introduction to some of the issues that have been raised in recent documents emanating from central government and more recently from a DES-sponsored project by Suffolk LEA. Secondly, I shall examine some of the methodological issues involved, the assumptions that are made and some issues that are overlooked, before turning to a colleagial model that might be used in teacher appraisal/assessment.

The social context of teacher appraisal

A brief glance at the popular press indicates that the teachers' pay dispute in 1985 has been linked to teacher appraisal. However, it is important to focus on some of the central themes involved which were summarized very clearly in *The Times* when it was stated that the major issue was concerned with:

> the management of the schools by linking ... the qualitative achievement of educational purpose, good teaching leading to palpable attainment for chil-
> dren at all intellectual levels, with the quantities of public money spent, in

which by far the most significant element is the cost of teachers' salaries.

Yet, as Wilby (1986) points out, while the central case for teacher appraisal has been linked to a contractual definition of teachers' duties, there has been little public presentation of the aims and objectives of teacher appraisal or of the *process* of appraisal. As a result, the press saw appraisal as a means by which Sir Keith Joseph might 'sack' or 'weed out' large numbers of teachers who 'fail' the appraisal 'test'. But we might ask: is this consistent with the available evidence?

While the press may see teacher appraisal as a major educational issue in the mid-1980s, it has a much longer history. A review of educational history in the nineteenth century indicates that Sir James Kay-Shuttleworth was concerned with the qualities of elementary school teachers which he defined in terms of reliability, competent social control and efficient pedagogic work. Further-more, reports on the qualities looked for in the school teacher were such that not only intellectual ability but also qualities of character and ideological stance were of vital importance. This evidence has been well documented by Grace (1985), who illustrates how the criteria that were used to evaluate teachers have changed over the last century. In these circumstances, context was seen as important. However, we might reflect on the ways in which values intrude into the assessment of the nineteenth-century teacher. Here, the value standpoint is apparent to the twentieth-century observer, but we might ask: how far have different value positions influenced the debates about appraisal and more importantly the way in which appraisal can be conducted? Turning to the twentieth century, Hartley and Broadfoot (1988) have outlined some of the main research that has been conducted principally by psychologists on teacher performance. They demonstrate how psychologists were united in their view that there were numerous problems associated with defining and measuring teacher performance. Indeed, by 1977, Borich indicated that there was no agreement on a definition of the criteria that could be used to assess teacher performance or to establish competency. With this evidence in mind we need to consider critically those criteria that are currently used in discussions of teacher appraisal. Here, we turn briefly to government documents produced in the last 3 years.

A key document is *Teaching Quality* (HMSO, 1983) where, in a section on 'management', the following comments were made:

> The Government welcome recent moves towards self-assessment by schools and teachers, and believe these should help to improve school standards and curricula. But employers can manage their teacher force effectively only if they have accurate knowledge of each teacher's performance. The Govern-ment believe that for this purpose formal assessment of teacher performance is necessary and should be based on classroom visiting by the teacher's head or head of department, and an appraisal of both pupils' work and of the teacher's contribution to the life of the school. (HMSO, 1983, p. 27)

This statement on the management of the teaching force focusses attention on *what* would be done and *by whom* under the heading of teacher appraisal. At this stage we could only speculate about the purpose, for it was 2 years before when questions about the purpose of teacher appraisal were addressed in the document *Better Schools* (HMSO, 1985a). Here, the account that had previously been given was re-presented as we are told:

> Only if this information [data from appraisal] relates to performance in post can LEA management make decisions affecting the career development of its teachers fairly and consistently. (HMSO, 1985a, p. 55)

A laudable statement, but one which is quickly qualified by the comment:

> Taken together, these decisions should result in improved deployment and distribution of talent within the teaching force, with all teachers being helped to respond to changing demands and to realise their full professional potential by developing their strengths and improving upon their weaknesses. (HMSO, 1985a, p. 55)

It is, therefore, with the publication of these two documents that the managerial model of teacher appraisal is presented in a series of short instalments. First, we are told that appraisal is to be conducted by the management team in a school (senior and middle management) who can deliver information to members of the LEA management team for the purpose of distributing the teacher force. However, we should note that this suggestion comes at a time of falling rolls in schools and when the management teams in schools and in LEAs are concerned with teacher redeployment. It is clear, as HMI have recently pointed out: 'Appraisal may serve many different purposes' (HMSO, 1985b, p. 1).

Despite all this documentation, little has been written about the *process* of appraisal apart from comments about the collection of information that is 'reliable', 'comprehensive' and 'up to date' through 'systematic performance appraisal' (HMSO, 1985a, p. 55). Nevertheless, the document *Quality in Schools* (HMSO, 1985c) takes us a little further into a discussion of process. It begins by providing a definition of appraisal in the following terms: 'appraisal emphasises the forming of qualitative judgements about an activity, a person or an organization (HMSO, 1985c, p. 7). In addition, it goes further by specifying the forms of staff appraisal when it states:

> staff appraisal involves qualitative judgements about performance and, although it may start as self-appraisal by the teacher, it will normally involve judgements by other persons responsible for that teacher's work – a head of department or year, the head teacher, or a member of the senior management team or an officer of the LEA. (HMSO, 1985c, p. 7)

While such statements tell us who would conduct the appraisal, little is said here about the approaches that are included in the term 'qualitative judgement'. It would seem therefore that the appraisal problem has to find a method or range of methods which would yield sets of reliable and valid data. A clear impression of this search for a method can be obtained from the DES-sponsored project on teacher appraisal which focusses on the conduct of appraisal.

Enter a torch-bearer

Alongside policy statements from the DES and HMI, 1985 also witnessed the publication of a report from the Suffolk LEA (Graham, 1985) with the tantalizing title *Those Having Torches* .... It is this report on the process of teacher appraisal that begins to focus on possible methods of investigation. Here, it appears there is little understanding of the problem that is to be the subject of study. In a brief introduction we are told that 'effective teaching' is at the heart of teacher appraisal, although no attempt is made to question what is understood by 'effective' or 'good' teaching – an issue that has been problematic for some years (cf. Hartley and Broadfoot, 1988). For example, Elliott (1980) found that LEAs emphasized different aspects of 'teaching' in their checklists. Furthermore, we are told that teachers' work cannot be measured – a point that is clearly demonstrated by Hartley and Broadfoot's (1988) review. Nevertheless, the Suffolk team argue that an appraisal scheme:

> must enable teachers whose performance falls below par to be identified so that steps can be taken by the school and LEA to rectify the situation, and exceptionally, to terminate employment. (Graham, 1985, p. 4)

Such a conclusion would seem to represent the value perspective of senior management both in the Suffolk LEA and in some schools as the team who conducted this study comprised the County Education Officer, the Deputy County Education Officer, Senior General Adviser and three headteachers in the Authority. Together they represent the management hierarchy in schools and in an LEA who are in a position of power relative to the teacher who is appraised – a situation that is not unusually endorsed by other headteachers (e.g. see Threadgold, 1984). However, we need evidence that these members of the educational hierarchy can clearly identify those criteria that are to be used in appraisal. Yet in the Suffolk document there is no specification of the term 'below par', so that the reader can only conclude that the team who conducted this study are able to recognize what constitutes being above and below 'par' (whatever that might be).

If this is not sufficient cause for concern there is more. Instead of specifying what exactly is to be examined under the term 'teacher appraisal', a move is quickly made to discuss 'appraisal skills' which are identified as interviewing and classroom observation. These skills are part of 'the process of appraisal' which is defined as seven distinct phases: 'Preparation; classroom observation; the appraisal interview; results, monitoring, moderation, evaluation' (Graham, 1985, p. 5). Here, the authors of the report have fallen into three common methodological traps. First, they assume that as teaching cannot be measured, qualitative approaches are most appropriate, but they fail to specify the problem that is to be examined or what constitutes qualitative work. Secondly, methods are equated with skills; a common error that they appear to have acquired from the management literature and which has been made by others (e.g. see Martin, 1980, who argues that approaches to appraisal can be easily acquired from a management 'primer'). Finally, they see the appraisal process as a set of stages rather than a process where the collection and analysis of data is permeated by theoretical, political, ethical and moral questions. In short, they appear ignorant (or have they just ignored?) the ideological influences upon the appraisal process. It is to some of these problems that we now turn.

Some problems in teacher appraisal

At the centre of the process of appraisal is methodology, but the authors of the Graham Report (Graham, 1985) appear to be confused about methodology. From their point of view, it would seem that methodology is a set of technical procedures which deal with techniques of obtaining information and collecting data. However, as Gouldner (1971) has argued, methodology is much more than that, as it involves ideological assumptions about the social world and about the researcher:

> When viewed from one standpoint 'methodology' seems a purely technical concern devoid of ideology; presumably it deals only with methods of extracting reliable information from the world, collecting data, constructing questionnaires, sampling and analyzing returns. Yet it is always a good deal more than that, for it is commonly infused with ideologically resonant assumptions about what the social world is, who the sociologist is, and what the nature of the relation between them is. (Gouldner, 1971, pp. 50–1)

In these circumstances, some clarification is required on terminology so as to avoid the kind of ambiguity that exists in the Suffolk document. In particular, some distinction needs to be made between general methodology, research strategy or research procedure, and research techniques. These terms have been defined by Burgess and Bulmer (1981, p. 478) as follows:

> *General methodology* denotes the systematic and logical study of the general principles guiding the inquiry. This is distinct from 'research methods' used in empirical inquiry, which may be subdivided. *Research strategy* or research procedure refers to the way in which one particular empirical study is designed and carried out. *Research technique* refers to a specific fact finding manipulative operation used to yield social data.

Within the Suffolk document, it is research techniques that are considered for use in appraisal; especially qualitative methods such as interviews and observation. As many methodologists and educational evaluators have indicated, such methods put the investigation (or in this case the appraiser) at the centre of the stage as these approaches demand that some consideration be given to the relationships involved between all those in the setting (cf. Burgess, 1982, 1984a, b, 1985c; Eisner, 1985).

Yet, in the account from the Suffolk team relatively little attention is given to the appraiser who will use observation and interview 'skills' to conduct the appraisal. Indeed, in all the documentation available we are only told that appraisers will be drawn from senior and middle management in the schools. Yet, if senior and middle management are involved in the appraisal of teachers this will reproduce the hierarchy already in existence in schools. Furthermore, if appraisers are drawn from these groups, questions of power and authority are clearly involved together with the value perspective used and the ways in which material collected in teacher appraisal may be reported and disseminated. The evidence that is currently available on teacher job interviews and shortlisting meetings, where similar sets of evidence are used by members of senior management in schools and LEAs, would lead us to have relatively little confidence in the same personnel being involved in appraisal based on hierarchical relationships, as it appears they are far from skilled when using 'evidence' to evaluate teachers (cf. Morgan *et al.*, 1983; Burgess, 1986a, b).

Several issues are involved here. First, there is the question of *who* conducts the appraisal. If we turn to statistical evidence on senior and middle management in primary and secondary schools, we can begin to see the problem (DES, 1983). In 1983, 77% of primary teachers were women but only 7.3% were heads. Indeed, men hold a greater proportion of middle and senior management posts from scale 3 upwards relative to their numbers. Similarly, in secondary schools in 1983, men were more likely to hold senior posts. Although women constituted 45% of the work force only 0.7% of women teachers were heads. Automatically this raises questions about gender and gender relations in the context of teacher appraisal. It appears that if senior and middle management are to conduct appraisal this will reproduce the male-dominated perspective that currently exists in schools. Furthermore, the concepts and categories that are used might well reflect the male world of the appraiser.

Yet there is another dimension here in terms of the perspective that is used. If, as has been suggested by HMI (HMSO, 1985b) that appraisal needs to be considered in relation to the conditions that influence teachers' work, it would seem unlikely that a headteacher will view a teacher's performance in relation to his or her inadequate management. For example, the DES (HMSO, 1985c) provide an illustration of a secondary school where appraisal took place but where appraisal of senior management was not involved:

> the head asked staff to complete a proforma with the title *Evaluation of senior management areas of responsibility*. This was regarded by the staff as an unsatisfactory document, in that it was concerned with 'areas of responsibility' and not with the performance of individuals. (HMSO,1985c, pp. 26–7)

In a similar way it would seem improbable than an LEA will establish criteria in relation to their own under-resourcing of individual schools. While HMI appear aware of the relative importance of social context in relation to appraisal it would seem that little thought has been given to the ways in which this will influence the perspective from which teacher appraisal is conducted or for that matter the practicalities of appraisal.

If we consider the appraisal interview it is important to ponder on the quality of the information that will be obtained. Clearly, much will depend upon the relationship between appraiser and appraised. However, if the individual who conducts the appraisal is part of the senior management team one might question the status of the 'confidentiality' of the appraisal interview. How, we might ask, will the information be used? If the information is to be used in the deployment and redeployment of teachers then it would seem unlikely that valid responses will be obtained from the teachers who are appraised. Some headteachers are aware of this problem. For example, Threadgold (1984) indicates that there is little formal, overt assessment, because teachers' superiors within and beyond the school constantly make judgements based on day to day observations and comments from colleagues – an approach that is far from systematic or reliable (cf. Burgess, 1986a, b). Here, much has been written by ethnographers and by observers who use systematic classroom observation schedules on the problems of observing in classrooms (cf. Spindler, 1982; Burgess, 1985a; Croll, 1986). Yet this is a literature that is absent from the Suffolk document. Indeed, the difficulties associated with classroom observation are reduced to a very simple level:

> Because many teacher express unease about this [classroom observation], feeling that observers are an intrusion in the classroom, their very presence changing the situation, and because any one lesson may not typify the generality, observational data must be gathered with particular care and on more than one occasion. (Graham, 1985, p. 5)

Such a statement is far too brief and fails to come to terms with the complexity of such issues as the unit of data collection, sampling in terms of time, people and events, the relationship between data collection and data analysis and the relationship between the observer and the observed. Indeed, there appears to be no account taken of the role of the appraiser to the problems that are posed, to the meanings that are attributed to social situations, or to the historical context in which classroom events may be located (for further discussion, see Burgess, 1984a; Eisner, 1985). In short, the discussion overlooks the basic methodological problems associated with the use of qualitative strategies in the conduct of educational research and evaluation, but this is hardly surprising since the computer-based literature search used the following key words: 'staff/teacher', 'review', 'assessment', 'appraisal' and 'evaluation'. In this sense, neither 'methodology' nor 'qualitative research' nor 'ethnography' was on the research agenda. Certainly, if the Suffolk team had followed this line of enquiry they would have quickly discovered that much work has been done on the use of qualitative strategies of investigation in schools and classrooms. Accordingly, much of the literature that was consulted came from commerce and industry, despite the fact that over a decade ago Taylor (1976) had warned of the dangers of importing industrial approaches into the study of schools and classrooms where roles and relationships are of a different order. Nevertheless, while Taylor's position has been defended by some researchers such as Hartley and Broadfoot (1988) and Stones (1986), others such as Threadgold (1984) and

Nuttall (1986) have argued that we have much to learn in education from the work that has been done on appraisal by industry and commerce. An assessment of the evidence provided would lead me to conclude that industry and commerce have made many of the methodological errors identified in the Suffolk report. In the circumstances, it would appear that educational appraisal should take a different approach.

An alternative approach

Clearly, there appear to be many basic flaws in the approach that is being advocated by the DES and by the Graham Report. Many of the difficulties stem from importing the male-dominated hierarchical power structure that is currently in existence in schools into the system of teacher appraisal. In such situations, power relations become important to the context of appraisal.

An alternative model for conducting appraisal might therefore be a colleagial system where colleagues in an institution (but from different status positions) might begin to examine their own practice. This approach has been advocated in relation to pastoral care (Burgess, 1985b), where heads of house or year might use qualitative strategies to research their own practice. Here, colleagues work together not only on the content but also on the form of the investigation. Furthermore, the approach is research-based in the manner advocated by Stenhouse (1975), where the teacher is put in the position of critical practitioner.

A further development involves collaboration between groups of teachers and individuals who are external to an institution where again a methodology is devised in relation to the problem in hand. Indeed, Cope and Gray (1979) have illustrated how quantitative techniques can be used by teacher groups to examine their own practice, while Burgess and Burgess (1985) have shown how different qualitative approaches may be used by teachers to examine classroom experiences. Here, the activities are research-based, where the objective is to develop a knowledge base so that teachers may evaluate their own teaching experiences with a view to developing and extending current practice.

Within both these models are a series of alternative conceptions to the current discussion of teacher appraisal. They are:

- non-hierarchical, as they assume a coming together of teachers who hold different statuses within schools – a learning process among colleagues;
- non-judgemental, as they are not intended to generate knowledge that might be used against a teacher;
- research-based, whereby groups of teachers work together to generate knowledge about teaching/learning experiences in schools (cf. Stones, 1986).

As such these characteristics suggest a move towards a democratic mode of teacher-based work where:

1 A problem is clearly specified.
2 A methodology is devised relative to the problem that is posed. It is not

automatically assumed that a particular technique will always be used; rather it is essential to consider those approaches that will be best equipped to deliver data that are reliable and valid.

3 The data that are generated are the property of the teachers and *not* some senior management team internal or external to the school.

4 Control over the dissemination and use of the data lies with those teachers and their collaborators who engage in the collection and analysis of the information that is generated.

All of this discussion suggests that teachers need to be given an opportunity to acquire the relevant methodological knowledge to conduct such work. The report by Graham and his colleagues suggests that in the USA this can be done within 3 days, yet the methodological naivete displayed in his report would lead me to cast doubt on this suggestion. Indeed, I would share the view of the authors of *Quality in Schools* (HMSO, 1985c), when they state that unless some training is provided in techniques of self appraisal, 'the assessment of classroom practice may be limited to checking the teachers' perceptions against those of the head' (HMSO, 1985c, p. 17).

In providing training for self-appraisal I would advocate a collaborative mode of research and evaluation concerned with teaching and learning, as this would facilitate an exploration of the methodological issues and problems that are central to classroom observation alongside a deeper analysis of teaching and learning (cf. Stones, 1986). These issues have to be resolved, otherwise teachers will have a system forced upon them which is far from systematic, objective and reliable. The current proposals lack depth of vision because the appraisal systems which are advocated often use one approach and are from one perspective – perhaps it is at this point we should leave the last word to Eisner, who in a timely warning states: 'Looking through one eye never did provide much depth of field' (Eisner, 1985, p. 199).

Postscript: Some light or more gloom?

Since this chapter was submitted for publication in the summer of 1986, there have been further commentaries on teacher appraisal (cf. Hartley and Broadfoot, 1988) and reports from pilot schemes that have taken place in local authorities and in some schools (e.g. see Bunnell, 1987; Blackburn, 1986). In addition, further work has been reported from the Suffolk team (Graham, 1987). The second Suffolk document, like the first, is not noted for its scholarly style. This time there appears no agreement on the title of the report as it is shown as *In the Light of Torches – Teacher Appraisal: A Further Study* on the cover, but becomes *Teacher Appraisal: Some Further Studies* on the title page. In addition, there is no evidence of wide reading and systematic research as the bibliography contains very few items (and hardly any that are directly related to appraisal in the UK or overseas).

The work in this second report was funded by a grant from the Department of

Education and Science for two purposes: first, to conduct courses and conferences in local authorities who were preparing for the introduction of formal appraisal systems and, secondly:

> to investigate in pragmatic and practical terms some topics not covered in 'Torches' where our work might assist those charged with establishing a national scheme, and with the pilot projects which are envisaged. (Graham, 1987, p. 4)

In this study, this task is covered through discussions of headteacher appraisal, classroom observation, training for appraisal, the cost of appraisal and some notes on a study visit to California. At first glance this work seems to have some potential, but close inspection reveals that little 'light' is cast on detailed questions of methodology that need to be addressed in any appraisal scheme.

In common with the first report, this material contains numerous assumptions about the units of study and the strategies to be adopted in studying them. In particular, terms like 'good teachers' and 'good teaching' continue to be used without careful specification. Indeed, we are told: 'All concerned [with visiting teachers in their classrooms] recognise good teachers and know what they should be achieving' (Graham, 1987, p. 15). The only problem appears to be that they 'lack a common set of guidelines, principles or criteria for appraisal' (p. 15). Furthermore, it is maintained that given the fact that student teachers are passed or failed it has been accepted by teachers that 'observers know what good teaching is and recognise it when they see it' (p. 15). Such statements are no more than assertions by the Suffolk team.

Such a stance prefaces discussions of styles of appraisal. At least in this report some account is given of the context of appraisal (at least as far as headteachers are concerned) and a whole chapter is devoted to classroom observation. However, there is little evidence of any understanding of this work. There is no discussion of the different styles of classroom observation. Instead, the reader is plunged straight into a discussion of observation checklists but with none of the scholarly detail provided by Croll (1986). Indeed, all the examples provided are presented without reference to their source and appear simplistic and crude. They are not good examples that will deliver information that is reliable and valid. For instance, a UK checklist is provided that can be used to analyse the work of newly qualified teachers in terms of it being 'good', 'adequate' or 'in need of improvement', yet no criteria are given to indicate the qualities associated with each term. Similarly, the section that deals with appraisal interviewing draws on none of the social science literature on strategies and styles of interviewing, a topic that has been the subject of much discussion among educational researchers in recent years (cf. Stenhouse, 1984; Burgess, 1984a; Measor, 1985; Powney and Watts, 1987). Here, the danger exists that those engaged in research on appraisal will reinvent the wheel. A clear example exists in this report when there is a discussion of models of headteacher appraisal which includes 'a triangle' approach using three headteachers (Graham, 1987, p. 7). Here, brief attention (in just over three lines) is drawn to the way in which different kinds of information can be used – a gloss on the topic of triangulation that has been explored in much detail by social and educational researchers (cf. Denzin, 1970; Burgess, 1984a).

The second report from the Suffolk team provides little systematic work on methods of appraisal. Indeed, as Hartley and Broadfoot (1988) have indicated, there is a need to recognize the difficulty of methods of assessing teacher performance, establishing variables on the teaching process and measuring them, handling subjectivity in the appraisal process, and so on. Research, therefore, needs to be conducted on the difficulties involved in handling these issues in appraisal systems. Certainly, there is much scope for systematic studies to be conducted in schools, in higher education and in establishments that conduct appraisal in non-educational settings.

References

Blackburn, K. (1986). Appraising teachers. In M. Marland (eds.), *School Management Skills*. London: Heinemann.

Borich, G.D. (1977). *The Appraisal of Teaching: Concepts and Process*. London: Routledge and Kegan Paul.

Bunnell, S. (1987). *Teacher Appraisal in Practice*. London: Heinemann.

Burgess, H. and Burgess, R.G. (1985). *Collaborative Research and the Curriculum*. Paper prepared for Sociology and the Teacher conference at St. Hilda's College, Oxford.

Burgess, R.G, (ed.) (1982). *Field Research: A Sourcebook and Field Manual*. London: Allen and Unwin.

Burgess, R.G. (1984a). *In the Field: An Introduction to Field Research*. London: Allen and Unwin.

Burgess, R.G. (ed.) (1984b). *The Research Process in Educational Settings: Ten Case Studies*. Lewes: Falmer Press.

Burgess, R.G. (ed.) (1985a). *Strategies of Educational Research: Qualitative Methods*. Lewes: Falmer Press.

Burgess, R.G. (1985b). Documenting pastoral care: strategies for teachers and researchers. In P. Lang and M. Marland (eds), *New Directions in Pastoral Care*, pp. 187–98. Oxford: Basil Blackwell.

Burgess, R.G. (ed.) (1985c). *Issues in Educational Research: Qualitative Methods*. Lewes: Falmer Press.

Burgess, R.G. (1986a). *Points and Posts: Teacher Careers in a Comprehensive School*. Paper prepared for Comprehensive Schooling Conference, King's College, University of London, February.

Burgess, R.G. (1986b). *Going for a Job: The Ethnography of Teacher Job Interviews*. Paper prepared for BERA Annual Conference, University of Bristol, September.

Burgess, R.G. and Bulmer, M. (1981). Research methodology teaching: trends and developments. *Sociology*, **15**(4), 477–89.

Cope, E. and Gray, J. (1979). Teachers as researchers: some experience of an alternative paradigm. *British Educational Research Journal*, **5**(2), 237–51.

Croll, P. (1986). *Systematic Classroom Observation*. Lewes: Falmer Press.

Department of Education and Science (1983). *Statistics of Teachers in Service in England and Wales*. London: HMSO.

Denzin, N. (1970). *The Research Act*. Chicago: Aldine.

Eisner, E. (1985). *The Art of Educational Evaluation: A Personal View*. Lewes: Falmer Press.

Elliott, G. (1980). *Self Evaluation and the Teacher*. Hull: University of Hull/Schools Council.

Gouldner, A. (1971). *The Coming Crisis of Western Sociology*. London: Heinemann.

Grace, G. (1985). Judging teachers: the social and political contexts of teacher evaluation. *British Journal of Sociology of Education,* **6**(1), 3–16.

Graham, D.G. (1985). *Those Having Torches... Teacher Appraisal: A Study*. Ipswich: Suffolk Education Department.

Graham, D.G. (1987). *In the Light of Torches: Teacher Appraisal: A Further Study* (or *Teacher Appraisal: Some Further Studies)*. London: The Industrial Society.

Hartley, L. and Broadfoot, P. (1988). Assessing teacher performance. *Journal of Education Policy,* **3**(1), 39–50.

HMSO (1983). *Teaching Quality,* Cmnd 8836. London: HMSO.

HMSO (1985a). *Better Schools,* Cmnd 9469. London: HMSO.

HMSO (1985b). *Education Observed 3: Good Teachers. A Paper by HM Inspectorate*. London: HMSO.

HMSO (1985c). *Quality in Schools: Evaluation and Appraisal*. London: HMSO.

Martin, D. (1980). Systematic performance appraisal for schools. *Secondary Education Journal,* **10**(2), 18–19.

Measor, L. (1985). Interviewing: a strategy in qualitative research. In R.G. Burgess (ed.), *Strategies of Educational Research: Qualitative Methods,* pp. 55–77. Lewes: Falmer Press.

Morgan, C., Hall, V. and McKay, H. (1983). *The Selection of Secondary Heads*. Milton Keynes: Open University Press.

Nuttall, D.L. (1986). What can we learn from research on teaching and appraisal? In *Appraising Appraisal,* pp. 20–8. Birmingham: BERA.

Powney, J. and Watts, M. (1987). *Interviewing in Educational Research*. London: Routledge and Kegan Paul.

Spindler, G. (ed.) (1982). *Doing the Ethnography of Schooling: Educational Anthropology in Action*. New York: Holt, Rinehart and Winston.

Stenhouse, L. (1975). *An Introduction to Curriculum Research and Development*. London: Heinemann.

Stenhouse, L. (1984). Library access, library use and user education in academic sixth forms: an autobiographical account. In R.G. Burgess (ed.), *The Research Process in Educational Settings: Ten Case Studies,* pp. 211–33. Lewes: Falmer Press.

Stones, E. (1986). Colleagial appraisal for the enhancement of pupil learning. In *Appraising Appraisal,* pp. 39–54. Birmingham: BERA.

Taylor, W. (1976). The head as manager. In R.S. Peters (ed.) *The Role of the Head,* pp. 37–49. London: Routledge and Kegan Paul.

Threadgold, M. (1984). Professional appraisal as a factor in school evaluation. Unpublished paper, School of Education, University of Birmingham.

Wilby, P. (1986). Teacher appraisal. *Journal of Education Policy,* **1**(1), 63–72.

4
Teacher appraisal, collaborative research and teacher consortia

Clem Adelman

Administrative schemes to appraise the quality, standard and efficiency of teachers' work have ebbed and flowed in England and Wales and the USA. In England and Wales under the Revised Code of 1862, the efficiency of teachers in elementary schools was measured by the pupils' results in annual tests. The reward was payment over the minimum for the particular subject in which the teachers had been appraised by pupil test scores. Teaching to the test and narrow curriculum were two of the consequences (Sutherland, 1973). Though some objected, teachers felt they had no initiative to go beyond the knowledge and skills rewarded through 'payment by results'. Schools, especially in im- poverished areas, received fewer rewards; they found it well nigh impossible to improve their results. By 1890 the Code was on the wane, and was abolished (or put into cold storage!) as part of the 1902 Education Act.

In the USA Boyce (1915) and Bobbit (1913) claimed that they could scien- tifically appraise teacher effectiveness, Boyce by observing and measuring teacher behaviour in the classroom, and Bobbitt by applying the time and motion studies of the founder of scientific management, (F. W. Taylor, 1911; see also Callahan, 1962; Travers, 1983). A glance at apparently declining test scores has provided some with sufficient excuse to accuse teachers of neglecting reading, spelling and mathematics: the competence as well as the efficiency of teachers has thus been questioned from Rice (1903) in the USA to Prime Minister Callaghan (1976) and Cox and Marks (1984) in the UK.

Teachers and teacher trainers in England and Wales are for the most part still confident that they are 'able to spot a good teacher', but do not systematically make explicit the criteria of 'good' or indeed 'bad' teaching (Adelman, 1988). This lack of serious interest in pedagogy in England as compared to the USA and Scotland has been commented on by Simon (1981) and Stenhouse (1975). Some attempts have been made to collaborate with teachers to help make explicit their pedagogic practice (Ford Teaching Project: Elliott and Adelman, 1975), and in the USA studies of the tacit assumptions of instructional pedagogy are in process (see Erickson *et al.*, 1984; Lampert, 1984).

The National Union of Teachers (NUT) issued its initial proposals on appraisal in *A Fair Way Forward* in 1981. In this document the NUT expressed the view that to use the same performance indicators for all schools would be invalid and unfair as each school has particular social and educational circumstances. The quality of the 'input' and 'output' of schools cannot be equated to that of an industrial process with inanimate materials (read pupils), using standard machines (read teachers). While the NUT placed the complexities of teaching at the centre of their memorandum, in 1984 the Secretary of State placed punctuality and dress as priorities one and two! This signifies the conceptual chasm between the Secretary of State's conception of teaching and that of the profession's largest union. However, the past and present record of the NUT would seem to favour a hierarchical model of teacher appraisal rather than one based on judgements by peers. In an effort to inform the debate on appraisal, the DES funded a study by Suffolk advisers and teachers (Graham, 1985) of teacher appraisal. In a Cook's tour of the USA and Europe, models of staff appraisal taken from industry and the civil service as well as teaching were considered. The report adds little to previous knowledge. Indeed, there is an alarming lack of context and history of conflicting interest in the account of the USA – the country with most experience of appraisal. In part this reflects the hurry with which the study had to be completed and partly the lack of background knowledge of advisers, including the LEA advisers commissioned to complete this study.

But it is worth noting that no national or local appraisal initiated by administrators has been based upon criteria from teachers' systematic research into their own pedagogic practices. Instead, adaptations of researchers' observations schedules and items from the 'findings' of experiments on learning are preferred by administrators. Using these as the means, administrators claim objectivity and fairness in application and analysis.

Appraisal instruments

However, close comparison of items from observation schedules reveals bias, not only in what is looked at but what is absent. Given the claims of objectivity for appraisal instruments, are they valid (do they target what they claim) and are they consistent in their target accuracy (are they reliable)? Reviews of the past 60 years of 'process–product' studies of teaching (Travers, 1983; Tom, 1984; Dunkin and Biddle, 1974) show meagre returns for considerable expenditure. What has been detected is that teaching that attends to the set task, giving students the opportunity to learn what is later tested, is weakly correlated to learning achievements (Rosenshine, 1979). Studies to match student learning 'characteristics' to the 'style' of teaching have not arrived at any substantive conclusions (Tobias, 1982). That the reviewers have found that the extent of teachers' knowledge of the topic being taught is not correlated to learning outcomes should not be surprising, as learning has but a contingent rather than a causal relationship to teaching (Borich, 1977). Tom (1984) summarizes the research on teacher effectiveness:

> So far no powerful concepts have emerged out of the data. All we have are some low-level empirical claims such as direct instruction or academic learning time, which are masquerading as conceptual models. The hope that the midpoint between poles of accuracy and generality might yield the advantages of each end point has been dashed by the conceptual simplicity and the technical orientation of the existing models.

Observation schedules were not devised for appraisal purposes but for research on teaching. However, competency-based teacher education and microteaching observation schedules have been adapted and devised for appraisal. Well known are the Stanford and those reviewed by Gage and Giaconia (1981). There is considerable doubt as to whether 'skills' practised, and subsequently tested by these appraisal schedules, transfer to the real classroom (McIntyre, 1980; Elliott and Labbett, 1974).

The compilation, administration and analysis of such schemes in schools is costly of time and money. If the scheme can be shown to be unreliable then its worth to the administrator, teacher and the taxpayer is in question. Questions to ask the administrators who commission such schedules might include the following: what correspondence is there between one observer's ratings and that of another at the same teaching events, and how are the observers trained? Further enquiries can then be made about the validity of particular items (What did that item seek? How does it relate to other items?). Given unsatisfactory replies, teachers may wish to suggest that the items included in the schedule be negotiated with them on the grounds of their professional knowledge of teaching. If, however, an appraisal scheme is sacrosanct, then cooperation from the teachers must be in doubt.

The reader will have recognized by now that I am writing about appraisal schemes used as a means to enforce predefined (but not necessarily publicly explicit) standards of teaching in the interests of administrative control. The values and purposes manifested through such control reflect the checks and balances of competing interest groups. Teacher promotion, salary increases, probation, retraining, even dismissal, can arise from the prosecution of such appraisal schemes and yet the schemes may be unreliable and invalid!.

Two examples of teacher appraisal schemes in practice serve to illustrate many of the problems mentioned above. In Michigan pupil achievement scores were to serve as the indicators of teacher effectiveness. In Oregon a far more complex scheme of cost-effective accounting for the school system was piloted. In neither State were teachers consulted prior to the introduction of these schemes.

In 1973 the State of Michigan issued details of a plan for administering speedily developed objective referenced tests to all fourth- and seventh-grade students in the State. On the basis of achievement in test scores, State money would be awarded to schools. Test scores were already published in local newspapers. Criticisms of the plan came from the Michigan teachers and from the National Education Association who commissioned an independent evaluation of its worth. The evaluation (House *et al.*, 1974) strongly criticized the way State goals were derived, the lack of participation by teachers and the unreliability of the tests and their various sources of invalidity. I quote House (1980):

> The Michigan authorities claimed that the 23 objectives in reading and 35 objectives in maths at the fourth grade level represented both a statewide consensus of opinion about what should be taught and minimal performance that every child in Michigan should be able to achieve at that grade level. The evaluators contended the objectives were neither consensual nor minimal, given their process of derivation. The specially constructed objectives tests based on these objectives were not adequately validated or field tested. Teachers were only minimally involved in the development of both.
>
> Furthermore teachers and schools received little or no help in implementing the tests and total system. The evaluators labelled the tying of funding to individual student test scores as 'whimsical' at best. The publication of such scores by schools has caused dismay and consternation throughout the state. Finally, the accountability system risked substituting state objectives and curricular for local ones, and posed the threat of the teacher teaching to the tests rather than to the child. The evaluation report concluded by making several specific suggestions as to how some of these defects might be remedied.

In 1969 the South Lane School District (Oregon) was selected as the site for a pilot project of checks in the efficiency and economy of teaching in the District. This was part of a more extensive check on the efficiency of the school system as a whole. The initiative and funding for this project had come from Federal Government and private organizations in cooperation with the University of Oregon and the School District authorities.

South Lane District had 3500 pupils in grades 1–12. Its size and proximity to the university made it an ideal site for the project. On returning from the summer vacation the South Lane teachers were informed they were involved in the pilot study. The superintendent (district education officer) of schools had made the decision, subsequently telling the teachers that it was a cooperative project. He then arranged many meetings upon which he subsequently modified the appraisal procedures.

In 1973 an independent evaluation of the project (Wolcott, 1977) traced the teachers' part in and their current objections to the project. Wolcott reports that 'The developers' view was that in spite of their resistance to the plan, teachers could eventually perceive its benefits to them.' The developers claimed that the plan provided teachers with data that would show what changes were needed in their curriculum and teaching. Indeed, some teachers agreed that the project's evaluation materials were useful, but almost all objected to the lack of consultation in the first place.

In 1973 the project expanded to involve additional school districts without sufficient evaluation of the strengths and weaknesses in the pilot longitudinal study. Compared to the Michigan plan, Oregon tried to examine most aspects of the school system. Appraisal of schools and teachers was to be made, but using a wide range of data. The values and purposes of this technocratic scheme clashed with those teachers. The scheme was introduced without prior consultation with the teachers, and its complexity of operation did not help individual teachers to locate their contribution to schooling in their district. Wolcott (1977) concludes:

> I think that teachers and technocrats agree in principle that there is always room for improvement in education; possibly both groups recognize that teaching requires such energy that major changes are unlikely to be initiated by teachers. But I think that teachers question why change must be introduced with such magnitude or with such frequency and why there appears to be so little regard for what they have accomplished. Teachers are particularly suspicious of adamant insistence on the status quo. Long-time teachers have experienced wave after wave of change attempts and have developed a large repertoire for coping with the relentless tides of change.

Where were the teachers' own professional judgements of self and peers, their criteria, valid or not, in all this?

In England and Wales, since Callaghan's (1976) Ruskin College speech, the Department of Education and Science has developed plans to appraise the effectiveness of teachers. Only since the advent of the premise that teachers can identify their 'needs' for the purposes of participation in TRIST and records of achievement has criteria of appraisal from work of the self-evaluating teacher been considered, rather than ignored, by DES and most LEAs. But the DES has not made explicit connections between these initiatives and the issue of appraisal. There is no sign that greater teacher autonomy will be allowed to result from the teacher's identification of needs, or of attainment criteria identified by teacher research. The key question is, who commands the definition of criteria, and the administration of appraisal? As in the USA the law courts will probably become the arena for many disputes. Individual teachers are on the receiving end of appraisal and in an appeal might need evidence of their competence, other than examination or test results. They turn to colleagues, who for the most part have never seen them teaching. What evidence would individual teachers draw on to challenge lack of promotion, tenure or even dismissal?

Teacher consortia

I think that reliable and valid evidence on the quality of teaching might be gathered by consortia of 30 or so teachers representing different types of schools and different subjects, collaborating in the long term. The consortia would be comprised of professional tutors, advisory teachers, senior and junior staff of schools. Members of the consortia would research their own teaching and management. The consortia would plan its research to focus on particular activities, such as teaching for pupil understanding, pupil profiling, and teacher–pupil social relationships. Staff development through self-evaluation would be the overall aim. After a minimum of 3 years, peer judgements of consortia members might be made regarding the overall development of individuals. The criteria upon which these judgements were made would be explicit and agreed on prior to the peer judgements. Upon these, teacher promotion and suitability for another type of post could be made. The grounds and criteria for satisfactory probation and dismissal could be decided through the action-research and deliberations of the consortia.

Those members of the consortia that had applied themselves to the tasks thoroughly and showed reflective sensibilities in their writing and discussion would be encouraged to pursue their work to help develop other consortia in the LEAs. Instead of normative appraisal schedules, insensitive to contexts of teaching and to change, the consortia's identification of issues from its action-research, discussion and reports would maintain and enhance professional standards of teaching. Teachers' consortia work and teachers' salary structures would have to reflect collaborative enquiry rather than hierarchical dictates.

The work of the teacher consortia would be 'moderated' by accreditation associations made up of members of higher education institutions, Examination Boards, HMI and local Inspectors. The aim of such moderation leading to accreditation would be to ensure that the standards demanded by each consortia were comparable, naturally, and in pursuit of 'improvement' rather than static or moribund.

Professional council

For this form of peer appraisal and accreditation to have credibility and influence requires the formation of a Professional Council on Teaching, comprised of teachers, teacher educators, LEAs and HMI representatives to grant licences to teach. All teachers irrespective of type of school would require a licence to practise. The Council would receive reports from accreditation associations upon the moderation of teacher consortia. The teachers' unions would continue to negotiate conditions of service and salary structure. Should the teachers' unions amalgamate (as in Scotland) in order to counter the present threat of central government control (of curriculum and pedagogy as well as resources), then the functions of the proposed Council and those of the unions would, in time, merge. However, the Teachers' Council in Scotland, which does not include accreditation through peer evaluation in its work, has not met the expectations of the majority of teachers. It has become dominated by Principals of Colleges of Education and has lost the support of the majority of the schoolteachers (Humes, 1986).

While the Secretary of State and the DES persisted in requiring agreement to national appraisal before negotiation of salaries and salary structure with the teachers' unions, the teachers are blocked from developing their own scheme for appraisal, or indeed from pilot studies. Meanwhile, in many LEAs, advisers are being pressed to plan and even carry out teacher appraisal using criteria that are *ad hoc* in the ways suggested above. National appraisal is now written into the conditions of employment of teachers in England and Wales.

Ironically, teachers have been asked to identify their criteria for the assessment of pupils in the GCSE examinations and to identify their in-service needs for TRIST/TVEI (Technical and Vocational Education Initiative Related In-service Training) – foreshadowing the customer–contractor in-service relationship post-1987. A glimmer of recognition by the DES and LEAs of teacher professional autonomy is evident in these latter developments, recognition that should be extended to peer appraisal accreditation and to the establishment of a Teachers' Professional Council. Whatever the future of appraisal, the tasks of policy and planning within larger schools will be considerably enhanced by the strengths and weaknesses revealed through appraisal – most fairly and validly conducted by an accredited consortium of teachers.

References

Adelman, C. (1988). *Looking at Teaching*. EP228. Milton Keynes: Open University.
Bobbitt, F. (1913). *The Supervision of City Schools: Some General Principles of Management Applied to the Problems of City School Systems*. Bloomington, Ill.: 12th Yearbook of National Society for the Study of Education.
Borich, G. (1977). *The Appraisal of Teaching*. Reading, Mass.: Addison-Wesley.
Boyce, A.C. (1915). *Methods of Measuring Teachers' Efficiency*. Chicago: University of Chicago Press.
Callahan, R. (1962). *Education and the Cult of Efficiency*. Chicago: University of Chicago Press.
Cox, C. and Marks, J. (1984). Educational attainment in secondary schools. *Oxford Review of Education*, **10** (1), 7–31.
Dunkin, M. and Biddle, B. (1974). *The Study of Teaching*. New York: Holt, Rinehart and Winston.
Elliott, J. and Labbett, B. (1974). *Teaching, Research and Teacher Education: Some Comments on Competency Based Teacher Education*. University of East Anglia: CARE, mimeo.
Elliot, J. and Adelman, C., *et al* (1975). *Ford Teaching Project*. University of East Anglia: CARE.
Erickson, F., Campbell, D. and Navarro, R. (1984). *Teachers' Conceptual Change in Practice*. Institute for Research in Teaching, Michigan State. Michigan State University mimeo.
Gage, N.L. and Giaconia, R. (1981). Teaching practices and student achievement: Causal connections. *New York University Education Quarterly*, **12**, 2–9.
Graham, D.G. (1985). *Those Having Torches . . . Teacher Appraisal: A Study*. Ipswich: Suffolk Education Department.
HMI (1985). *Quality in Schools: Evaluation and Appraisal*. London: HMSO.
House, E. (1980). Accountability in the USA. In A. Finch and P. Scrimshaw (eds), *Standards, Schooling and Education*, pp. 663–9. London: Hodder and Stoughton.
House, E., Rivers, W. and Shufflebeam, D. (1974). An assessment of the Michigan accountability system. *Phi Delta Kappa*, **55**(June).

Humes, W. (1986). *The Leadership Class in Scottish Education.* Edinburgh: Edinburgh University Press.

Lampert, M. (1984). *How Do Teachers Manage to Teach? Perspectives on Problems in Practice.* Michigan State University, Institute for Research in Teaching, mimeo.

McIntyre, D. (1980). The contribution of research to quality in teacher education. In E. Hoyle and J. Megarry (eds), *Professional Development of Teachers: World Yearbook of Education,* pp. 293–307. London: Kogan Page.

National Union of Teachers (1981). *A Fair Way Forward.* London: NUT.

Rice, J. (1903). *The Public School System of the United States.* New York: Century.

Rosenshine, B. (1979). Content, time and direct instruction. In P.L. Peterson and H.J. Walberg (eds), *Research on Teaching,* Berkeley, Calif.: McCutchan.

Simon, B. (1981). Why no pedagogy in England. In B. Simon and W. Taylor (eds), *Education in the Eighties.* London: Batsford Academic and Educational.

Stenhouse, L. (1975). *An Introduction to Curriculum Development and Research.* London: Heinemann.

Sutherland, G. (1973). *Policy Making in Elementary Education.* Oxford: Oxford University Press.

Taylor, F. (1911). *The Principles of Scientific Management.* New York: Harper.

Tobias, S. (1982). When do instructional methods make a difference? *Educational Researcher,* **11**, 4–9.

Tom, A. (1984). *Teaching as a Moral Craft.* New York: Longman.

Travers, R. (1983). *How Research Has Changed American Schools.* Kalamazoo, Mich.: Mythos Press.

Wolcott, H. (1977). *Teachers versus Technocrats.* University of Oregon: Center for Educational Policy and Management.

5
Problems in teacher appraisal: an action-research solution?

Richard Winter

Introduction: contradictions in teacher appraisal

The DES has responded to criticisms of its proposals concerning teacher appraisal with some degree of self-righteousness:

> In the course of their daily work, teachers appraise their pupils continuously. . . . Yet by comparison with other professions, teachers have been slow to accept the need to appraise each other and themselves. . . . It would be strange if a profession which is dedicated to drawing out the full potential of the young decided to neglect this means of developing both the individual members and the collective potential of the profession. (Hancock, 1985, paras 21–2)

Clearly, Hancock, Permanent Secretary at the DES, thinks there is a contradiction here. But what, where, and whose is it? Keith Joseph (then Secretary of State for Education), referring to what he suggested was the 'fundamental quality' required by teacher appraisal, reminded teachers that 'It takes moral courage to admit that you can do better . . . [to] face up to our weaknesses and seek others' guidance and help in overcoming them' (Joseph, 1986, p. 10). Is 'moral courage' really the issue between the Secretary of State and the teaching profession? Presumably not; but if not, what is?

To begin answering these questions, let us look at the different forms of benefit which the DES expects to result from a teacher appraisal scheme. First:

> [It would] help all teachers realise their full professional potential by providing them with better job satisfaction, more appropriate in-service training, and better planned career development. (Joseph, 1985, para. 44)

That this is a key passage is suggested by the fact that he repeated it in a later speech (Joseph, 1986, p. 9), as did his junior minister Angela Rumbold (1986, p. 4). Rumbold (1986, p. 7) continued:

> We want to encourage teachers and help them to work to the best of their ability, to review their job, what they do and how to do it better, to build on their strengths.

In a similar vein, Hancock suggests that appraisal aims 'to keep alive [teachers'] sense of purpose and zest for the job' (Hancock, 1985, para. 22).

Why, then, the opposition from the teacher unions, which the DES bemoans? The answer is not hard to find. Another aim of a teacher appraisal system will be to provide 'employers' with 'accurate knowledge of each teacher's performance' as part of a set of arrangements for 'effective staff management' (Hancock, 1985, paras 4 and 6). 'Staff management' here means not only decisions concerning appropriate INSET and career development, but also concerning the 'deploy-ment' of teachers (ACAS, 1986, para. 3) and the response to teachers 'experienc-ing performance difficulty'. In this context 'appraisal records' would provide 'relevant information' for 'disciplinary procedures' (ACAS, 1986, para. 3, v).

Already then we can see a profound ambivalence built in to the aims of the proposed appraisal scheme. The DES-commissioned Suffolk report spells it out:

> Clearly, the appraisal process must assist teachers in their career development and can help them acquire the skills and experience to further their aspirations . . . (but) . . . The scheme must enable teachers whose performance falls below par to be identified so that steps can be taken by the school and LEA to rectify the situation and, exceptionally, to terminate employment. (Graham, 1985, p. 4)

The opening quotations from Hancock and Joseph can thus be seen – at best – one-sided. The moral qualities needed to admit to one's own shortcomings are of a different order from those involved in a response to someone else's decision that one's performance is below par. And teachers know that while their appraisals of learners may indeed be part of 'drawing out full potential', they may also be the documentary justification of 'failure'. In other words, there is a potential threat within the appraisal process proposed, namely the threat contained within the central contradiction of schooling itself: at school, learners develop their individual potential, but they are also authoritatively graded for differential rewards. For different learners the balance between these two is very different, and it is on this balance that their motivation ('zest' or otherwise) depends. We may assume that the same will be true for teachers in relation to appraisal. Hancock (1985, para. 7) stresses that appraisal should be seen *not* as a threat but as a series of opportunities, but it is clear that the threat is potentially just as real as the opportunities – it all depends on what sort of process is envisaged.

If the details of the process do not allay the sense of threat, some teachers may well respond to appraisal with the same mixture of anxiety, resentment, cynicism and anger as pessimistic fifth-formers facing GCSE assessments. Similarly, just as for some pupils school assessments are an ineffective ritual, the Suffolk report warns:

> There is some evidence to show that staff appraisal can degenerate into a paper exercise in which worthless reports are compiled and filed simply to comply with procedural instructions. (Graham, 1985, p. 6)

Let us then look at some of the procedures and rationales envisaged for teacher appraisal, and consider how far they are likely to offer opportunities to develop professional skills and thus to enhance 'zest for the job', and how far they are likely to pose the threat of negative evaluation, that well-known 'turn-off' for learners of any age in any context.

Some models of the appraisal process

The target output model

The procedure here is that a set of objectives is agreed with a teacher, whose professional work is then compared with those objectives (see Joseph, 1986, p . 12; ACAS, 1986, p. 4). The objectives may be derived from a job description or from attainment targets for learners (Delaney, 1986, p. 77). Appraisal thus takes the form of measuring how far targets have been achieved. The process, clearly derived from commercial models, involves teachers in a commitment to a sort of productivity contract. It could be termed a 'quota-fulfilment' model.

However, the problem with teachers' objectives is that they are both highly specific (to this learner in this lesson) and highly mysterious (internal to the emotional and cognitive processes of learners). Attempts to express objectives in a general and public form usually leads to an idealistic vagueness whereby any practical evaluative function is lost, since the judgements at issue are side-stepped. The following, for example, is an extract from an appraisal instrument presented to the *Better Schools – Evaluation and Appraisal Conference*:

> Organization should show evidence of: good classroom organization, and appropriate arrangements of space, resources and time . . . creativity and enthusiasm for own curriculum area . . . the demonstration of a well-balanced curriculum. (Taylor, 1986, p. 105)

To attempt to negotiate an 'objective' appraisal around such targets seems destined to end either in contentious semantics or a paper exercise. Perhaps it is to avoid such problems that we have seen the proposed introduction of national attainment tests. Only by means of testing pupils can targets for educational processes be manipulated in the same way as the targets for the other types of organization from which this model of appraisal is derived. But then, of course, the balance between opportunity and threat is decisively tilted towards threat. Consequently, in order to manage this threat, teachers may be tempted to preserve the required harmony between target and output by focussing on the negative aspects of their professional situation, and especially on the 'low ability' or 'poor background' of their pupils. A process less likely to stimulate the development of professional zest or skill could hardly be imagined. And this is doubly ironic, since the DES themselves point out, in *Better Schools*, that unsatisfactory standards are closely linked with teachers' underestimation of pupils' capacities (DES, 1985, p. 6). Appraisal by means of target pupil attainments thus actually provides a strong motive for making such underestimations as a way of legitimating current practices and outcomes.

The performance criteria model

In this model, teaching is conceived as a skill-based performance, analysable into a list of constituent 'competencies' represented by observable 'indicators' or criteria. In relation to this list of competencies, the judgement is made as to 'whether teachers can satisfy the agreed criteria' (DES, 1986, p. 71). In their presentation of this model, entitled *Techniques for Appraising Teacher Performance*, the DES gives an example of such a list, including:

Competency VII – Communicates with Learners
- Indicator 4 Gives directions and explanations related to lesson content . . .
- Indicator 6 Uses responses and questions from learners in teaching.
- Indicator 7 Provides feedback to learners throughout the lesson.
- Indicator 8 Uses acceptable written and oral expression with learners.
  (DES, 1986, p. 75)

The complete two-page list of such 'objective' indicators of adequate performance has a formal resemblance to an MOT checklist of criteria for vehicular adequacy, but with a crucial difference: the criteria listed always need a further level of criteria before they can be utilized. Sometimes this is implicitly recognized (we can easily see that we will have to discuss and agree the meaning of 'acceptable' – Indicator 8), but usually this problem is disguised by the adoption of 'value-free' phrasing; for example, even a comment such as 'Not like that, you oaf' would otherwise seem to fulfil the requirements of Indicator 7, 'Provides feedback to learners . . .'.

The point is that, as the author of the DES contribution says, 'Research has not unearthed any simple or comprehensive indicator of effective teaching performance' (DES, 1986, p. 70). Hence, as the Suffolk report argues, attempts to measure teachers' performance with any precision are highly questionable (Graham, 1985, p. 2). And in the absence of reliable and effective criteria, professional development along these lines is more likely to be inhibited than supported by the provision of checklists which are 'objective' only because they are vacuous. Further, the use of such dubious instruments for an assessment process (rather than as a preliminary agenda to stimulate open-ended critical discussion) is likely to render such assessments both implausible and also, once again, threatening, because it will be recognized that, since they lack precision, they must, in the end, be arbitrary.

The diagnostic model

According to the ACAS Appraisal and Training Working Group's *Agreed Principles* (ACAS, 1986, para. 3, iii), diagnosis of 'potential' will enable:

> individual teachers, their head teachers and their employers to see when a new or modified assignment would help the professional development of individual teachers and improve their career prospects.

On the other hand, a diagnosis that a teacher is 'experiencing difficulty' will lead to 'help . . . guidance, counselling, and training' and, possibly, 'disciplinary procedures' (para. 3, v). Quite apart from the threat of dismissal, quite explicit in the literature, diagnosis always cuts both ways: teachers will not welcome being diagnosed as *not* having potential for a particular career step. It is for this reason, presumably, that diagnosis is to be linked with classroom observation (ACAS, 1986, para. 7, iii) and carried out by a superior (ACAS, 1986, para. 5), so that contentious judgements as to need, potential or merit can be adjudicated in the light of 'evidence'. There is thus no doubt that diagnosis of need and potential could be experienced as threatening, especially as part of a universal scheme of appraisal. For example, teachers whose deeply-held educational philosophy leads them to adopt a particular teaching style may fear that an appraisal observation by a superior holding opposed views could trigger a 'guidance and counselling' procedure which would be at best unwelcome, and at worst might damage their career. And, given current economic differentials, coupled with a widespread ideology of success-as-promotion, it would be hard for all concerned to act on a diagnosis that, say, a head of department needed a couple of years' respite from administrative responsibility in order to straighten out aspects of his or her own teaching. In other words, certain beneficial forms of 'new or modified assignment' would be ruled out by the link between career (as a series of professional experiences) and a hierarchical structure of salary and status.

The product model of appraisal: a bureaucratic principle

Although the three models just discussed are conceptually distinguishable, they are in fact being proposed together as part of a single set of procedures serving a diverse range of purposes. Thus the St Edmunds scheme (Delaney, 1986, pp. 16–18) is based on a job description, professional need, career discussions, standard of classroom performance, curriculum targets and pupil attainments. The diversity of DES aims for appraisal schemes has already been set out above. All this is quite surprising since there is a readily available body of evidence and argument suggesting that a plurality of aims renders appraisal schemes ineffective.

Judith Whyte, for example, in a comprehensive review, cites work from the 1960s and 1970s, as well as the early 1980s, which concludes that 'reward reviews, performance reviews, and potential reviews' should be served by separate procedures, and generally that procedures for evaluation and for development should not be mixed (Whyte, 1986, p. 142). There is nothing surprising about this point; it emerges quite clearly from the consideration above of the potential threats present, alongside undoubted 'opportunities' in each of the appraisal procedures advocated. The work reviewed by Whyte is given full weight in the Suffolk study which concludes: 'A precise definition of the purpose of the appraisal system is an imperative; failure to do this can be not only inhibitory but also downright disastrous (Graham, 1985, p . 18). (Notice that they refer to 'the purpose' – singular.)

That the DES also are fully aware that different appraisal procedures are suited to different purposes is shown in their contribution to the *Better Schools – Evaluation and Appraisal Conference* (DES, 1986), where it is noted that self-appraisal and peer appraisal are most effective for professional improvement, and that pupil attainment and pupil ratings are most effective for the assessment of performance. And yet they place all their emphasis on superordinate appraisal, even while listing half a paragraph of unanswered questions, and stating that 'the difficulties are evident' (DES, 1986, pp. 71–3). So, while the DES notes the contradiction that teachers are unwilling to submit themselves to a process which they impose on pupils, we can note the contradiction that the DES seems to be impelled to recommend a set of procedures which they know are unlikely to achieve their avowed purposes. How can this be explained?

Underlying all three models outlined above is what could be called a *product model* of appraisal. In other words, the main value of the appraisal process lies in the value of the product which it will generate. This product is, in the first instance, 'accurate and up-to-date information on performance in post' (Hancock, 1985, para. 6, ii); 'a new comprehensive and up-to-date information base on teacher performance for the use of LEAs and governing bodies' (Joseph, 1986, p. 14). This information base will then be used to achieve the purposes of appraisal, namely to improve professional 'standards' through recommendations as to promotion, remediation or training.

In the next section I will contrast this *product* model with a *process* model of appraisal, but first it is worth pondering why the DES should embrace the product model when there are clearly so many queries about the quality and reliability of the information the recommended procedures are likely to generate, quite apart from their inevitable problematic side-effects.

The DES is part of a bureaucracy. The ancient function of a bureaucracy is to render effective over a wide territory the demands of a central political power (see Poggi, 1978, p. 74ff.). Its effective structure is hierarchical, and its fundamental instrument is information travelling 'up' the system so that 'informed' decisions can then travel 'down'. In principle, its overriding effort must be to convert the activities over which it has jurisdiction into information which can be filed and thus used (later, and by any official) to justify administrative decisions (see Winter, 1976). Bureaucracies must always be able to justify their decisions, because they spend public money for which they are accountable. Hence the opening of *Better Schools*, with its immediate reference to 'securing the best possible return from . . . resources' (DES, 1985, p. 1), and hence the quaint 'value-added' image of the educational process (DES, 1986, p. 70; Joseph, 1985, para. 43), reminding us that the original bureaucracies were concerned with effective taxation. The DES's emphasis in its appraisal proposals may thus be seen as part of an ancient historical tendency.

The professional principle: a process model of appraisal

There is another, equally widespread and more recent historical tendency at work – the growth of professions. Whereas bureaucratic workers draw on authority for their decisions from above – ultimately from the state, which gives them their powers and duties – professional workers possess a personal licence to practise, having demonstrated their mastery of a body of knowledge. Their allegiance is therefore not upwards but downwards – to their clients – and inwards – to the specialism which they practise. Clients' cases are complex and unique; they cannot be decided upon by the application of general rules (given from above) but only by the discretionary interpretation of specialist knowledge in the individual instance. This means that professional workers are continually learning (increasing their knowledge and enhancing their skills) through the actual practice of their profession. Now, although this is in principle the ideal relationship between professional practice and professional knowledge, it is a process which can be inhibited – by low morale, inadequate resourcing, excessive case-load (class-size), etc. And it is for this reason that a *process* model of appraisal has relevance for professional work: to encourage the realization of that process – which is the hallmark of the professional role – of learning more about one's practice through the examination of that practice as it occurs.

In a process model of appraisal, the value resides in the process of carrying it out. It is the process itself which will result in professional development. Any outcomes are unique to the individual practitioner and the specific context. Whereas the product model seeks to generate authoritative ('accurate') assessments of teacher performance (so that learning experiences can be prescribed, subsequently, *for* the teacher), the process model seeks in itself to stimulate effective learning *by* the teacher. It would not generate information about teachers' work, but insight for those teachers themselves to use in improving their work.

We can now return to the contradictions with which we started. The DES's contradiction is that they are a bureaucracy presiding over a profession, and thus haunted by ideals of professional practice and development (hence their references to zest, job satisfaction and moral courage). The teachers' contradiction is that they are professional educators operating within a bureaucracy, and thus haunted by fears of bureaucratic regulation and accountability (i.e. by DES references to performance assessment). Both parties may indeed sincerely be seeking to improve the quality of education, but the practical problem is that no single scheme can do justice to both principles. Hence the current conflict and confusion.

Ways forward: action-research and the process model of appraisal

An obvious solution would be to set up *three* separate policy initiatives, rather than one scheme.

First, it is easy to agree that improved promotion procedures are needed. The 'Peter Principle', i.e. that people are promoted from one set of tasks to another until at last they reach and become stuck at a set of tasks at which they are incompetent (see Faber, 1980, p. 26), neatly articulates the widespread cynicism concerning current arrangements. As an improvement, one might envisage setting up a 'pre-promotion' programme, whereby those aspiring to a particular type of post can:

- discuss with experienced holders of that post the skills involved,
- make arrangements to have opportunities to exercise such skills, and
- document their possessions of these skills, so that when a post comes up they can present a portfolio of materials in support of their case.

Secondly, we might agree that improved procedures are needed to respond (in one way or another) to that minority of teachers whose shortcomings cause frustration for their pupils and embarrassment for their colleagues. This is a sensitive issue, exacerbated by the harshness of current employment and welfare policies; who will blow the whistle on a colleague when it might mean precipitation into wastage and poverty, rather than careful retraining for work more in line with that colleague's abilities? This is a legal, moral, political and economic nettle which employers and unions *must* grasp; it cannot be evaded. There is a real lack of moral courage (cf. p. 44) entailed in attempting to conceal the difficult decisions involved in this problem within a general appraisal scheme in which those decisions will, supposedly, emerge from the system – at the cost, as I have argued, of a universal anxiety which will render the other purposes of appraisal ineffective.

Once these two issues have been separated out, the way is clear to pursue directly the third purpose of appraisal, the general enhancement of professional commitment and satisfaction, skill and effectiveness. For this purpose I have proposed a process model of appraisal, which will now be elaborated through a brief consideration of the nature of educational action-research.

The comparison of outcomes with objectives and the analysis of a complex activity into constitutive elements are merely two (by now rather dated, and always rather ponderous) ways in which a professional worker can adopt an analytical stance towards their practice. There are others, e.g. the triangulation of accounts between collaborating colleagues, the critical analysis of tape-recorded sessions, comparative studies of two pupils or two classes.

The advantage of action-research is its flexibility. Its claim to validity is that of fresh and usable insight within the particular context. It seeks contrasts and surprises, which can stimulate learning and innovation. It defines an analytical effort which *accompanies* (but does not *prescribe*) professional practice. Action-research can thus be effective on a small scale, achieving its purposes through intensive work on a small amount of critical evidence.

Of course, it requires preparation, time and support, but this is envisaged as available for the appraisal scheme: 'A successful appraisal scheme will depend on teachers being properly prepared and trained, and having sufficient time to allocate to the appraisal process' (Joseph, 1985, para. 47). How much is 'sufficient' time? Taylor (1986, pp. 99–107) reported that for each teacher appraised the time required was (apart from the teacher's contribution) 4 hours by the head teacher and 4 days by an outside observer. The difference, however, is that an action-research approach would not involve outside observers, and could thus give relatively more time to the teachers, and take up less time of the 'superordinate appraiser', who would thus become, as Delaney says, 'a helper or co-worker, rather than judge' (Delaney, 1986, p. 19).

Collaboration as a principle and as a means for professional development is implied (albeit ambiguously) by Hancock's suggestion that appraisal offers 'the opportunity to share professional problems'(Hancock, 1985, para. 7, iii). More explicitly, it is proposed both by the Fish Report on provision for special educational needs (Fish, 1985, p. 202) and by the Hargreaves Report (1984, p. 106). The latter also notes the power of effectively planned self-evaluation:

> Self-evaluation . . . may challenge teachers' assumptions about their class-room practice . . . . Changes and modifications in teaching practice brought about by self-evaluation are likely to be maintained. (Hargreaves, 1984, p . 105)

The urgency of the argument in favour of an action-research approach to appraisal is demonstrated by a recent report in the *Times Educational Supplement* (Surkes, 1987), which details the long list of possible performance indicators which the DES might propose to collect for its 'comprehensive information base', including measures of lateness, attendance and demeanour! There is a vital issue at stake here, concerning the social organization of knowledge, which lies at the heart of what is meant by educational research. The construction of supposedly 'objective information' according to some form of positivist rationale, derived from natural science, embodies the aspiration to understand phenomena by controlling them (see Fay, 1975). The previous arguments have shown how likely it is that this epistemology will fit neatly into DES thinking. The educational research community, however, knows the limitations of positivism as applied to social affairs and can advise the DES accordingly:

- that indicators of social phenomena are always contestable, since they must always rest on a long series of individual interpretive decisions;
- that general conclusions derived in this way are thus always open to question;
- that such conclusions, therefore, can only have the most indirect relevance for practice (either at the level of general policy or the individual context); and hence

Table 5.1 Tabular summary of the argument

Model of appraisal	Product	Process
Educational function	Assessment	Learning
Outcome	Information	Individualized in-service education
Purpose	Accountable decision making	Development of practice
Institutional principle	Bureaucracy	Professionalism
Epistemological principle	Positivism	Practical hermeneutics
Associated research mode	Observation	Action-research

- that the vast resources expended in collecting 'comprehensive objective information' will therefore in the end only provide *valid* justification for quite modest and tentative conjectures – which may not seem like 'value for money'!

In contrast to the positivist epistemology which serves the inherent task of bureaucracy, action-research embodies an alternative epistemology, (it might be termed 'practical hermeneutics'), which serves the inherent task of professional work, i.e. development through a dialectic between practice and reflection. Elsewhere (Winter, 1987), I have argued at some length that a self-consistent set of methodological principles can be formulated for action-research and that action-research can thus begin to resolve many of the ambiguities which otherwise beset social research so often undermined by the unacknowledged problems in its positivist heritage. My argument here is that action-research's principles and procedures can inform that aspect of the teacher appraisal proposals which is unambiguously concerned with the enhancement of teachers' professionalism, leaving the other aspects to be dealt with separately. One LEA is already experimenting in this direction.

It would be a pity if attempts to kill several professional birds with one bureaucratic stone led to the choice of a rough unwieldy boulder, when the shining pebble of widespread school-based professional development lies there before us waiting to be picked up.

References

ACAS (1986). Teachers Dispute ACAS Independent Panel: Report of the Appraisal and Training Working Group. London: ACAS CAI.
Delaney, P. (1986). *Teacher Appraisal in the Primary School*. Leamington Spa: Scholastic Publications.
Department of Education and Science (1985). *Better Schools*. London: HMSO.

Department of Education and Science (1986). Techniques for appraising teacher performance. In *Better Schools – Evaluation and Appraisal Conference Proceedings*. London:
HMSO.

Faber, H. (1980). *The Book of Laws*. London: Sphere Books.

Fay, H. (1975). *Social Theory and Political Practice*. London: Unwin.

Fish, J. (1985). *Educational Opportunities For All?* London: ILEA.

Graham, D.G. (1985). *Those Having Torches . . . Teacher Appraisal: A Study*. Ipswich,
Suffolk Educational Authority.

Hancock, D. (1985). Staff appraisal in schools and colleges – a view from DES. Education
for Industrial Society Conference Speech, London, 25 February.

Hargreaves, D. (1984). *Improving Secondary Schools*. London: ILEA.

Joseph, K. (1985). Better Schools – evaluation and appraisal. Conference Speech.
Birmingham, 15 November.

Joseph, K. (1986). Industrial Society Conference Speech, 14 April.

Poggi, G. (1978). *The Development of the Modern State*. London: Hutchinson.

Rumbold, A. (1986). Educational Inspectors and Advisers Conference Speech. Bristol,
25 September.

Surkes, S. (1987). 'Assess schools by behaviour' says DES. *The Times Educational
Supplement*, 28 August, pp. 1 and 5.

Taylor, F. (1986). Watergall Junior School, Peterborough. In *Better Schools – Evaluation
and Appraisal Conference Proceedings*. London: HMSO.

Whyte, J. (1986). Teacher assessment: a review of the performance appraisal literature
with special reference to the implications for teacher appraisal. *Research Papers in
Education*, **I**(2) 137–63.

Winter, R. (1976). Keeping files: aspects of education and bureaucracy. In G. Whitty and
M. Young (eds), *Explorations in the Politics of School Knowledge*, pp. 75–86. Driffield:
Nafferton Books.

Winter, R. (1987). *Action-Research and the Nature of Social Enquiry: Professional Innovation
and Educational Work*. Aldershot: Gower.

6
Teacher appraisal

Ernest R. House and Stephen D. Lapan

In a recent Montana legal trial the validity of the teacher appraisal system of one school district was at issue. School administrators had devised interviews for assessing teacher competence. Each interview consisted of 10–20 questions, half of which were 'knowledge' questions and half 'situational'. For a special education teacher a knowledge question might be: 'What is the Montana definition of learning disabled?' A situational question might be: 'Suppose a student in one of your classes had a body odor problem. What would you do?' Each question had prescribed answers and the teacher was interviewed jointly by two administrators, each of whom scored the teacher separately on the acceptability of the answer. The scores were then combined and compared to those of others who had been interviewed, thus providing a ranking of the teachers.

The Missoula school district had been using this procedure in the hiring of new teachers but a legal conflict ensued when a teacher with 13 years teaching experience returned from a leave of absence, was subjected to the interviews, fared very badly, and was fired by the school district for incompetence. She invoked her legal rights and a 2-day hearing was held to judge the district's actions. During the hearing the teacher's attorney presented evidence of competent teaching in the form of ratings of her actual classroom performance by her supervisors, as well as testimony by colleagues and parents that she was a good teacher. The attorney for the school district argued that the supervisor ratings were invalid as evidence of effective teaching, as were the testimonies of colleagues and parents.

Eventually, the court declared that the process used for dismissing the teacher was itself invalid because the district ignored evidence about her actual teaching performance, a criterion more relevant to teaching than the interviews. This incident illustrates the pressures that currently exist for teacher appraisal and also the disagreement about how to accomplish it.

In their examination of teacher appraisal practice in 32 US cities, Wise *et al.* (1984) associated the type of teacher appraisal with the way one conceives the job of teaching. They posited four fundamental views of teaching: as labor, as craft, as profession, and as art. If one conceives teaching as essentially labor, then the teacher's job is to implement preset, prescribed procedures and routines, and the appraisal system includes direct inspection of the teacher's work, such as monitoring lesson plans, classroom performance and performance results. Adherence to set procedures is the overall criterion, just as in a factory assembly line, and the school administrator is the teacher's supervisor.

The second conception of teaching is to see it as a craft. This means that teaching requires a repertoire of specialized techniques and knowledge, including knowledge of how to apply these skills. The teacher is expected to carry out teaching without close supervision or direct instruction. The administrator acts as a manager who holds teachers to general performance standards. Teaching as a craft assumes that there are specific techniques and general rules for applying them. Evaluation determines indirectly whether the teacher has the requisite skills.

Teaching as a profession, the third conception, requires not only the repertoire of skills but also the exercise of judgement about where the skills should be applied. Presumably this requires theoretical as well as technical knowledge that the teacher be a doctor rather than a lab technician. Standards of performance are developed and determined by peers. The administrator is one who marshalls the necessary resources so that the professionals can do their job. And, increasingly, knowledge is presumed to be based upon empirical research.

Finally, in the conception of teaching as an art, the techniques and procedures of teaching are personalized rather than standardized because the teaching situation is seen as unpredictable, requiring a frequent departure from set rules and techniques, and these departures are expressions of the personality and personal insight of the individual teacher. Evaluation involves self-assessment as well as peer assessment, relying more on holistic judgements rather than analytic qualities, more on the overall pattern of events rather than discrete behaviours. The administrator is a leader who inspires and encourages.

The Missoula teacher appraisal scheme seems to us to fit the teaching as craft perspective. Teachers are presumed to need certain knowledge and skills, which can be ascertained from structured interviews, but not to require close supervision, as in the teaching as labor perspective. The latter might be represented by schemes like management by objectives, which prescribe rather precise tasks the teachers must accomplish. In the 32 school districts surveyed by Wise and his colleagues, all of which were districts reputed to have effective teacher appraisal systems, the typical evaluation procedure was a pre-evaluation conference between the teacher and evaluator (usually the principal), followed by classroom observation by the evaluator, a post-evaluation conference, and finally a written agreement as to what the teacher should do next. Only 12 of the districts had any provision for self-evaluation and only 8 had any peer review. During the classroom visit the evaluator-principal usually filled out a form rating the teacher from 1 to 5 on specific classroom behaviours. Items on the rating forms varied from district to district but the checklists contained items like 'teaches the curriculum', 'ability to motivate', 'develops plans', 'has mature understanding of own and other's problems', and 'evidence that student is working at task'.

Most of these teacher appraisal schemes are based upon the teaching as craft perspective. Teachers are expected to carry out their duties without close supervision and the role of the administrator-evaluator is to hold them to performance standards by visits, conferences and written agreements. It is presumed that the principal is able to see the proper techniques in action during occasional visits to the classroom. Two major complaints about these systems were that principals lacked sufficient resolve and competence to evaluate accurately and that teachers were either resistant or apathetic to the evaluation.

Dimensions of merit

No one has been more critical of the classroom visit as a means of evaluating teachers than has Scriven (1986, p. 25):

> Classroom visits not only violate every tenet of sampling theory (too small, non-random, reactive, biased observer, etc.) but can only look at what is essentially irrelevant in all but the most bizarre cases, namely teaching style. This is ritualistic evaluation at its worst, the bait-and-switch technique of substituting something worthless for what is advertised to the community as serious accountability.

Scriven's reason for this harsh judgement is that both the quality of content presented to the student and the amount of learning inspired by the teacher are invisible in the occasional visit by the principal, and that the active procedure is rife with potential bias. Teachers and administrators alike feel the inadequacy of the process. We believe that classroom visits can play an important role in the overall evaluation if properly done as part of a more global strategy, but they cannot bear the brunt of teacher evaluation alone.

Ironically, research on teaching styles may have contributed to inappropriate teacher evaluation because the temptation is to construct checklists of characteristics correlated with efficient teaching and to use those to assess teachers in the classroom visits. To take a silly but real example, eye contact has been correlated with effective teaching and used to judge teachers. For puposes of summative personnel evaluation this is hardly an adequate criterion; one can easily find excellent teachers who do not maintain eye contact in the classroom. In general, statistical indicators cannot reasonably be used for summative evaluation even though they may be statistically 'valid' indicators of good teaching. (Their use in formative evaluation is another matter.)

Criteria used for summative personnel evaluation should have either a logical or legal connection to teaching performance. That is, they must be necessary for good teaching (Scriven, 1986). Characteristics such as eye contact and amount of teacher talk are at best only secondary indicators of good performance. They would indicate good teaching only if one had no other information about the teacher, and summative personnel evaluation should hardly proceed on such a flimsy information base. To cite a positive example, in the districts studied by Wise *et al.*, the most common reason for declaring a teacher incompetent was the teacher's inabililty to control a class. This criterion is obviously necessary for effective teaching and a legitimate one for summative evaluation. It is also one that principals can judge relatively easily. To repeat, related criteria should be necessarily and directly related to teaching: controlling the classroom is; eye contact is not. The teacher's actual characteristics in 'producing valuable learning while using proper procedures' supervene over the indirect evidence of statistical indicators (Scriven, 1986).

Scriven suggests four dimensions of merit for summative teacher evaluation:

- quality of content taught;
- success in imparting/inspiring learning;
- mastery of professional skills; and
- ethics.

Quality of content taught is not the same as quality of the content known, although the two are obviously related. Quality of content taught is directly and necessarily related to teaching; content known is only indirectly related. Thus, we have some reservations about judging teachers by testing them for content knowledge. Clearly, teachers must have knowledge of what they are teaching but it is also critical how and whether they apply that knowledge.

According to Scriven, success in imparting/inspiring learning also includes learning outside the cognitive domain. However, non-cognitive development is perhaps not adequately captured by this wording. In our opinion, there must be concern for personal development in the larger sense. Professional skills, such as how to construct a test properly or how to control a class, are obviously important as well. Again some characteristics are directly related to good teaching and some are not: constructing lesson plans, a commonly used one, is not critically related; grading papers is. Finally, ethics involves avoidance of racism, favouritism, and the like.

Scriven contends that these four dimensions of teaching merit are separately necessary and jointly complete. That is, the teacher must be competent along each dimension to be minimally competent, and serious failure on any one would be grounds for dismissal. A teacher could not make up in knowledge of subject matter an inability to control a class or seriously unethical behaviour. On the other hand, a reward for good teaching would have to include all four dimensions to be complete.

Most current teacher evaluation schemes are concerned primarily with minimum competency, perhaps because most are for the purposes of account-ability rather than for recognizing good teaching or for improving teaching. Unfortunately, schemes aimed at discerning minimum competence, and thus allaying the fears of an anxious public, are employed with all teachers. Thus, all teachers may be visited by the principal, an approach that may identify those who cannot control a classroom but does not highlight good teaching. Or all teachers may be required to take relatively primitive tests to weed out the illiterate. Such teacher testing schemes are often perceived as onerous and insulting by the majority of teachers and are of little help in improving instruction. This is not to deny the legitimacy of sometimes evaluating teachers for minimum competence but this is at best a partial approach and one that may be counterproductive in that it discourages good teaching. The worst schemes treat teaching as labour or craft, without concern for teaching as profession or art. A high-quality teacher appraisal scheme would provide for excellent teaching as well as for eliminating incompetence.

Causal inference and action

Our own conception of teaching is rather different from the perspectives underlying most teacher appraisal schemes. First, consider how teachers learn to teach successfully. After graduation from college, the beginning teacher enters the classroom and is pretty much left to her own devices to learn how to teach. Most beginning teachers, for example, do not know how to handle discipline in high school classes. For most teachers, the first weeks and months are difficult as they struggle to control their classes. They receive little help from their colleagues or administrators. If the administrator visits, he or she is likely to file a report saying that discipline is lax. Over time the successful teacher learns what she can do to maintain control. She may learn that it is essential to be firm during the first few weeks of school in order to establish control and that eventually she can relax her disciplinary grip somewhat. The visiting administrator can discern the results of this learning by the teacher in the ruliness of the class.

But many other things the teacher learns to do are not so evident. What poetry 'works' with this particular type of student or how to handle a class discussion are things good teachers learn. These causal connections come mostly from the teachers' classroom experience. Some teachers are good at discovering these things and some are not. In both cases the teacher's personal causal inferences serve as the basis of her classroom practice in the future. Some teachers are highly successful because of what they have learned and others are not. There is great individual variation in teachers' ability to discover the causal connections particular to their own situation. Teachers who are not able to discover how to control a class, for example, lose their jobs in a short time regardless of what else they know. Good teachers learn far more subtle and complex things on the job. The best teachers keep on learning indefinitely, but many teachers settle into fixed patterns after 4–5 years.

Some practical knowledge that the teacher discovers, generates, or creates is explicit, and the teacher may be able to explain or at least provide rough guidelines as to how to do it. Much of this knowledge is tacit, however, like riding a bicycle. The teacher may not be able to explain how to do something, even though she knows how to do it. There is a significant difference between 'knowing how' and 'knowing what'. Of course, one can see immediately whether someone knows how to ride a bicycle. Good teaching is more difficult to demonstrate. Much teacher knowledge is 'how to'.

Furthermore, teachers often know more than they are aware they know. Tacit knowledge often emerges only in specific situations. The teacher may encounter a particular situation and only in that context realize that she knows how to handle it, whether by combining elements from previous learnings or from long forgotten experience. Professional know-how in the form of tacit knowledge presents a particularly difficult problem for evaluators, since this knowledge cannot be readily seen by the observer or explicated by the teacher. The traditional methods of evaluating teachers – by testing, interviewing, and classroom observation – all leave much to be desired. They do not directly tap the true basis of teaching and hence the classroom observer is forced into indirect and correlational methods of assessment rather than ascertaining what is directly responsible for good teaching.

Teaching rests in large part upon the individual teacher's inference structure and one key to appraising teachers is to assess the inference structure the teacher has developed. The teacher's causal inference structure is directly and causally related to her teaching in a way that many measures of teacher performance are not. Of course, how one might discern the inference structure, let alone assess it, is no easy task. Three possibilities are worth exploring. One way is to ascertain whether the teacher is still actively experimenting with teaching. Really excellent teachers will keep trying out new things to improve their teaching and to adjust to new students and changing times. Mediocre teachers, on the other hand, develop a set pattern that they do not change in spite of changing circumstances.

A second possibility is to investigate whether the teacher can explicate and justify the teaching moves she is making. Although we have argued that much teaching knowledge is tacit, we think that good teachers will be able to give reasons for the things they are doing in the classroom and poor teachers will not. Admittedly, much teacher knowledge will not be explicit but much can be elicited through inventive techniques. The challenge is to develop such techniques.

A third possibility is to check the teacher's inferences against those of the teacher's peers. The teacher's peers will share many of the teacher's underlying assumptions and although this will not help tacit knowledge become explicit, it will help the teacher test her ideas against those facing the same situation. We can envisage a set of evaluation procedures that would be based upon the teacher's own personal causal inferences and that would help teachers test their own inferences.

Minimum and maximum performance

We base our view of teacher appraisal on two assumptions. The first is that evaluations should emphasize major dimensions of teacher performance, di-

Table 6.1 Views and assumptions about teaching and appraisal[a]

| View of teaching | Underlying assumptions | | |
	Accepted perfor-mance pattern	Source of standards	Evaluation of performance
Labour	Existing pre-specified skills	External authority and detailed specifications	Direct inspection and constant monitoring
Craft	Prescribed skills gained through practice and imitations of masters	External authority and general rules	Indirect inspection and periodic monitoring
Profession	Different patterns of performance lead to success	Developed by peers, possibly self	Quality judged by peers
Art	Each pattern of per-formance is unique	Developed by self, possibly peers	Quality judged by peers, self, reputation

[a] Adapted from Wise *et al.* (1984).

mensions that can be logically equated with teaching success. We hold with Scriven (1986) that too much of current practice reflects a trivialized perspective allowing evaluators to praise or condemn on the basis of characteristics *not* fundamental to successful practice. Detailed behavioural criteria, such as amount of teacher talk or appropriate use of examples or illustrations, are not necessary to good teaching, although sometimes associated with it. Teachers failing these criteria could still be performing acceptably overall. Scriven's 'dimensions of merit' provide a framework for guiding the appraisal of teaching and thus holding the evaluator to more comprehensive and logical views of the teacher's performance.

Our second assumption is that teacher appraisal approaches should consider teaching at its highest levels of quality, not as a minimum standard pass/fail situation. Conventional teacher appraisal is oriented toward a labour/craft view of teaching characterized by minimal standards for success. Little distinction is made between acceptable and outstanding performance. Evaluation should reflect the more comprehensive view of teaching as a profession and as art, thus providing for finer delineations between levels of success. In this perspective the idea of prespecified skills is replaced by the assumption that different and even unique patterns of performance can lead to successful practice. Standards are more often set by the professionals themselves and evaluations are usually carried out by peers rather than managers. A summary of how the labour/craft view versus the professional/art perspective can alter assumptions and approaches in teacher evaluation is presented in Table 6.1.

Some may interpret the labour, craft, profession and art distinctions as a hierarchy through which all teachers must progress. This is not our intention. Rather, we consider each designation as a different way of viewing what teaching can be. Thus, if evaluators perceive the work of teaching as primarily labour or craft, they will use quite different standards than would appraisers who are guided by professional or artistic assumptions.

Too much attention has been given to poor indicators of teaching. Focussing on artifacts of teacher performance such as written lesson plans, room arrangement, dress, and the like, seldom reflects how teachers become good practitioners. More direct teacher performance such as grading practices, test construction, and classroom control better distinguishes between successful and unsuccessful teachers. These practices more closely represent what teachers must do to become successful.

Teacher thinking is an important component of performance that directly reflects what teachers need to know or work on to improve. The way teachers work and improve practice across teacher performance dimensions can be revealed in their causal inference structure. Teacher thinking can be used to identify important areas of a teacher's strengths and weaknesses. One technique used for learning about teacher thinking is called 'stimulated recall' (Shavelson and Stern, 1981). Using this approach, evaluators ask teachers to discuss what they did as they monitor an audio- or video-recording of a lesson just taught. Portions of several different lessons can be studied to obtain representative samples of the teacher's reasoning during instruction. The evaluator usually listens to small segments of a lesson, stops the tape so that the teacher can share her reasoning about the events that transpired, and finally asks the teacher questions to stimulate her recall and reasoning about events observed.

Another source of evidence is the teacher portfolio. Many expert teachers can decide which kinds of data best reflect their abilities. This approach has particular merit for the 'teacher as artist' who is allowed the opportunity to present her unique pattern of performance. Teachers could begin early in their career in developing samples to place in the portfolio. Refinement and replacement of portfolio items would be an important part in developing and improving as a teacher. This approach has met with failure in the past primarily because teachers were required to develop the portfolio all at once. Also, restrictions have been placed on what can be included.

Evaluation data must be comprehensive enough to represent teaching performance that is essential to good teaching. Teaching viewed as a professional and artistic endeavour is well worth promoting. Direct evidence of teacher performance should take precedence over indirect evidence such as written plans, courses taken, and years of teaching experience. Finally, the role of teacher thinking in teacher appraisal is undervalued. Experiments with this approach to teacher evaluation might lead to more effective teacher appraisal for both formative and summative purposes.

References

Scriven, M. (1986). New functions of evaluations. *Evaluation Practice,* **7**(1).

Shavelson, R.J. and Stern, P. (1981). Research on teacher's pedagogical thoughts, judgments, decisions and behavior. *Review of Educational Research,* **51**(4), 455–98.

Wise, A.E., Darling Hammond, L., McLaughlin, M.W. and Bernstein, H.T. (1984). *Teacher Evaluation: A Study of Effective Practices.* Santa Monica, Calif.: Rand Corporation.

7
Criterion-referenced assessment of teaching

Donald McIntyre

This chapter does not report empirical research or development but is rather concerned with identifying some of the issues that would need to be involved in developing any satisfactory procedure for assessing teaching. Such a preliminary analysis is still necessary despite decades of work by many people to develop reliable and valid ways of assessing teaching; most of this work, unfortunately, has been entirely fruitless, largely because it has been directed towards the highly ambitious – probably hopelessly ambitious – goal of perfecting valid norm-referenced assessment schemes. Only when one focusses on the less ambitious goal of criterion-referenced assessment is it possible to begin to disentangle the complex and neglected issues which have to be resolved before any kind of valid assessment is possible.

Justifications for choice of criteria

It is suggested that three general types of justification are necessary for the selection of a set of criteria in terms of which any human activities or attainments are to be assessed.

1 *Justification of the way in which the assessed activity or discipline is construed.* What sort of activity is teaching? What kinds of knowledge or attributes is it taken to involve? Is it, for example, primarily a social role governed by a set of *conventions* about appropriate behaviour? Or, is it an activity which primarily involves the display of certain *personal characteristics*, such as warmth, extroversion and social dominance? Is it a *skilled craft*, like carpentry or plumbing, in which intellectual knowledge and reflection is of minor importance in comparison to the sensitive use of practical skills which neither are, nor need to be,

consciously articulated? Or, is it a theory-based *technology*, in which the decisions made are derived from, and monitored against, a coherent and well-established body of theory? Or, is it best conceived as a *political activity*, in which the individual more or less consciously, and with more or less social skill and political awareness, plays a part in ongoing negotiations and struggles in which different social groups attempt to impose their wills, and their conceptions of reality, on each other?

Teaching might be conceived as none of these types of activity or as some complex synthesis of several of them. Or, one might believe that teaching is primarily one of these types of activity, but that it *could and should* be another type. But whatever the way in which teaching is construed, this will to a large extent determine the specific criteria in terms of which teaching is assessed; and these specific criteria cannot adequately be justified without a justification of the way in which teaching as a whole is construed. Although discussion of the assessment of teaching is rarely conducted at this level, it is frequently because of disagreements at this level that confusion and divergence in the assessment of individual teachers' activities occurs.

2 *Justification of the applicability of criteria to observed performance.* Irrespective of one's views about which criteria are important, criteria have to be justified in terms of the validity with which they can be applied to the information accessible to the assessor.

The issues which arise here will depend upon the purpose of assessing teaching, but if we focus on the purpose of making judgements about teachers' or student-teachers' competence, the central problem presents itself as one of applying criteria of *competence* to evidence about *performance*. Can criteria concerned with what X is capable of doing be related in justifiable ways to instances of what X does? If, for example, a criterion were that a teacher should be able to use group teaching methods in appropriate circumstances, two central questions would have to be asked about the use of this criterion in relation to any observed teaching. First, does the teacher have the *opportunity* to use group methods when they might be thought to be appropriate? Opportunity depends, among other things, on having access to all the information on which effective use of group methods would be based, on having access to the resources necessary for such effective use, and on having the power to decide to use these methods without any danger of 'punishment' by others. To be confident that an observed teacher does indeed have such an opportunity, the assessor must have an extremely sensitive understanding of the social and material context, as experienced by the teacher, within which the teaching occurs.

The second question which has to be asked is whether the teacher and the assessor have shared ideas about the conditions in which, and the purposes for which, it is appropriate to use group methods. A teacher who is competent in the use of group methods and who has the opportunity to use these methods, may well make different judgements from an assessor about when it is appropriate to use them. Once again, the assessor must have an extremely sensitive understanding of the teacher's thinking about teaching to be confident that such a shared perspective exists.

It is, then, far from easy to justify the feasibility of applying criteria of competence to observed performances. One way of resolving this problem – a resolution which is implicitly in widespread use – is for the assessor not only to assert criteria of competence but also to assert that the observed teacher *ought* to perceive the context and to make judgements about appropriateness in the same ways as himself or herself; but that is to raise issues about the rights and powers of different individuals in the process of assessment, which leads us to the third type of justification which is generally necessary.

3 *Justification of the accounting relationships involved in the assessment.* Any educational assessment is made in the context of a socio-political obligation of one group of people to account to others for what they do or have achieved. Either the performer is saying to the accountant 'See what I can do', and thus asserts the criteria in relation to which he or she wants to be assessed or, more frequently in practice, the accountant determines the criteria and demands that the performer demonstrates the extent to which he or she can meet these criteria. Often, however, the situation is more complex in that the accountant is acting on behalf of other social groups and is obliged to assert the criteria which reflect the interest of these groups.

What one is talking about here, then, is the power relationships within which assessment is embedded; but if the criteria are to be justified, these power relationships cannot be taken for granted and must themselves be justified. Thus it might be argued, emphasizing the public service function of the schools, that it should be the elected representatives of society who determine the criteria for assessing teachers. Or, emphasizing the shared professional expertise of teachers, one might argue that the teaching profession should determine the criteria. Or, emphasizing the personal understanding and commitment on which teaching depends, one might argue that each individual teacher should articulate the criteria in terms of which he or she should be assessed, perhaps with the proviso that other social groups should have the right to evaluate the acceptability or adequacy of an account offered in terms of these criteria. This latter example makes clear the need to distinguish the issue of who should initiate an account (and choose the criteria) from the issue of who should evaluate the account (and the criteria in terms of which it is offered).

These three types of justification, which have been suggested as necessary for the selection of criteria, cannot in practice be independent one of another. If, for example, one were to adopt and justify a view of teaching as the application of a theory-based technology, it is likely that one would be obliged to argue that only experts in the relevant theories and their application are equipped to articulate the criteria in terms of which teaching should be assessed. One might further argue that such experts are typically to be found on the staff of colleges of education. This view would also be likely to lead one into asserting that good teaching involves the formulation of explicit plans, that the effects of implementing these plans should be systematically monitored, and that modifications should be introduced in the light of the feedback obtained; and this type of analysis might lead to the view that judgements about a teacher's competence can quite readily be based on evidence that the teacher should be able to produce about his or her performance.

In order to pursue this discussion further, I shall have to adopt a specific standpoint in relation to the issues which have been raised, although I shall not attempt an explicit justification of this standpoint. I assume then that teaching, as it is commonly conducted in our schools, can best be characterized as a skilled craft carried out in social contexts in which there are powerful conventions about appropriate behaviour; that, while these craft skills and some of the social conventions have to be learned and respected, teaching *ought* also to be approached with the sensitivity and reflectiveness necessary for what Stenhouse calls 'induction into knowledge' and what Freire calls 'consciencization', and is thus crucially dependent on high levels of appreciation of the nature of the knowledge discussed, of social awareness in the classroom, and of political consciousness on the part of teachers. And I take it to follow from this that the criteria in terms of which teaching should be assessed are of three broad types:

1 Minimal consensual performance criteria, applicable to all teachers in a given type of context, relating to the social conventions of schooling and the craft skills of teaching, e.g. being present in the classroom, speaking in audible and comprehensible ways, showing enthusiasm for what one is teaching, listening to, and manifestly taking account of, what pupils say.
2 Criteria initiated by each individual teacher or student-teacher in relation to his or her own teaching; these criteria should reflect the teacher's personal conceptions of the knowledge with which his or her teaching is concerned, of his or her purposes in teaching, of the social processes of teaching, and of the extent and range of his or her professional responsibilities.
3 Higher-order criteria in terms of which others to whom the teacher or student-teacher is obliged to account may justifiably evaluate the accounts offered to them, e.g. adequacy of evidence that the teacher is meeting his or her own criteria, the coherence and internal consistency of the conception of teaching from which the teacher's criteria are derived, the clarity with which the criteria are formulated, and the sensitivity which the teacher's choice of criteria shows to the concerns of others who will be affected by his or her teaching.

Clarification of criteria

Different issues arise in the clarification of criteria of each of the three types outlined above. To explore these issues I shall focus on one example from each of the three categories.

1 The first category is of performance criteria which, I suggest, might legitimately be applied to any teacher's performance irrespective of his or her own preferences or perspectives. Taking as an example 'showing enthusiasm for what one is teaching', what kinds of clarification are necessary and possible?

Perhaps the most obvious point is that while this is presented as a performance criterion (i.e. it is concerned with what the teacher does), it is expressed in language which seems to refer to the teacher's mental state. It is the manifestation of enthusiasm, not the teacher's experience of enthusiasm, which has to be assessed; but this leads to the question of to whom the enthusiasm must be manifest. Is it sufficient, and is it necessary, that an observer perceives the performance as enthusiastic? Is it necessary that the pupils are conscious of the teacher's manifestation of enthusiasm? Or, does the value which we place on teacher enthusiasm depend not on pupils' consciousness of it but rather on the ways in which they are likely to be affected, possibly unconsciously, by it?

My own answer to these questions, and to comparable questions for other criteria, is that the selection of 'manifest enthusiasm' as a criterion implicitly asserts a minor theory which relates a purpose of manifesting enthusiasm to a range of conventional behaviours for expressing enthusiasm (through voice, gesture, prepared materials, etc.), and through these both to a perceived general effect of appearing enthusiastic and to effects on pupils' behaviour, minimally that pupils will tend to be attentive. If this is correct, then the application of the criterion in a way which focusses on one element of the theory to the exclusion of others would be to distort it.

This same interpretation of the criterion is relevant to another way in which clarification is necessary, the issue of the situations to which it is appropriate to apply the criterion. If pupils do appear attentive and interested, it would not be appropriate to criticize a teacher for his or her lack of manifest enthusiasm. On the other hand, if a teacher does appear manifestly enthusiastic, it would be inappropriate to object, on this criterion, that the pupils do not appear to be attentive. Furthermore, even if the teacher does not give an impression of enthusiasm *and* the pupils do not appear attentive, it would be inappropriate to criticize the teacher unless the observer can specify types of behaviour, such as voice variation or the use of gesture, which would be likely to give an impression of which the teacher is not making use. The situations to which the criterion is relevant are those in which the theory is 'working' and, on the other hand, those in which it can be diagnosed to be necessary but manifestly not being used.

2 The second category is of criteria initiated by the teacher. In many ways clarification of these criteria is facilitated by the fact that they are an actor's, not an observer's, criteria. For example, if a teacher's account makes use of the criterion 'asking thought-provoking questions', the teacher can identify the situations in which it is or was his/her intention to ask such questions, identify the intended characteristics of these questions, and point out the nature of, and the evidence for, the desired outcomes of asking these questions. Clarity,

however, comes only from abstraction; and for the teacher to clarify clearly the criteria in terms of which he/she wishes to give an account of his/her teaching, he/she must treat specific instances as examples of more abstract categories.

The major problem to be faced by a teacher here is that of defining criteria, and specifying the types of situation to which these are applicable, in such a way that these criteria can be consistently applied without injustice to him/herself. Part of this problem concerns the extent to which a teacher claims responsibility for what happens: if one attributes to one's teaching the good relationships between oneself and one's pupils, the imaginative ideas produced by pupils or their thorough mastery of new concepts, must one not also attribute to one's teaching any absence of these goods on specific occasions or with specific pupils? Or, can one specify clearly the circumstances in which one is not able to accept responsibility for the effects of one's teaching? It seems likely that most teachers would be best advised to accept responsibility only for meeting criteria relating to their own activities, justifying these criteria partly in terms of their probable or normal outcomes.

Even the clarification of such limited criteria is, however, likely to raise problems, especially since teachers not only initiate classroom activities but also respond to them. The generation of clear criteria would depend on each teacher making explicit his or her intuitive categorization of classroom situations and of his or her ways of dealing with these situations, and on each teacher examining the clarity of the distinctions made among these categories as well as his or her justifications for distinguishing among them.

3 The third type of criterion mentioned was of higher-order criteria in terms of which others might evaluate the accounts offered to them by teachers. Since these accounts and the criteria in terms of which they are offered are likely to vary in idiosyncratic ways, it may be difficult to specify higher-order criteria in anything other than very general terms. Certainly, there is no possibility that they could be applied in routine ways.

One suggested higher-order criterion was 'sensitivity in the teacher's choice of criteria to the concerns of others who will be affected by his or her teaching'. This exemplifies very well both the kinds of clarification that are necessary and the limited extent to which clarification in general terms is possible. Concepts such as 'affected', 'concerns' and especially 'sensitivity', obviously require elucidation. Thus, sensitivity would have to be clearly distinguished from acquiescence to others' views and also from mere awareness of others' views. Its elucidation would have to involve the articulation of positions on how teachers' criteria should be judged in relation to the efforts they would make to keep themselves informed about the concerns of their pupils and others in relation to their commitment to explicit or implicit negotiation of acceptable patterns of teaching, and in relation to the circumstances in which they would deliberately engage in conflict.

The positions adopted in the formulation of such higher-order criteria would necessarily imply views about the social relations of schooling. I would argue that they should be so formulated as to accommodate teachers whose perspectives on their teaching were widely divergent, provided that these perspectives were fully articulated and coherently defended. One likely consequence of this would be that no system of rules could be established for the application of these criteria; any evaluation made at this level would be open to debate.

Reliabililty of assessments

The reliability of assessment in relation to any criterion depends first on the appropriateness of the criterion to the nature of the thing being assessed. No reliable assessment is possible, for example, in relation to the criterion 'effective use of audio-visual aids' if a stable pattern is not even temporarily apparent in the effectiveness with which a teacher uses visual aids. It is for this reason that assessment of teaching is only likely to be reliable if it is concentrated primarily on the second of the types of criteria outlined, for only then are the criteria likely to be matched well with individuals' patterns of teaching.

Given appropriate criteria, the reliability of assessment depends on the degree of relevance of available evidence to the criterion under consideration and on the number of independent bits of such evidence. Thus assessments of aspects of teaching about which direct evidence cannot be available (such as teachers' decision making) or which are relevant only to relatively rare events (such as overt rebellion by pupils) cannot be expected to be very reliable. Assessments of more frequently relevant and more directly observable aspects of teaching are limited in their reliability only by the inevitably partial account of them which can be given by one observer. Where an observer can make explicit the limited perspective he can and will adopt towards a selected aspect of teaching, and where this limited perspective provides evidence directly relevant to the criterion under consideration, high reliability can be achieved most fully through the use of systematic observation procedures. Where such a limited perspective would not fully provide the evidence relevant to the criterion, reliability can often be achieved through the negotiation of a shared understanding of events by people taking different perspectives, something which is most fully exemplified by the technique of triangulation among teacher, pupils and an external observer.

Summarizing accounts of teaching

There would seem to be three main ways in which summary accounts of teaching could be produced:

1 *Selectivity:* One might decide to provide an account only in relation to a limited set of criteria, for example, minimal consensual criteria of performance, or a subjective selection of the criteria formulated by a teacher, including perhaps an account of those criteria perceived to be most im-

pressively met, those criteria met which are perceived to be most ambitious, and those not met. Any such selective account would, however, be distorted by the absence of criteria considered significant by the teacher.

2 *Use of higher-order criteria:* One might provide an account of teaching in terms of the abstracted higher-order qualities of the set criteria met in the teaching. While such an account would not be distorted, on its own it might well be experienced as unhelpful by the audience to whom it was offered.

3 *Theoretical structure:* The conception of teaching from which a teacher derived his or her criteria might be theoretically structured so that sets of criteria were interrelated. For example, various criteria relating to classroom discussion might all be seen as contributing to a defined characteristic of the discussion. In such circumstances, if the patterns of assessed teaching performance corresponded to these theoretical groupings, then summary accounts could be provided in terms of the teacher's personal theory for his teaching. While this would provide the most desirable kind of summary, it would be over-optimistic to expect that the conditions necessary for it could easily be met.

No other possibilities present themselves. In particular, there are no general theories of teaching competence which could provide a basis for summarizing accounts, and it is not plausible to expect that any such theories will be developed.

Final note

This chapter has been concerned with aspects of criterion-referenced assessment of teaching. Yet, although all the examples considered have related to teaching, all the principles and general arguments advanced are equally relevant to the assessment of any other areas of human competence. With only minor changes this same chapter could have been written with equal validity about, say, the assessment of secondary school mathematics attainments.

8
Evaluation of competences of teaching practice supervisors within the naturalistic paradigm

Franz Kroath

This chapter focusses on a specific aspect of teacher appraisal: the problem of how to assess the competences and abilities of teaching practice supervisors in a centralized educational system. I attempt to outline the profile of tutorial skills of a supervisor, describe the structure and programme rationale of the INSET course, and discuss some salient problems of course evaluation and competence assessment in the light of naturalistic teacher appraisal.

Political context

Austria has recently introduced a new reform programme for initial secondary teacher training with a 3-month teaching practice period as its core curriculum. Student teachers with a 2-year training background in their academic fields are assigned to an experienced teacher (supervisor) who guides and monitors their first teaching practice experiences. The supervisor is considered to be the key figure in the professional development of student teachers as he/she helps them to develop their own subjective theories about teaching. Thus the question of how to train and assess competent supervisors is a crucial factor for the successful implementation of such a scheme.

Aims and intentions of teaching practice

In order to develop a profile of supervisors' competences it is necessary to define the objectives which can be realistically achieved within a short teaching practice period of 3 months. The results of our pilot studies which we have conducted over the last 3 years suggest the following aims to be achieved within 3 months of teaching practice:

1 To enable students to self-assess critically their abilities for a teaching career.
2 To enable students to get to know their strengths and weaknesses as teacher trainees and to acquire basic teaching skills through their own practical experiences and by observing an experienced teacher.
3 To expose students to teaching situations where they can freely experience and test their own concepts and ideas about teaching.
4 To sensitize students to the complexities and dilemmas of a teacher's role.

Basic qualifications and competences of supervisors

Having established the aims of teaching practice some basic competences and personality traits of supervisors conducive to guiding and monitoring student teachers can now be specified. The following categories have been developed during the pilot study involving 50 students and more than 100 teachers. The categories are considered to be tentative ones; they do overlap and are primarily of heuristic value.

Personality traits and properties

- Communicative properties (open-mindedness, tolerance, flexible personality structure).
- Capability of criticizing oneself and being able to accept criticism from students.
- Capability of coping with students' clashing ideological views on teaching and handling students with mixed abilities with respect to teaching competence.
- Capability of expressing one's own opinion on teaching objectives based on rational arguments.

Competences in the art of teaching and in special didactics

- To be able to demonstrate various forms of teaching concepts and skills necessary to cope with standard classroom situations (e.g. formal–informal teaching; how to change from class teaching to group work, etc.).
- To be able to apply reflectively various strategies of intervention and control in unexpected situations (e.g. discipline problems).
- To be able to discuss the pros and cons of one's own teaching methods with regard to one's aims and values.
- To be able to help students to acquire basic teaching skills (e.g. lesson planning and evaluating, summarizing group work results, etc.) by providing them with the necessary amount of support needed.
- To be able to encourage students to probe their own teaching concepts and ideas by sensitively responding to their different levels of competence.
- To be able to give the students the kind of feedback needed to develop a capacity for realistic self-assessment.

Academic knowledge and expertise in one's fields

- Expertise in one's subjects, especially in foreign languages.
- Willingness to tackle new concepts in methods of teaching (e.g. a communicative approach to language teaching, etc.).
- To be able to demonstrate the application of a wide range of teaching aids and to be able to discuss critically their usefulness.
- To be able to discuss critically with students the values and objectives of curricula, syllabuses and textbooks used.

Programme rationale and activities of the training course for supervisors

In order to provide prospective supervisors with opportunities to develop and assess the above mentioned tutorial competences, the Department of Education at the University of Innsbruck in cooperation with the local LEA has designed an INSET course for experienced secondary teachers interested in the supervising job. The following are some details about course structure, programme rationale and activities of the INSET course.

Course structure
Eight experienced secondary teachers, a method tutor, a teacher educator and four advanced student teachers form a working group with weekly meetings for a term (3–4 months). The teacher educator, a member of the Education Department staff, functions as facilitator whose task it is to provide experiental learning situations for the teachers in the form of on-the-job training conditions.

Programme rationale and learning activities
The course programme is based on elements of self-directed, inquiry-oriented learning attempting to qualify future supervisors for the following competences:

Classroom observation and analysis: feedback competences
Participant teachers have the opportunity to mutually observe, analyse and critically assess their teaching; they can develop and modify their competence of how to give and accept valid feedback. For many teachers this is a crucial and risk-taking enterprise, especially challenging when they are confronted with blunt, unmasked student feedback which they hitherto had not experienced.

Lesson planning competences
All participants are required to present a lesson plan on the same topic which they had democratically agreed upon (e.g. how to introduce calculus in a fifth form; photosynthesis in a sixth form). Teachers can learn about different

didactical concepts and lesson-planning criteria, and they can discuss lesson-planning standards required from students: What should a student's lesson plan contain? How elaborate should the format be?

Assessment and evaluation competences
The most important competence of a supervisor is his/her way of relating and communicating with students, especially in a context of permanent implicit appraisal. Teachers, therefore, must find out whether their communicative style, feedback and assessment behaviour is conducive to a student's development of self-evaluation capacities.

In the final phase of the course one student and two teachers collaborate to plan, perform and evaluate a student's lesson. The post-lesson talk is held publicly in a plenary session to make teachers aware of the vast spectrum of adequate and inadequate assessment styles and different response patterns of the assessed.

The main rationale behind the training scheme is to introduce experienced teachers to situations where they can freely experiment with various aspects of a supervisor's role. The tasks and activities in which teachers are engaged throughout the course provide two kinds of self-evaluating situations:

1 *Selective situations.* In these situations teachers can find out in a selective way (yes or no decision) whether they regard themselves qualified enough for the supervisor job. Implicit self-assessment questions are asked with regard to basic personality traits which can hardly be modified within the period of the training course: Do I like this kind of job? Do I feel competent enough? Do I have enough self-esteem and flexibility to work with different students' basic personalities? Such selective situations are:

   • The teachers' response to critical feedback about their teaching by other course members, including students: Do they defend themselves constantly? Are they incapable of just listening and accepting negative feedback without justifying themselves? Are they capable of maintaining a balance between an open-minded learner and a self-assured expert?
   • The teachers' style of discussing and evaluating a student's teaching performance: Can the supervisor communicate with students holding different ideologies, especially those antithetical to his own? Can an atmosphere conducive to mutual learning and professional development be established?

2 *Developmental-learning situations.* These situations enable the teachers to develop and acquire new tutorial skills and competences such as:

   • cooperative lesson-planning;
   • reflecting on differences between the lesson-planning of a beginner and an expert;
   • classroom observation and analysis skills based on objective evidence and subjective appraisal.

The teachers can diagnose strengths and weaknesses in their role as supervisors without selective implications and can modify routines and strategies which they themselves find inappropriate.

The assessment of tutorial competences: how the qualification of a supervisor is established

The assessment of a teacher's qualification for a job as supervisor is based on a two-stage procedure, the principles of which have been democratically negotiated between LEAs and Departments of Education.ᐧ

Stage 1: probationary supervisor

A teacher is admitted as a probationary supervisor on the following criteria.

Fulfilment of course requirements
Each teacher must participate in all course activities (mutual classroom observation, public assessment of a colleague's performance in a written format, preparing an elaborate lesson plan) and is required to write a critical report on the personal value of the course.

Critical self-assessment
In addition to their reports, teachers are encouraged to reflect on their prospective role as supervisors. They are asked to assess their strengths and weaknesses and write about their feelings, expectations and role concepts. These reports are strictly confidential, accessible only to the facilitator and other course members on request. The main purpose of this self-account is to document the teacher's willingness and commitment to self-evaluation as an essential supervisor's competence.

Here is an example of a teacher's self-assessment taken from his report:

First some preliminary thoughts about the usefulness of this task:

- For the course leader: he can compare his observations with the self-assessments of course members. What does he do if the two accounts differ? Does he modify his observations or does he doubt the writer's reflective capacity and sincerity?
- I consider this 'forced' self-reflection an advantage for me. I know quite well I wouldn't have taken the time to think about my teaching in depth; besides, there is an additional chance of comparing myself with other teachers.

  Before I went to this course I was quite uncertain about my role as a teacher. I didn't know exactly what was really important for me, partially because I didn't bother to find a personal definition of school and teaching. I found myself dedicated to a concept of good teaching taken on from colleagues without reference to reality: learning objectives, quantifiable knowledge, learning products, etc. At the same time I intuitively followed a more pupil-oriented path. I knew about this ambiguous stance but I didn't suffer much because I tend to take things easy.

I think this course helped me to see much clearer now where I stand, although there are still uncertainties left, e.g. with regard to pupil assessment: I still don't know how to put my concepts into practice. I'll try to describe the important issues briefly:

1 The pupil is in the centre of my deliberations. It's the teacher's task to help the pupil to enter into the adults' world. Knowledge taught can only be justified under this perspective. It's the teacher's task to select important information from the vast information pool. In order to do that he must have more than just average academic knowledge.
2 The essential precondition for a teacher to help a pupil to become an autonomous adult is that the pupil accepts and trusts him. Trust can only be gained through openness and a human mind: admitting one's own mistakes, taking pupils seriously, are essential demands on every teacher.
3 Starting point for every teacher is the fact that most pupils can be influenced by pedagogical measures. If, therefore, a pupil doesn't show a certain desired response the teacher firstly has to blame him/herself.

Do I fulfil these requirements listed in a rather fragmentary way?

1 I consider my expert knowledge as mediocre, but I am eager to improve it.
2 My relationship with pupils is quite good; I am willing to develop it further.
3 Pupil assessment, especially giving bad marks, has never been my strength (perhaps, because I myself was always a bad pupil!).

Sometimes I am worried whether my pupils know as much as my colleagues' kids. I hope I can answer this question myself. How do I assess my capabilities in dealing with students? I think I am capable of establishing a good relationship with students; I also think I can make them aware of the various problems of being a good teacher; I think I can encourage them and make them happy about their role as a teacher.

What I am a bit doubtful about:

Whether I am capable of teaching 'model lessons', seen from a didactic perspective; I lack the necessary management skills to be a model teacher.

Whether I can live up to the students' academic expectations; and what I certainly don't know: Are the issues I raised relevant at all?

This report is a good example of the self-reflective potential of teachers which is often underestimated, but fully exploited and surfaced as a consequence of stimulating course experiences. The third source of assessment is the facilitator's appraisal of teachers' qualification as supervisors.

Appraisal by course leader (facilitator)

The course leader's evaluation and assessment is based on observations and evaluation of participants' performances in the three essential tasks: mutual classroom observation and appraisal, lesson planning, and evaluation of a student's performance. The course leader's assessment criteria are made explicit to the teachers throughout the course (e.g. a teacher must be able to give subjective feedback based on objective evidence). The facilitator's assessment role is restricted to guarantee that basic and minimal tutorial competences do exist within each teacher and to screen out extreme cases of incompetence. His judgement is always validated against the teacher's self-account and is open to negotiation in instances of severely differing appraisals.

Stage 2: Final qualification as supervisor

The final assessment and appointment as supervisor is based on students' feedback on the supervisors' communicative and counselling competences after the first term of teaching practice. Each student has to write a report reflecting on his/her experiences throughout the teaching practice period. The report is part of the credit requirements and must contain a critical comparison of planned and actually performed lessons and an evaluation of the supervisor's competences. Since the students are made aware of how significant their appraisal of their supervisors is, most of the reports are written with depth and attempted fairness. A teacher is only rejected as a supervisor at this stage if the majority of his/her students are dissatisfied with him/her. Out of 50 teachers who acted as supervisors in our training scheme, only 2 had to be dismissed from further applications.

Here is an extract from an English student's report describing her experiences with her supervisor:

> The post-lesson discussions with my supervisor were on the whole con-structive, even the talks about his own lessons were quite fruitful. I consider Mr M a very good supervisor. His lessons vary in an interesting way, that means he does not behave the same way in all his classes which makes him open to criticism which is important for us. In all his formal discussions with us he was open minded, told us episodes from his teaching practice and was very useful in his constructive criticism on our own performances. I found it especially valid that he didn't interfere with our activities; there were no restrictions; we had a free hand in planning and performing our lessons. If you wanted to do something you could do it but you had to do it yourself. I think this was good for me.

Features of naturalistic evaluation in the assessment of tutorial competences

The following characteristics of naturalistic evaluation can be identified in the outlined training model:

1 The opening up (making transparent) of each teacher's performance, values and competence development with all its positive aspects (new experiences, potential of change and development, etc.) and negative aspects (vulnerability through exposure to criticism, threat to one's self-esteem, destructive competition among group members, etc.).
2 The appraisal of competences from multiple perspectives and criteria (self-assessment, students' feedback, external appraisal collected from various data sources and situations).
3 Holistic judgement on final qualification based on numerous accounts and evidence in a two-stage procedure.
4 External appraisal (course leader, LEA) is always validated against self-appraisal through consensus-seeking negotiations.
5 Most of the appraisal situations are learning situations with a potential of change and development.

Some assessment dilemmas arising from the naturalistic paradigm

Despite all the evidence that the evaluation procedure in this training model is based on principles of naturalistic inquiry, there remain some fundamental conflicts for any evaluator operating in a hierarchically structured, selection-oriented school system:

- the dilemma between assessing for selection and assessing for professional development;
- the conflict between external assessment and self-assessment in instances where appraisals and sources of validity are questioned (e.g. a teacher's self-account vastly differs from the course leader's account).

How can these dilemmas be solved?

The first dilemma reveals a conceptual weakness of the training model: it quickly sifts out the competent teacher from the less competent one. The competences of the 'good' teacher are strengthened and significantly enhanced during the course, while there is no provision in the course for any extra help for the less competent one. One way of tackling this problem is the idea of a probationary status: the supervisors, while working with students, can detect new competences hitherto unknown to them or they can reconsider their aspiration for this job in the light of fair and realistic working conditions.

The second problem, a clash between external assessment and self-assessment, can be solved by taking students' accounts and feedback data as a criterion for final assessment.

Both solutions are based on the ideal concept of equal distribution of power, a phenomenon which rarely exists in a centralized, hierarchically structured school system. Thus, what remains is the hope that more and more people in powerful positions become convinced of the idea of naturalistic inquiry in educational evaluation so that external and internal assessment are realistically considered to be equal procedures in teacher assessment.

9
Appraisal of performance or appraisal of persons

John Elliott

Introduction

Increasing State intervention in the control and distribution of resources in schools and higher education institutions has placed teacher appraisal high on the agenda of educational debate within the UK. One of the few attempts to systematically review appraisal schemes in existence was made by a team in the Suffolk Education Department. The report *Those Having Torches ...* (Graham, 1985) was commissioned and funded by the DES following the publication of its White Paper on *Teaching Quality* (1983). It focusses on studies of implementation issues, particularly in the USA, from which it derives recommendations for policy development in the UK.

The Suffolk team argue that the primary purpose of appraisal should be the professional development of teachers. They tend to view this process as the improvement of specific performance skills implicit in teaching tasks rather than the development of personal qualities. Such a view fits the dominant political assumption that poor standards in education are caused by deficiencies in teacher performance. This assumption implies that good teaching largely consists of technical or craft skills.

The view that professional development is about improving performance skills rules out other conceptions of teaching. On its very first page the Suffolk report lists four quite distinct concepts of teaching: the first two – 'teaching as labour' and 'teaching as craft' – being comparable with the view of professional development depicted above. The third view, 'teaching as a professional activity', is very close to what I would call 'reflective practice' based on conscious self-monitoring of situation and self. The fourth view is 'teaching as an art'. The Suffolk report describes this view as follows:

teaching techniques may be unconventional, improvisatory, highly personal.

... The teacher makes use not only of a body of professional knowledge and skill but also of personal resources which are possibly unique and almost certainly uniquely expressed according to the teacher's personality and the interactions between him and individual pupils or whole classes. (Graham, 1985, pp. 1– 2)

The Suffolk team quote approvingly from Wise *et al*. (1984), who argue that:

Teaching competence may be conceived as a continuum. The further one moves along the continuum from minimal competence to excellence, the more wide-ranging and inferential the source of data and the less uniform and generalisable the specific indicators. . . . The demands of evaluation differ along this continuum.

The implication of all this is that the four concepts of teaching they identify constitute stages of professional development from minimally acceptable levels of competence to excellence. One might have some reservations about this. 'Teaching as labour' might not be considered as a professional view of teaching at all since its essential dependence on externally imposed standards of practice and evaluation negates the autonomy which is a central element in any professional culture.

However, one can make out a case for a developmental continuum from 'craft teaching' to 'teaching as an art' via 'teaching as a reflective practice'. At each stage of the transformation in practice there is nevertheless a retention of continuity with the previous stage(s). Reflective practice focusses on problematic areas while leaving the unproblematic to the tacit craft knowledge of the teacher. Teaching as art depends on a whole range of personal qualities but does not totally negate the reflective and craft aspects of teaching. The Suffolk team do not point out the inconsistency between the view of teaching competence they describe in the first section of the report and the way they later rule out the appraisal of personal qualities. They fail to recognize that the form of appraisal they recommend 'screens out' any acknowledgement of teaching competence at the highest level of its development. In fact Doll (1984) argues that the use of the term competence to refer to low-level performance skills at all is a departure from customary usage:

Competence refers essentially to a state of being or to a capacity . . . performance is the outward and public manifestation of underlying and internal powers.

I would argue that the different levels of competence suggested by the Suffolk team reflect different kinds of powers and capacities. At the level of externally standardized and controlled performance, it is the capacity to follow and correctly apply a programme of rules and procedures which is the source of competence. At the level of craft skills, the source of competence resides in the capacity for processing contextual and situational information as a basis for performance. For 'reflective practice' competence resides in a teacher's capacity to control his or her performance through self-monitoring. This capacity is at the basis of performances which are regulated by conscious decisions and action–plans. But its exercise reveals that decisions and plans do not always take effect as the teacher wants and intends. Performance is affected by emotional and motivational states of which the teacher may be unaware, and whose manifestations in action make him or her powerless to effect decisions and plans. In this context, competence involves the development of emotional and motivational states which are appropriate to the teaching task. Hence, personal qualities can justifiably be viewed as a fundamental source of teaching competence.

One reason which might be used to justify the exclusion of any evaluation of personal qualities from a process of teacher appraisal aimed at professional development is that the motivational and emotional tendencies of individuals cannot be easily improved. Appraisal for professional development should focus only on improvable performance. Such a focus must assume that one is dealing with individuals whose background motivational and emotional tendencies are appropriate for the job. The appraisal of personal qualities should be a quite separate process operating at the point of entry (selection) into the job.

The assumption that motivational and emotional tendencies cannot be improved is one of the legacies of an individualistic trait psychology, which posited them as elements in relatively fixed and unchangeable structures. As Harré (1983, pp. 199–200) points out, for example, Eysenck explained dispositions and tendencies as properties grounded in physiological structures. But Harré argues that emotional and motivational tendencies are grounded in systems of belief developed about oneself and others which are acquired in the social process of personal development. If this is correct, then emotional and motivational tendencies can be improved by modifying and changing the beliefs which underpin them.

But how might such changes in belief be accomplished? Do individuals possess the capacities to develop themselves into the sort of person they want to become? Harré makes a rough distinction between 'powers to do' and 'powers to be'. The former are the capacities individuals acquire to perform their tasks and roles. So we can ask, what personal qualities do teachers need to acquire to teach well? In my view, this question is central to any consideration of what constitutes teaching quality in education. The quality of teaching cannot be assessed in terms of performance-referenced criteria, but only in terms of the personal qualities displayed in the performance.

Personal and professional development

'Powers to be' are the *reflexive capacities* individuals acquire in relation to the emotional and motivational core of their personal being. The object on which they are exercised is not 'performance' but 'the self'. Harré (1983) lists such powers as those of *self-knowledge* and *self-control*. His distinction points up an ambiguous use of the concept of the self-monitoring teacher. In one sense, it can simply refer to the self, consciously monitoring its performance: it refers to a non-reflexive power. But in another sense, the concept is used to refer to the self, consciously monitoring the quality of being manifested in performance: it refers here to a reflexive power; to the power to develop the self's knowledge of itself.

This analysis of competence illuminates what professional development involves. First, it involves the acquisition of capacities necessary for the successful completion of a set of professional tasks, e.g. recording student progress, bringing about learning, planning the curriculum. Such capacities refer to information-processing skills, abilities to make decisions, formulate plans, and self-monitor performance. Secondly, it involves the acquisition of appropriate emotions and motivations and the theories about human nature and conduct which underpin them. These capacities cannot be derived from an analysis of tasks, since what are defined as tasks in the first place are determined by the exercise of such powers. For example, one cannot identify the abilities involved in bringing learning about unless one has an understanding of the nature of learning. What counts as learning will depend on a set of beliefs about human nature and the attitudes it is appropriate to adopt towards students on the basis of such beliefs. In as much as the acquisition of attitudes constitutes a source of competent practice, in addition to performance skills, then professional development implies personal development: the acquisition of emotional and motivational tendencies which constitute the core of personal being.

However, personal development itself, at least in our culture, involves self-development, i.e. a process in which individuals accept responsibility for changing the personal core of attitudes and motivations manifested in their performances. This process involves the development of powers of self-determination, e.g. reflexive self-monitoring and self-control. The higher levels of professional competence will draw on these powers as an important resource. In summary, then, the development of professional competence involves the acquisition of (1) skills and abilities which are implied by performance tasks, (2) appropriate beliefs and attitudes, and (3) reflexive powers.

The appraisal proposals of the Suffolk team define professional development as the acquisition of capacities which can be directly derived from an analysis of performance tasks (job descriptions). I would claim that even the development of relatively low-level cognitive capacities will depend upon and be shaped by the exercise of a teacher's reflexive powers. As the teacher becomes reflexively aware of the attitudes and motivations manifested in his or her performance and renders problematic the structures of belief which underpin them, he/she is able to control the sort of person he/she wants to become in the teaching role. The changes effected in this way result in new conceptions of teaching tasks and the skills required to perform them well. An exclusive focus on improving professional performance skills is ultimately self-defeating as a process of professional development. Such an approach tacitly transfers control over performance from the teacher's self to others. It enables management, for example, to exercise control over performance by preventing teachers from reflexively developing new understandings of the nature of teaching and learning tasks.

The process of developing professional competence, as I have outlined it, involves self-appraisal. Appraisal by others is often contrasted with self-appraisal. This distinction is made in the Suffolk report. In the Government's 1983 White Paper on *Teaching Quality*, self-appraisal is dismissed with faint praise in favour of appraisal by others. The assumption underlying this contrast is that self-appraisal is a private activity conducted in solitude and isolation from other people. I want to argue that this is not necessarily so. I will begin by trying to explain how this contrast between two kinds of appraisal is drawn.

Self-appraisal or reflexive self-monitoring is a central feature of the process of personal development. This process is basically social in nature. According to Harré (1983, pp. 259–61) public conversations play a fundamental role in this process. Personal or private conversations with oneself are also a feature. What we need to understand are the relationships between private and public conversations in the development of persons. Harré *et al.* (1985) attempt to explain these relationships in terms of a four-quadrant model based on two axes. One axis is called *display* and the other *location*. The display dimension marks the distinction between public and private space. In public space, individuals manifest or provide accounts of their psychological states; in private space, they keep these states to themselves.

If we look at the Suffolk appraisal proposals in this light we can see that they impose restrictions on the assessment of psychological states manifested in a teacher's performance. The focus of observation and the appraisal interview is on low-inference performance data rather than psychological data.

The location dimension marks a difference in the way psychological states and processes are realized. Is it realized in a collective of individuals or the individual? Harré *et al.* question the assumption that cognitions, emotions and motivations are exclusively the properties of individuals. Collectives can reason or think, express emotion, etc. He makes much of the idea of 'psychological symbiosis', in which the psychological states of individuals are dependent upon their interactions with each other. For example, a husband believes certain things but these beliefs are taken from his wife rather than developed by him. Harré *et al.* illustrate 'psychological symbiosis' by reference to Martin Richards' analysis of tape-recordings of conversations between mothers and their children. The analysis revealed that most mothers address their infants 'as if the infants had well-developed psychological repertoires of intentions, wants, feelings and powers of reason from the moment of birth'. The infants develop as persons by acquiring psychological states supplied by the mother.

It is only when individuals begin to take responsibility for their own development by exercising reflexive powers of self-monitoring and self-mastery, that we can talk about the individual as the location of psychological states and the processes of realizing them. According to Harré *et al.*, human beings rarely appear as psychological individuals but are usually in a situation of psychological symbiosis in which each supplements the psychological defects of another or others.

From the two axes of display and location Harré derives a four-quadrant model of personal development:

1 public–collective space;
2 private–collective space;
3 private–individual space; and
4 individual–public space.

Quadrant 1 marks out the process of 'psychological symbiosis'. Quadrant 2 marks out a process in which the individual develops a sense of personal identity by appropriating beliefs, emotions and motivations operating in the collective as his or her own. Quadrant 3 constitutes the realm of the personal in which the individual privately converses with him or herself. Reflexive self-monitoring appears to fall into this quadrant. The individual creates a private space in which to reflect about his or her psychological states in terms of their origins, their location, and their relationship to the sort of person she/he wants to become. Quadrant 4 is the domain in which the individual publicly manifests the 'self' in action, or accounts for the 'self' so manifested. The accountability process constitutes a form of reflexive practical discourse because it presupposes that the individuals involved exercise a capacity for reflexive self-monitoring. It is a form of self-assessment which operates in a context of public dialogue.

For Harré *et al.* (1985), personal development involves a series of transitions across these quadrants in the direction of 1 to 4. But this does not imply that individuals as totalities can be unambiguously located in a particular quadrant at different points in their life histories. In accomplishing a transition the individual does not necessarily leave one dimension of psychological space behind. For example, in moving from private self-reflection to an involvement in reflexive public discourse, the individual may continue to create future private space for self-reflection. Discourse in the public domain, however, constitutes an important resource for developing powers of self-knowledge and self-control.

Let's now look at the Suffolk proposals in the light of this model of personal development. A naive view of the appraisal process would be that it ought to facilitate a transition from a situation of symbiotic dependence on others as a source of psychological support for personal deficiencies, to one of psychological independence in which the appraisee has appropriated certain beliefs, attitudes and motivations as aspects of his/her personal identity. This would involve appraisers providing appraisees with feedback in the form of moral assessments of their personal qualities. Rather than being viewed as a helpful and beneficial process of fostering psychological independence in teachers, so that they can perform their professional roles more effectively, the process is often seen as a primitive and harmful one aimed at destroying the appraisee's sense of personal identity and creating a form of psychological symbiosis.

What is really at stake here, I believe, is not the value of external appraisals of personal qualities, but the quality of the organizational climate in which they are made. In contexts where relationships are characterized by lack of respect for persons, competitive individualism and mistrust, external moral assessments of psychological states are highly threatening to individuals. In contexts where relationships are governed by respect for persons, cooperation in pursuit of common goals and mutual trust, external appraisals are likely to be perceived as supportive rather than destructive of personal identity.

The ruling 'out of court' by Suffolk of a form of appraisal which would facilitate personal development from quadrants 1 to 2 is a sad reflection on the prevailing climate in education today. It suggests that the major problem of enhancing teaching quality in such institutions lies not so much in the psychological deficiencies of individuals as in the moral climate which prevails in the wider collectivities of educational institutions and systems. The Suffolk report, and indeed the whole subsequent debate about teacher appraisal, suggests that priority should be given to the improvement of organizational and policy-making structures within the educational system.

The Suffolk report appears to make provision for personal development construed as a transition between quadrants 3 and 4. It proposes that teachers produce self-assessments on the basis of solitary and private reflection and then make them available to the appraiser prior to the external appraisal. The espoused aspiration is to create a dialogue. Does this indicate an awareness of public discourse as a medium of self-appraisal? Perhaps, but it is a distorted awareness. The focus should be, it is argued, on low-inference performance data rather than personal data. Self-assessment and external assessment are both understood as appraisals of observable performance rather than the states they manifest. As such, they can contribute little to the personal development of teachers.

We must therefore conclude that the Suffolk proposals, if implemented, will do little to foster the development of personal qualities in teachers, and therefore little to raise teaching quality to reflect the highest levels of professional competence. By screening personal development out of the appraisal process, the proposals construct a dangerous contrast between the professional competence and personal qualities. In the context of the large-scale ill-health they presume to exist in the educational system, the proposals may be interpreted as a justifiable means of safeguarding the personal identities of teachers from destructive manifestations of managerial and bureaucratic intent. But they can also be interpreted as a means of legitimating the use of a power-coercive strategy for establishing bureaucratic control over the performance of teachers. Such an appraisal process would not only discount teachers as persons but foster a process which segregate their professional from their personal identities. The professional identity simply becomes a social identity – a 'being-for-others' from which the core of the personal-self has disengaged.

Perhaps the most significant political manifestation of mistrust of teachers was the publication in 1983 of Sir Keith Joseph's White Paper on *Teaching Quality*. In this document, the DES blamed individual teachers for deficiencies in the quality of educational provision. It proposed appraisal as the means of rectifying them. Within the White Paper the purposes of appraisal are starkly and clearly pinpointed in terms of the training, deployment and dismissal of individual teachers. Moreover, all these purposes are viewed as management functions:

> The Government believe that those responsible for managing the school teacher force have a clear responsibility to establish, in consultation with their teachers, a policy for staff deployment and training based on a systematic assessment of every teacher's performance and related to their policy for the school curriculum.
>
> Concern for quality demands that in the small minority of cases where, despite in-service training arrangements, teachers fail to maintain a satisfactory standard of performance, employers must, in the interests of pupils, be ready to use procedures for dismissal . . . unsatisfactory performance can be sufficient reason for dismissal. (DES, 1983)

The overriding model of 'management' which emerges in the White Paper is a power-coercive one. This is not because appraisal is seen as serving management functions but because of the form of appraisal envisaged. The White Paper (DES, 1983) dismisses self-assessment with faint praise in a single sentence:

> The Government welcome recent moves towards self-assessment by schools and teachers, and believe these should help to improve school standards and curricula. But . . .

The paragraph (92) then proceeds to legitimate hierarchical control over the collection, analysis and release of data about each teacher's performance.

> . . . employers can manage their teacher force effectively only if they have accurate knowledge of each teacher's performance. The government believe that for this purpose formal assessment of teacher performance is necessary and should be based on classroom visiting by the teacher's head or head of department; and an appraisal of both pupils' work and of the teacher's contribution to the life of the school.

The assumption here is of a hierarchy of credibility in which the appraisals of managers are presumed to be more accurate than those of the appraisee, professional peers and his/her students. If this assumption is a questionable one, as I believe it to be, then there is no necessary reason why management decisions could not be based on the assessments of the appraisee, professional peers and students. Decisions about training, placement and dismissal do not have to be based on a form of hierarchical surveillance which effectively empowers managers to exercise control over the details of performance.

The Suffolk project was established by the DES to develop proposals for *appraisal* within the framework set out in the White Paper. The focus on classroom performance, and the acceptance of appraisal as a tool of management, which emerged in the project report, are fully in line with the White Paper's statements of intent. But it builds into its proposals a measure of protection for individuals against the intrusion of bureaucratic control into the personal domain. It attempts a formal linkage between self-assessment and formal appraisal, rules out 'personal qualities' as criteria of assessment, and claims standards cannot be defined in terms of a set of generic skills (since skills are context-bound). Instead of coming up with criteria or standards as part of its brief, the project team defined 'areas of teacher action' which contribute to effective performance, namely, climate, planning, management, subject knowledge, the act of teaching, and interpersonal relationships. These provide the major categories in which low-inference performance data is to be collected and skills-in-context assessed.

In claiming that multipurpose appraisal did not work and that professional development, focussed on improving classroom performance, should be the primary overriding purpose, the Suffolk team also built in further protections against bureaucratic intrusion into the realm of the personal. It did not rule out 'placement' and 'grounds of dismissal' as purposes, but made them subordinate by restricting the database to a form which limits the extent to which it can be used for such purposes. It is difficult to see how one could dismiss individuals entirely on the basis of low-inference performance data. Deficiencies in performance require explanation before they constitute relevant grounds for dismissal. Faulty training, inadequate development opportunities, and external constraints on the exercise of acquired skills could all be cited as reasons for non-dismissal. Grounds for dismissal normally have to refer to undesirable character traits, personal attitudes and motivations. Placement decisions about individuals are normally based on predictions of successful and unsuccessful performance on tasks other than those they are currently performing. Data about performance skills in relation to specific tasks and contexts is hardly likely to be very relevant to placing and developing individuals on other tasks in other contexts. What is relevant is data about personal qualities, which although manifested in current performance, are deemed relevant to task performance in other contexts.

We have recently completed a study of the personal qualities competent police constables display in their handling of incidents on the streets (Elliott and Shadforth, 1987). In the course of cross-checking our analysis of behavioural event interview data with the formal appraisals of the officers interviewed, we discovered that supervisors' assessments largely referred to 'personal qualities' as opposed to specific performance skills, e.g. relates well to peers and public, well-organized approach to work, interested in activities beyond work, enthusiastic, ambitious, self-motivated, self-confident, mature, takes pride in appearance, respectful and polite to others, pleasing and cheerful personality, committed, takes initiative, intelligent, efficient, persistent, conscientious, adaptable, industrious, willing to learn, respects discipline, sense of integrity and honesty, open-minded, empathetic towards others, loyal. A separate analysis of the appraisals of officers who were either dismissed or 'forced' to resign revealed that negative assessments referred to deficiencies in the qualities listed above. The appraisal files of patrol constables did not indicate any intrinsic conflict about the purposes for which the data could be used. The same information appeared to be relevant to decisions about training, placement and dismissal. Personal qualities were not seen as fixed traits incapable of development through training. Looking at the regular appraisals of individuals over time, it was clear that perceived improvements were acknowledged and judgements modified. Dismissal was indeed only contemplated after a period of time in which improvements could reasonably be expected.

I would argue that appraisal can serve a variety of purposes when it takes the form of an assessment of personal qualities. This kind of qualitative data is relevant to decisions about training, placement and dismissal. Intrinsic conflict only arises when the data about performance is confined to low-inference data about task-specific skills. This renders it unusable for purposes of placement and dismissal. One can therefore conclude that the Suffolk proposals produce a conflict of purposes in order to legitimate a policy of excluding the assessment of personal qualities from the appraisal process.

The appraisal of personal qualities in police organizations

Some would no doubt argue that police organizations are quasi-military institutions in which the performance of constables is controlled through the rank structure. The appraisal of personal qualities is simply a means of shaping the individual psychologically into a form which guarantees compliant performance. But all this ignores the nature of police work. Patrol constables are expected to be capable of working alone on the streets and independently from close supervision. The nature of their work calls for high levels of skill. Observational studies of patrol practice suggest that the following abilities are generic to good policing (see Fielding, 1984):

(i)   sensitive observation and a capacity to impute motive on the basis of deep local knowledge;
(ii)   the ability to convey power in a tangible but generally understated manner; and
(iii) a refined capacity for negotiation.

The 'personal qualities' extracted from police appraisal files are highly congruent with these broad clusters of abilities. They constitute the psychological characteristics individuals need to possess in order to exercise such abilities. Moreover, they are the converse of the 'dependent qualities', which would enable the organization to control the details of performance. Observational research by Fielding and others portrays the police 'as massively competent social actors'. They are not simply reproducing in performance sets of formal rules whose application is rigidly controlled and monitored by supervisors. The formal rules are continuously interpreted in the light of the requirements of action within the working environment. Fielding (1984) argues that: 'the apparently rigid hierarchy of authority was notional in the face of its circumvention by members who were granted various degrees of discretion'. He contrasts the formal rules of the organization with the occupational culture which emerges as a response to the everyday working situation, and suggests that one of the major competencies required in officers is the ability to offer satisfactory accounts of practice within the organization in those areas of discretion and licence it permits. This requires 'a thorough knowledge of the justifications available to ensure an account is honoured'. Fielding claims that unlike other occupations enjoying professional licence, 'officers are continuously obliged to account for (or disclaim) their action or inaction and must do so variously in relation to peers and supervisors'.

Management appraisals of police constables are not based on direct observation of patrol work. In describing the form they take I shall draw largely on the 'notes of guidance' produced by a particular force. But I have no reason to believe the process it describes is in any way untypical.

Part 1 of the appraisal report consists of a pen picture report of the officer's work in the context of his/her life beyond it. The notes of guidance state that: 'It would be quite unfair to judge performance at work without taking into account other pressures.' The report also consists of gradings against a lot of personal qualities 'which are felt to be of basic importance in all people'. These are 'appearance', 'professional ability', 'report writing', 'ability to work alone', 'initiative', 'judgement'. The report is completed by the constable's senior work supervisor, the unit or shift Inspector. Its focus is on the constable's work over the past 12 months, but includes 'any recommendations for employment, training and suitability for any expressed job preference'.

Although the Inspector is expected to have a detailed knowledge of each constable's work this is not so much based on close surveillance of his/her patrol practice as on the written and verbal accounts he/she produces back at the station. The supervisor's appraisals constitute 'audits' of self-appraisals, perhaps cross-checked against appraisals provided by peers and members of the public. In considering various justifications for action or non-action, a supervisor not only takes into account the forms of license permitted by the organization, but also the motives, attitudes and beliefs cited as reasons and explanations. As Fielding (1984) again points out, in the frequent absence of tangible results, the quality of police action is assessed in terms of the attitudes manifested in action rather than the action itself. The notes of guidance claim that: 'It is of more importance in any assessment of character, of motivation or vitality, not so much to know what a person did but rather why and under what circumstances.' This explains why data about life beyond work is considered relevant:

> It is not unknown for an indifferent performer on duty to be a bundle of energy and full of resourcefulness when pursuing off-duty interests. We might ask ourselves if we can harness these assets during duty time and so reap the benefit of much that is good in the officer.

In addition to the reasonableness of the justifications provided by an officer during the course of his or her work, the supervisor will want to assess the authenticity or credibility of their account in the light of his/her knowledge of the person. In this informal 'accounting' context the constable has opportunities to disagree with the views of the supervisor and to convince him/her of the merits of the course of action in question. The work supervisor's formal report must be viewed against the background of this continuous accountability process. It is read and signed by the constable: 'By seeing the report a person can correct any mistatements of fact and give views on any aspect of behaviour that may have been misunderstood.' It is then used as the basis for Part 2 of the process: the appraisal interview with a senior officer (Chief Inspector or Superintendent), and a further report.

The main purpose of the interview is to assess 'the officer's needs and to see that the best use is made of personnel'. Whereas the supervisor's primary task is to assess the personal qualities manifested in performance, the senior officer's primary task is to discuss this assessment with the constable in order to identify his/her needs and potential within the organization, and to make recommendations about future placement and training. The constable is expected to make a major contribution to the discussion:

Discuss the report giving the officer ample opportunity to put across points of view. Establish a rhythm of 'talk' and 'listen'.

Expand on the job preferences of the officer. Are they realistic and capable of fulfilment?

Police appraisals appear to be two-tier. The first tier, at the level of the supervisor, is the outcome of an 'accountability' discourse about practical incidents, between patrol constables and their supervisors at the work-face. At this level the appraisal process is not managerially controlled, and it calls for the display of considerable competence by the appraisee in reflectively self-monitoring practice in the light of organizational goals and norms. It is the supervisor's responsibility to mediate these goals and norms through calling his/her constables to account for their actions.

The second tier in the appraisal process, at the level of management, is grounded in the outcome of the first-tier. But its purposes are different. The supervisor has the role of ensuring high-quality patrol practice. The senior officer's management role involves placing individuals in positions where their personal qualities benefit the organization and make it more effective.

I have made much of appraisal in police organizations because their hierarchical nature is frequently presumed to imply the suppression of individuality. What I have tried to show is that hierarchical appraisal systems in police organizations are not necessarily power-coercive. The two-tier model I have outlined, if implemented properly, can foster the development of dynamic and reflexive qualities in appraisees.

This integration is made possible by structural features of police organizations which do in fact limit and restrict the operation of power-coercive control over police practice. The nature of the constable's work places the supervision function in an accountability rather than surveillance context. And within the hierarchy the supervisory function is differentiated by roles from management functions. The two-tier model of appraisal which obtains in the police reflects these organizational characteristics. The result is an appraisal system which leaves little room for the development of observational systems of hierarchical surveillance – that major device of power-coercive control – and quite a lot of room for self-appraisal as a central feature of the process.

The appraisal of individual constables in police organizations by managers is grounded in data that emerges from interactions in what Harré *et al.* (1985) call 'the individual-public space' (quadrant 4). It consists of assessments of the psychological states manifested by officers in publicly accounting for their actions to supervisors and peers within the organization. The appraisal interview with a senior officer (manager) need not simply be a mechanism which makes the individual accountable to the organization. It can also enable the organization to be responsive to the individual. Such responsiveness would indicate a direction of influence from 'individual-public' (quadrant 4) to 'public-collective' (quadrant 1) space. The personal development of individuals can, in principle if not practice, influence the organizational development through the manner in which the management responds to the accounts of individual practitioners during quadrant 4 interactions at both levels of the appraisal process.

The hierarchical appraisal of individuals in police organizations is certainly concerned with promoting the acquisition and maintenance of desired psychological states. But as I argued earlier, such appraisal is a feature of the process by which personal identities are developed generally. One must make a clear distinction between the fact that personal identities are socially acquired and the kind of identities so acquired. It is not the exercise of hierarchical influence over identity formation which can reasonably be objected to, but the manner in which it is exerted and its ideological content. One can object to a form of influence which prevents the individual from having a say in the appraisal process, since this would stifle those reflexive powers and capacities upon which the higher levels of personal development depend. One can also object to the promotion of psychological states which are inconsistent with the values embodied in our concept of personhood, e.g. passive qualities as opposed to the dynamic qualities which characterize human agency.

Toward a two-tier model of teacher appraisal

From my study of police appraisal, I would conclude that hierarchical appraisals of teachers by managers in the educational system need not be incompatible with the development of dynamic personal qualities within the professional role. The belief that they are, stems from the style of management teachers read into the appraisal proposals and the ideological content embedded in them: a power-coercive style which entails the acquisition of passive and dependent psychological states as opposed to personally empowering dynamic qualities. I think there is little doubt that schoolteachers were correct to interpret the White Paper in terms of a passive and dependent view of their role (see Elliott, 1985, for a critique of the theory of teaching implicit in the White Paper). But this does not necessarily entail that the three management functions of appraisal, as outlined in the White Paper, cannot support a process whereby the professional practices of teachers are empowered with personal qualities. It is not the government's view of the functions of management which lies at the heart of the problem but its power-coercive model of how those functions are to be carried out.

During the teachers' dispute with the government over conditions of service, and following the publication of *Some Having Torches . . .* , the ACAS Independent Panel negotiated an agreed set of principles for appraisal between the teachers' unions, the government and local authority employers. I shall now examine those principles with a view to comparing them with the proposals in the White Paper (see also Elliott, 1987) and the Suffolk report.

The ACAS document outlines six functions of appraisal covering the identification of training and professional development needs, the assessment of potential for career development, the selection of staff for new posts, and the 'recognition of teachers experiencing performance difficulty'. They do not differ in many respects from the purposes stated in the White Paper, although they are rather more specific. They might be seen merely as clarifications of the latter, as 'negotiated' shifts of emphasis, or as obscurations of real intent. For example, 'deployment' was used in the White Paper to refer to the involuntary relocation of teachers to different schools. In the ACAS document the term is used in a general statement about the functions of appraisal, but when these are put in specific terms there is no clear implication of involuntary relocation. The only functions which appear to cover the term are those of identifying potential for career development, and staff appointments. But do these rule out involuntary relocation. The NUT raised this point in their response to the ACAS document's use of the phrase 'deployment of teachers' (ACAS, 1986):

> Whilst the words can fit, quite precisely, one aspect of successful and acceptable career development, for most teachers and LEA's it will bring to mind the process of redeployment . . . it remains for most people a disagreeable and threatening process. One must seriously question the necessity for retaining the words, if one believes that successful Teacher Appraisal will have its own beneficial effect on the more sensitive placement of teachers.

This is just one example of an attempt to get sufficient precision of language to rule out power-coercive uses of appraisal by management.

The White Paper clearly saw dismissal as a possible disciplinary action following from appraisal. The ACAS document argues that disciplinary procedures would remain quite separate from appraisal, emphasizing constructive purposes in relation to defective performances. However, having said this, it then proceeds to connect the two processes by stating that disciplinary action may 'need to draw on relevant information from the appraisal records'. If appraisal is used as such a basis for disciplinary action then surely this is one of its functions. Again, an apparent shift of emphasis may turn out to be a mere glossing over of intent. The NUT was on to this one as well, although one might doubt if appraisal is necessarily power-coercive because it is linked with disciplinary procedures. As the Union admits, 'appraisal could work to the advantage of a teacher faced with disciplinary procedures'. It goes on to argue that there should be no connection between appraisal and discipline in order to maximize the acceptability of the former. This sounds like quite unwarranted professional protectionism. The individual can come to see the reasonableness of the sanctions brought against him or her, and surely appraisal can be an important means of demonstrating this. The real issue is the fairness of the appraisal process and not its connection to disciplinary procedures.

The ACAS document addresses this issue by outlining a number of procedural principles:

- everybody in the system should be appraised at all levels of the hierarchy;
- each appraisal should benefit from a 'second opinion';
- the appraisal should, where possible, be agreed with the appraisee and any remaining points of disagreement reported;
- appraisal reports would have a limited life-span on file, be kept by head and appraisee, and made available to the appraisee and others authorized by the Chief Education Officer;
- all those involved – appraisers and appraisees – should be trained.

The NUT expressed reservations about the possibility of unspecified but wide access to records which it felt the ACAS document (1986) allowed. The Union stated its view that appraisal records:

> should be confidential to the appraiser and appraisee; that it should have an agreed 'life' to better inform the subsequent appraisal processes between the appraiser and appraisee; that its use for any other purpose was entirely a matter for the appraisee; that for the purpose of school-based management decisions (e.g. INSET planning; school organisation) an *appropriate separate extract* be made available to the Head Teacher.

The ACAS document develops the proposals in *Teaching Quality* (DES, 1983) in a form which appears to eliminate much of the power-coercive intent evident in the latter document. The outcome was no doubt influenced by the arguments and views vehemently expressed by teachers and their associations in response to the government's original proposals.

I have argued elsewhere that as it stands the ACAS framework can be interpreted as open to a form of appraisal which empowers rather than diminishes teachers as professionals (see Elliott, 1987). But I have also argued that it is open to a rather different interpretation; as enabling direct hierarchical control over teacher performance. The document lacks the precision necessary to reassure teachers completely that the proposed framework describes a real shift of intent, rather than a glossing over of very real issues about the use of power. Certainly, the ACAS report is far less protectionist towards teachers than the Suffolk report. Like the White Paper, the ACAS report makes classroom observation by appraisers an essential feature of teacher appraisal. I believe that hierarchical surveillance of classroom performance is a pretty good indicator of power-coercive intent. The ACAS document introduces an ambiguous element by specifying the appraiser as either a head teacher, *or* an experienced teacher appointed by him or her. What is implied by 'experienced' is left open to interpretation. Does it imply someone in a middle management position or simply an experienced peer? The ambiguity perhaps represents an attempt to tone down the hierarchical surveillance of performance clearly proposed in the White Paper. However, the connection with this form of observation remains. The appointment of the appraiser is to be hierarchically determined.

The Suffolk report deals with the powert-coercive implications of hierarchical surveillance in a different way. It accepts it but limits its focus to low-inference measures of performance; thus screening off the person as an object of scrutiny. This protection offered to the person could, as we have seen, create very negative effects by alienating the person from his or her performance. The ACAS document makes no stipulation about the nature of the data to be collected. The framework as it stands is quite open to the appraisal of personal qualities. Combine such openness with the possibility it allows for hierarchical surveillance through classroom observation, and we must conclude that, while in many respects offering a better framework for promoting teacher development than the Suffolk report, it leaves too many loopholes for the exercise of power-coercive control.

In my view, the NUT's suggestions that the appraisal process be separated into two quite distinct but connected processes with different functions offers a possibility for the constructive development of the ACAS framework. One process involving appraiser and appraisee would be aimed at fostering the self-development of the teacher. The records would remain confidential to both parties. Another process of appraisal, for the purpose of making management decisions, would be based on extracts selected by the appraiser of the first process and his or her appraisee, in terms of their relevance to the particular decision-making domain. This suggestion separates the classroom observation role of the appraiser at the first level from a necessary location in the formal hierarchy, and even if the appraiser is a member of management she/he is prevented from utilizing observational data for management purposes. Management is given indirect access to practice through the accounts of practitioner and observer, selected and agreed by both parties in the light of the legitimate functions of management, e.g. training, selection, placement, etc.

This model, which has much in common with the police appraisal system, is also remarkably similar to more detailed proposals developed in 1985 at the Cambridge conference on educational evaluation (see Bridges *et al.*, 1986). The report of the conference outlines a non-power-coercive appraisal system which can genuinely foster the personal development of teachers by promoting a reflexive discourse about their practices with peer observers and students. The accounts of practice generated from this discourse can be drawn upon by the practitioner when compiling a further account for the purposes of appraisal by management. Appraisal by management should not simply be concerned to fit the person to the organization, but to discover how the organization might utilize and develop further the personal qualities evidenced in the appraisal data. Subsequent management decisions about training requirements, placement in the organization and career potential can serve the purposes of both organizational and personal development. Moreover, in the accountability context of this second level of appraisal, the teacher can draw on the accounts produced at the first level to argue for certain training, placement and career opportunities. The fact that these are ultimately management decisions in no way implies he or she has no right to influence them. And it is the reflective production of accounts at the first level which empowers the teacher to take this responsibility for his or her own development.

What has been sketched above is a variant of the two-tier model of appraisal which supports the self-development of the individual in his or her professional roles, and the development of the organization by those responsible for its management. It respects both the professional discretion of the teacher at the work-face and the organizational functions of management. And it reconciles the professional licence or discretion of the practitioner with the right of the management to call him or her to account.

At the policy level we still wait to see such a model of schoolteacher appraisal developed. Perhaps it will emerge from the national pilot projects which are currently attempting to implement and evaluate schemes in the light of the ACAS framework. Or, it could emerge as a model for teachers in universities where the appraisal debate has also emerged.

In search of criteria

One of the things the teachers' unions have almost let go of in the negotiations over a framework for appraisal is the view that the source of a teacher's professionalism lies in the personal qualities he/she manifests in his or her practice. It is often argued that the agreement on such qualities is impossible. People will pick out different attributes on the basis of their own personal prejudices. And so one searches for more objective 'criteria' derived from either theory or task analysis. The problem with both these approaches is one of the validity of the criteria rather than their reliability as measures of performance. What is attractive about both is their instrumental value in facilitating external regulation over performance. If one can derive specific performance rules from behaviourist, or even humanistic, psychology, then one prescribes the details of performance externally and monitors the extent to which it conforms to these prescriptions. Similarly, if a job can be broken down into performance tasks, and the specific skills involved in each specified, then one can externally control the performance through assessing the range of skills performed, and identify deficiencies to be remedied through structured training programmes.

However, as Spencer (1979) points out, detailed lists of job tasks are of little use 'without supplementary information about the competencies a superior job incumbent uses' to accomplish the tasks successfully. And, with respect to theory-based approaches, he points out that they 'lack supporting empirical data to show that the knowledge or skill characteristics they posit are in fact related to on-the-job performance'. Spencer argues that there are also problems with respect to the validity of intuitive and commonsense theories about the personal qualities manifested in good practice. He argues that they tend to reflect idealized images of professional identities derived from the folklore of the occupational culture.

So where do we go in search of valid criteria of performance appraisal? McBer and company in the USA have pioneered empirical research aimed at discovering the personal competencies which are generic to 'good' as opposed to 'marginally acceptable' performances in a variety of professions. The method of sampling is to select a group of practitioners which a range of people, in a close working relationship with them, agree to be superior performers. This group is then compared with a group of practitioners who receive an agreed average rating from peers, clients and immediate supervisors. The main research method is the behavioural event interview. Each practitioner is asked to describe in narrative detail how they handled one or more difficult and complex work situations. The interviewer does not pre-structure his or her questions, but probes the interviewee's handling of the incident responsively in a search for explanations of various aspects of the performance. The interview data is then analysed, with a view to extracting those competencies which characterize the superior performers and differentiate them from average ones. The analysis can be validated by cross-checking against a further sample, and follow-up observations of the performance of members from each subsample.

To my knowledge, no such study has been carried out on teachers in the UK. Most of this kind of research has been carried out in the USA by McBer and Company, who have now identified competencies which appear to be generic to good practice in a variety of occupations (see Klemp, 1977).

Elliott and Shadforth (1987) recently completed a study which identified four fundamental competencies that are generic to good patrol police officers; namely, competence in 'assessing the total situation', 'self-monitoring one's own conduct', 'empathizing accurately with the concerns of others', and 'exercising power and authority in a manner consistent with organizational goals and the professional ethics'. Moreover, the analysis identified a number of criteria for assessing the extent to which these competencies are evidenced in behaviour. The analysis was consistent with the cross-professional findings reported by Klemp (1977), but a number of more job-specific qualities were identified as generic to good policing. The latter did, however, presuppose one or more of the four more generalizable competencies. These appear to constitute 'the deep structure' of professional competence upon which the other job-specific qualities depended. Research into generic competencies offers to provide a basis for making objective and valid assessments of the quality of professional practices. Such assessment avoids the tendency to reduce judgements of competence to measures of performance, and thereby protects professionals from forms of assessment which foster external regulation and control.

It also avoids the atomization of competence into checklists of dozens, or even hundreds, of specific skills. Generic competencies consist of broad clusters of abilities which are conceptually linked. Research suggests that they are relatively few in number compared with the results of atomistic task analyses.

An assessment system based on generic competencies would also avoid the fears which accompany intuitive assessment of personal qualities. While such a system acknowledges the significance of personal qualities for competent practice, it minimizes the element of personal prejudice which often operates in impressionistic and intuitive selections of criteria.

The major problems with this form of assessment are methodological, and are connected with gathering a sufficient qualitative database on which to make fair and valid inferences. Since it is based on high-inference data, procedures for involving more than one person in the appraisal are necessary. Inferences made by one assessor will need to be cross-checked and challenged by others, including the appraisee. Moreover, the database can only be generated by those who work closely with the appraisee over prolonged periods, e.g. work-face supervisors, peers and clients. This form of competency-based assessment has to originate from those involved at the work-face. As a basis for appraisal by management it has to operate as a two-tier system.

'Generic competency' research on teachers, at all levels of the educational system, could mark a significant breakthrough in the development of a valid professional model of staff appraisal. Research projects can be carried out on the basis of very small samples fairly inexpensively. Two of us (myself and a police officer) interviewed 22 constables operating in a variety of policing environments, and then cross-validated our analysis against the cross-professional findings reported by Klemp (1977), observational studies of policing competence reported by Fielding (1984), and the provisional results of research in progress on a much larger sample. We concluded that one could make valid generalizations using the behavioural event interview method using relatively small samples.

References

ACAS Independent Panel (1986). *Report of the Appraisal and Training Working Group* (including NUT comment). Mimeo.
Bridges, D., Elliott, J. and Klass, C. (1986). Performance appraisal as naturalistic inquiry. *Cambridge Journal of Education,* **16**(3), 221–33.
Department of Education and Science (1983). *Teaching Quality*. London: HMSO.
Doll, W.E. (1984). Developing competence. In E.C. Short (ed.), *Competence*, pp. 123–38. New York: University Press of America.
Elliott, J. (1985). Evaluating teaching quality. In Review Symposium on the White Paper 'Teaching Quality'. *British Journal of Sociology of Education,* **6**(1), 102–7.
Elliott, J. (1987). *Knowledge, Power and Appraisal.* Paper delivered to the Annual Conference of the British Educational Research Association. Centre for Applied Research in Education, School of Education, University of East Anglia, mimeo.
Elliott, J. and Shadforth, R. (1987). *Qualities of the Good Patrol Constable: A Report for*

Discussion. Centre for Applied Research in Education, School of Education, University of East Anglia, mimeo.

Fielding, N. (1984). Police socialization and police competence. *British Journal of Sociology*. **XXXV**(4), 568–90.

Graham, D.G. (1985). *Those Having Torches . . . Teacher Appraisal: A Study*. Ipswich: Suffolk Education Department.

Harré, R. (1983). *Personal Being: A Theory for Individual Psychology*. Oxford: Basil Blackwell.

Harré, R., Clarke, D. and de Carlo, N. (1985). *Motives and Mechanisms: An Introduction to the Psychology of Action*. New York: Methuen.

Klemp, G.O. (1977). *Three Factors of Success in the World of Work: Implications for Curriculum in Higher Education*. Boston, Mass.: McBer and Co.

Spencer, L.M. (1979). *Soft Skill Competencies*. Oxford: Oxford University Press.

Wise, A.E., Darling-Hammond,, L., McLaughlin, M. and Bernstein, H. (1984). *Teacher Evaluation – A Study of Effective Practice*. Santa Monica, Calif.: The Rand Corporation for the National Institute of Education.

10
Perspectives on teacher appraisal and professional development

Mary Louise Holly

Introduction

Given current demands to improve the quality of schooling provided to young people, educators may be embracing policies and practices which inadvertently work against this aim. With, for example, the demand for competency and accountability from teachers, there is often a failure to provide them with the support necessary for personal and collegial reflection and systematic self-critical enquiry which are the bases for professional knowledge and behaviour. Images of teachers and teaching, of the conditions of life in schools, and of progress and time, are undoing change. They are the focus of competing forces as we move from previous conceptions of teaching and learning to future ones.

In this chapter, perspectives and interrelationships of teaching, professional development and appraisal are explored. Appraisal is defined as 'the forming of qualitative judgements' and, as such, is central to teaching and professional development. Journal writing and collegial discussion, it is argued, are useful aids to professional reflection, dialogue and documentation for critique of practice.

The premise underlying this chapter is that to improve the quality of schooling, it is necessary to improve the quality of support given to teachers. To do this, there needs to be a greater understanding and appreciation of teachers as they try to make sense of the complexities of human development and learning within their classrooms. With greater understanding, appraisal schemes can be designed which support teaching and professional development, enhance personal and collaborative enquiry, promote critique, and contribute to an evolving pedagogy.

Making sense

From the earliest moments of existence human beings try to make sense of life. We both define our worlds and are defined by them through adaptation, learning and growth in social contexts. For the most part, these processes make sense as we reflect on them; we can see how our experiences flow one into another and have rhythm and direction. As we live them, these experiences may or may not seem to flow, have rhythm or direction. In times of obvious transition, when comfortable ways seem inadequate, many aspects of our lives do not make sense or have stability:

> Life itself consists of phases in which the organism falls out of step with the march of surrounding things and then recovers unison with it – either through effort or by some happy chance. And, in a growing life, the recovery is never mere return to a prior state, for it is enriched by the state of disparity and resistance through which it has successfully passed. If the gap between organism and environment is too wide, the creature dies. If its activity is not enhanced by the temporary alienation, it merely subsists. Life grows when a temporary falling out is a transition to a more extensive balance of the energies of the organism with those of the conditions under which it lives. (Dewey, 1934, p. 14)

According to Dewey (1934, p. 14), the 'world is full of things that are indifferent and even hostile to life; the very processes by which life is maintained tend to throw it out of gear with its surroundings'. Attempting to understand, bringing order, integration and a sense of aesthetic wholeness to life, often requires overcoming opposition and conflict, thus transforming ideas 'into differentiated aspects of a higher powered and more significant life' (Dewey, 1934, p. 14).

Whether we are talking about the infant adjusting to life outside the womb, the 5-year-old to school, or the 21-year-old to that first professional position, the whole organism particpates in the process. Joining the social, psychological and aesthetic worlds of humanity, institutional and educational groups, and work are milestones in adaptation and identity formation. They differ only in magnitude from the continuing changes of everyday existence. Bringing order, or making sense, is necessary for life:

> Order cannot but be admirable in a world constantly threatened with disorder – in a world where living creatures can go on living only by taking advantage of whatever order exists about them, incorporating it into themselves. In a world like ours, every living creature that attains sensibility welcomes order with a response of harmonious feeling whenever it finds a congruous order about it.
>
>   For only when an organism shares in the ordered relations of its environment does it secure the stability essential to living. (Dewey, 1934, pp. 14–15)

While we strive to bring coherence and order in our lives, it is the very uncertainty, incompleteness, suspense and open-endedness that brings purpose, meaning and engagement to life. The 'moment of passage from disturbance into harmony is that of intensest life' (Dewey, 1934, p. 17). By reaching into ourselves and our surroundings to explore and integrate the tensions necessary for meaningful life, we live consciously the exhilaration of the journey as well as experience its products. There is no end to sense-making – only continuing differentiation and openings to new curiosities and challenges.

According to Erikson (1950), it is not only the person who falls out of step with the march of surrounding things, but also whole societies and social groups. Persons reflect societal conditions and societal conditions can mirror personal dilemmas. Take, for example, a person's continuing identity formation. In an agrarian society where social roles are relatively well defined and historically determined, where ritual and routine are stable and have significant influences on development, the young person rarely has difficulty defining identity in terms of culture and work. In a society in which transition from an agrarian way of life to a technological way of life is pronounced, however, identity formation becomes a more difficult task. There are options, but no clear paths to follow. The young person must make decisions and is often caught between what was and what will be. The person can hold on to the past, use it to guide identity; the person can break with tradition and move optimistically into 'whatever happens'; or, the person can construct identity by integrating the past and future slowly and interactively through the present. If a person is to join in the creation of society, 'a whole new orientation which fuse[s] a new world image . . . with traditional theoretical assumptions' is necessary (Erikson, 1975, p. 44).

To move into the unknown means to risk falling out of step with the person's surroundings. To venture willingly, trust in one's self, and trust in the environment, are important assets.

Teachers in transition

Teachers are persons in time and culture. As Erikson might say, they are persons whose personal coherence and role integration within the group, whose guiding images, ideologies and life histories exist within historical moments. In other words, teachers' 'life histories are inextricably interwoven with history' (Erikson, 1975, p. 20). While each teacher has a unique life history based on biology and experience, each has characteristics in common with all other teachers as well as with immediate colleagues (Runyan, 1984).

Teachers today find themselves in a state of transition from trained instructors to educated professionals, and from dispensers of information and skills to facilitators of knowledge, attitudes, values and skills. As teacher preparation and continuing professional development became a reality for all teachers, the terms professional and staff development began to replace in-service training. In-service training ('to form by instruction, discipline or drill') of teachers which characterized the last century, reflected, above all else the prevailing and partially valid assumption that the immaturity, meager educational equipment, and inexperience of the teacher rendered him unable to analyze or criticize his own teaching, or, unless given direction, to improve it. (Richey, 1957, p. 36)

Although teachers are more highly educated and experienced than ever before, the attitude of remediation persists (Edelfelt and Lawrence, 1975). The training of teachers in 'instructional techniques', 'strategies' and 'technological expertise' as preparation for helping students cope with the 'knowledge explosion' seemed to little enhance the image of teachers. Conveying the sentiments of many teachers, Devaney and Thorn (1975, p. 7) wrote:

> Teachers must be more than technicians, must continue to be learners. Long-lasting improvements in education will come about through inservice programs that identify individual starting points for learning in each teacher; build on teachers' motivation to take more, not less, responsibility.

Ten years earlier, during a period of rapid expansion of schools, concern for social equity and civil rights, new developments in curriculum, and increasing numbers of teachers entering the profession, Combs called for a new professionalism in the education of teachers on both the pre-service and in-service levels. He called for attention to the person who teaches:

> really important changes will come about as teachers change. Institutions are made up of people, and it is the behaviour of teachers in classrooms that will finally determine whether or not schools meet or fail to meet the challenge of our times. (Combs, 1965, p. 5)

Many other teachers and teacher educators agreed; the 'beliefs, feelings, and assumptions of teachers are the air of the learning environment' (Postman and Weingartner, 1969, p. 33). Teaching, it became clear, demanded more than conveying information and skills. Schools could not solve society's ills. Nor could teachers with special instructional knowledge, skills and competencies (even with the help of prepared curriculum materials by specialists outside the field of education) meet the broader challenges of teaching. New images of teaching and of teachers were emerging.

Teachers are researchers

As it became apparent that no one method of teaching was superior, and that teaching and learning were complex, dynamic, transactive, and context- and person-specific endeavours, researchers looked more closely at teachers and classrooms: 'Research on teaching', 'effective schools', 'teachers' thinking' and 'knowledge use' in the USA paralleled 'action-research' in England and Australia. In the USA, research *on* teachers slowly grew into cooperation *with* teachers and then to collaboration *with* teachers for research. Presently, the concept of 'teacher as researcher' is gaining attention. Not surprisingly, the notion of 'teachers as researchers' first gained credibility in England where teachers have a greater responsibility for curriculum development than do teachers in the USA. Standardization of textbooks, instructional materials and tests, as well as the use of special teachers for music, art, physical education, remedial reading and speech at the primary and elementary school levels in the USA, has meant that teachers have less responsibility for these areas than teachers in England. In England, teachers *had* to be curriculum 'researchers' and 'developers', it was implicit in 'teacher' and 'teaching'.

Curriculum development, regardless of who takes major responsibility for it, is by nature hypothetical. Even with highly structured materials the teacher must test ideas, and interpret and change them to suit the classroom.

In *An Introduction to Curriculum Research and Development* (1975), Stenhouse describes how teachers are and can be educational researchers. He devotes a chapter to 'The Teacher as Researcher', stating that:

> For me this chapter is of central importance. In it I shall try to outline what I believe to be the major implication for the betterment of schools. ... Stated briefly, this is that curriculum research and development ought to belong to the teacher and that there are prospects of making this good in practice. I concede that it will require a generation of work, and if the majority of teachers – rather than only the enthusiastic few – are to possess this field of research, then the teacher's professional self-image and conditions of work will have to change. (1975, p. 142)

For Stenhouse, it was not enough that teachers' work should be studied; teachers had to study it. Their classrooms would be professional laboratories; teachers would be members of scientific communities, hypothesizing, testing and theorizing about teaching. In the Ford Teaching Project, for example, Elliott and Adelman worked closely with teachers and advisors in action-research designed to better understand inquiry/discovery methods in class-rooms. Acting as support persons for a team of teachers from different schools, grade levels and subject areas, they worked from the premise that 'action, and reflection on action, are the joint responsibilities of the teachers' (Elliott and Adelman, 1973, p. 12).

By providing support to teachers and advisors as they focussed research on practice, the university researchers helped to strengthen participants' self-confidence as well as to build a colleagial milieu within which research could continue. They fostered 'a capacity for autonomous professional self-development through systematic self-study, through the study of the work of other teachers and through the testing of ideas by classroom research pro-cedures' (Stenhouse, 1975, p. 44).

For Stenhouse, using research meant doing research. He defined research as 'systematic and sustained enquiry, planned and self critical, which is subjected to public criticism and to empirical tests where these are appropriate' (Sten-house, 1981, in Rudduck and Hopkins, 1985, p. 18). 'As an enquiry', he wrote:

it is founded in curiosity and a desire to understand; but it is a stable, not a fleeting, curiosity, systematic in the sense of being sustained by a strategy . . . fundamental to such persistence of enquiry is a sceptical temper of mind sustained by critical principles, a doubt not only about the received and comfortable answers, but also about one's own hypotheses. (Stenhouse, 1981, in Rudduck and Hopkins, 1985, p. 8)

Because curiosity involves risk and change, it is dangerous. Stenhouse argued that teachers needed support; that they would have to see themselves as professionals capable of nourishing and critically assessing their own and each others' enquiry. To make public their enquiries, teachers would need confidence to engage in the critique that would enrich their studies and contribute to their professional knowledge. Professional action and knowledge, he hoped, would lead to pedagogy – not research *on* education or teaching, but *educational research*:

could we have an educational science? . . . could we have a study of educational phenomena which opted neither for the common language of education nor for the language of social science theory, but instead for a theory which related directly to educational practice? Not a psychology, nor a sociology, but a pedagogy? (Stenhouse, 1981, in Rudduck and Hopkins, 1985, p. 13)

Developing a pedagogy takes time – time for teachers, like artists, to develop processes of self-monitoring and to make teaching a conscious art. Elliot Eisner advocates much the same aim, when he speaks of teachers becoming connoisseurs of teaching. Like Stenhouse, he calls for teachers to be critics, professionals who publicly disclose and discuss significant aspects of practice (Eisner, 1985). 'The most serious impediment to the development of teachers as researchers – and indeed as artists in teaching – is quite simply the shortage of time' writes Stenhouse, 'teachers teach too much' (Stenhouse, 1981, in Rudduck and Hopkins, 1985, p. 16).

Educational reflection, theorizing and knowledge

Unfortunately, 'teaching too much' usually means that there is less time to engage in sustained enquiry, to cogitate over teaching, and to reflect on its consequences and meaning. 'No experience having meaning', writes Dewey, 'is possible without some element of thought' (1916, p. 144). In today's world of 'the hurried child', teachers often find themselves teaching more, sooner, faster, and feeling less satisfied with their teaching and children's learning (Elkind, 1982).

More information can translate into less meaning. Activity can replace experience. While one can imagine how 'more knowledge' can translate into 'more teaching', and in breaking down knowledge and skills to more manageable tasks for 'mastery', it is difficult to understand how it all fits together to support children's evolving understanding and definition of themselves and their worlds. Even if the 'what' and 'why' questions of teaching are answered (e.g. 'teacher-proof' curriculum materials), there remains the professional challenge of helping students to make sense of the curriculum, to make the connections necessary to make knowledge useful. Time for observation and reflection becomes more, not less, important, as more is expected of teachers:

> All that the wisest man can do is to observe what is going on more widely and more minutely and then select more carefully from what is noted just those factors which point to something to happen. (Dewey, 1916, p. 146)

Most teaching decisions are made without conscious attention to how or why they are made. They occur normally during the course of events. When asked 'Why did you do that?', teachers often cannot put their reasons into words: 'I just knew what to do', or 'I had a feeling', or 'I sensed what to do'. As one teacher put it: 'How do I know? I can't put it into words. You know, teaching is like breathing, you just do it!' Personal knowledge, tacit knowledge, routine knowledge, knowledge that is not put into words, guides 'sense making' and commits teachers to action when conscious thought is not permitted the time to percolate and inform practice (Polanyi, 1967).

The danger in 'hurrying' and teaching 'more' is that time for gathering information and reflecting on practice and the implicit and explicit theories that guide it can evaporate easily into the busyness of increasing demands. We come to rely on 'autopilot' (Tripp, 1984). This 'teaching as breathing' at first sounds appealing, almost natural. After all, how many artists take time to explain what they are doing while, or even after, they are doing it? Upon reflection we realize that teachers do not paint on canvases; their work is not done in isolation. Children do not hold still, nor are the consequences of effort always immediately apparent. Teachers' work is social and moral.

As Dewey (1916, p. 146) noted, the opposites to conscious enquiry and thoughtful action,

> are routine and capricious behavior. The former accepts what has been customary as a full measure of possibility and omits to take into account the connections of the particular things done. The latter makes the momentary act a measure of value, and ignores the connections of our personal action with the energies of the environment. It says, virtually, 'things are to be just as I happen to like them at this instant,' as routine says in effect 'let things continue just as I have found them in the past.' Both refuse to acknowledge responsibility for the future consequences which flow from present action. Reflection is the acceptance of such responsibility.

In accepting the responsibility of teaching others, the teacher agrees to be reflective, to behave intentionally and observe the consequences, and to alter behaviour and circumstances as professional judgement indicates.

Whereas for years researchers worked under the assumptions that teachers were atheoretical, and that teachers needed to apply 'theory' to their teaching, current thought holds that teachers do apply theory – their own and others (Bussis *et al.*, 1975; Schon, 1983; Clandinin, 1985; Elbaz, 1983). Though far from resolution, several questions continue to be debated. Do teachers use research findings? Should they? Does theory inform practice? Should it? What kinds of theories? Whose theories? How do they? And, how do teachers theorize?

There is a difference between private and public theories. Publically available theories, such as Erikson's theory of psychological development and Piaget's theory of cognitive development, are 'systems of ideas published in books', whereas:

> Private theories are ideas in people's minds which they use to interpret or explain their experience. These may be inferred from observing someone's behaviour; but they must be at least capable of explicit formulation. (Eraut, 1985, pp. 1–2)

To theorize, Eraut continues, 'is to interpret, explain or judge intentions, actions and experiences'. The theoretical notions underlying professional decisions and actions are public and private, and depend for their articulation on the teacher's perceptual field at the time.

The perceptual field is the person's 'universe of naive experience', including how the person thinks and feels about herself or himself, the circumstances and the relationship of self to circumstances (Combs and Snygg, 1959). The perceptual field is influenced by the person's life history, the present, and the perceived future as well ('If I do this, this might happen'). It is characterized by stability; the person seeks equilibrium. It also has fluidity; it adapts and changes. It has direction and coherence. Behaviour is purposeful and reasonable, even though the actor, or an observer, may not be immediately aware of these at the time of action; hence, the complexity of teaching. Each person has a unique perceptual field, a unique life history. Teaching involves communicating with others, finding common ground on which to connect and make sense of experience.

Schön (1983, pp. 49–51) illustrates how professionals theorize as they work:

> When we go about the spontaneous, intuitive performance of the actions of everyday life, we show ourselves to be knowledgeable in a special way. . . . Our knowing is ordinarily tacit, implicit in our feel for the stuff with which we are dealing. It seems right to say that our knowing is *in* our action.
> . . . the workaday life of the professional depends on tacit knowing-in-action. . . . In his day-to-day practice he makes innumerable judgments of quality for which he cannot state criteria, and he displays skills for which he cannot state the rules and procedures. Even when he makes conscious use of research-based [public] theories and techniques, he is dependent on tacit recognitions, judgments, and skilful performances ...
> Although we sometimes think before acting, it is also true that in much of the spontaneous behaviour of skilful practice we reveal a kind of knowing which does not stem from prior intellectual operation.

Schön suggests that we are in a time of transition, what Kuhn (1962) might describe as a paradigm shift. Practitioners are caught in a conceptualization of professional practice as technological rationality when reflection-in-action might provide a more appropriate, illuminating and comprehensive theoretical framework. Schön argues that professional practice moves beyond problem solving and the application of knowledge, to problem definition and improvisation, which are more akin to artistic creation than to technological management. He asserts that 'professional practice has at least as much to do with finding the problem as with solving the problem found' (Schon, 1983, p. 18). Most problems confronting the professional are unique. Though previous experience and knowledge are useful, they are not in themselves sufficient to identify, define and solve the problem. In the real world of teaching:

> problems do not present themselves to the practitioner as givens. They must be constructed from the materials of problematic situations which are puzzling, troubling, and uncertain. In order to convert a problematic situation to a problem, a practitioner must do a certain kind of work. He must make sense of an uncertain situation that initially makes sense. (Schön, 1983, p.40)

Defining problems requires seeing them. Teachers, caught in a tradition of technological rationality in which knowledge acquired during schooling is studied predominantly for its replicative and applicative functions, are not encouraged to explore the more complex interpretative and associative uses of knowledge (Broudy *et al.*, 1964; Eraut, 1985). Stable, constant knowledge can be taught. Standards can be developed, taught and tested. Standardized curriculum materials and instructional strategies and techniques can bring perceived, albeit simplistic, coherence to a complex set of relationships and tasks. Knowing-in-practice becomes increasingly tacit, spontaneous and routine. The narrowness of focus and expectation as to what should happen in the classroom narrows the possibilities of what could happen. Problems and challenges outside those which upset routine are not seen. Consequently, rigidity of practice contributes to what Schön refers to as boredom and 'burnout' (it also relates to a lack of intellectual stimualtion among experienced teachers – Nias, 1983). 'The practitioner may miss important opportunities to think about what he is doing' (Schön, 1983, p. 61) – practice that initially makes sense continues to do so.

Reflection acts as an antidote to the anaesthesia that slowly suffocates teaching and professional judgement:

> Through reflection, he can surface and criticize the tacit understandings that have grown up around the repetitive experiences of a specialized practice, and can make new sense of the situations of uncertainty or uniqueness which he may allow himself to experience.

Practitioners do reflect *on* their knowing-in-practice. Sometimes, in the relative tranquillity of a postmortem, they think back on a project they have undertaken, a situation they have lived through, and they explore the understandings they have brought to their handling of the case. They do this in a mood of speculation, or in a deliberate effort to prepare themselves for future cases. (Schon, 1983, p. 61)

Reflection has different forms and purposes: thinking, discussing, writing, re-reading what has been written, and reviewing materials, conversations and ideas as well as experiences. Reading is often a reflective process, especially when the reader is 'wide awake' (Greene, 1982) and 'searching' (Percy, 1980). The teacher may:

> reflect on the tacit norms and appreciations which underlie a judgment, or on the strategies and theories implicit in a pattern of behavior. He may reflect on the feeling for a situation which has lead him to adopt a particular course of action, on the way in which he has framed the problem he is trying to solve, or on the role he has constructed for himself within a larger institutional context.
>
> Reflection-in-action, in these several modes, is central to the art through which practitioners sometimes cope with the troublesome 'divergent' situations of practice.
>
> When the phenomenon at hand eludes the ordinary categories of knowledge-in-practice, presenting itself as unique or unstable, the practitioner may surface and criticize his initial understanding of the phenomenon, construct a new description of it, and test the new description by an on-the-spot experiment. Sometimes he arrives at a new theory of the phenomenon by articulating a feeling he has about it. (Schön, 1983, pp. 62–3)

Questions of support

In teaching, reflecting and theorizing are responsibilities, obligations and necessities. The question is, 'How can teacher reflection be supported?' In what ways can their questions be extended into 'systematic self-critical enquiry?' Do their theories-in-use become known to them? In what ways can teachers be supported in developing professional and collegial environments that can sustain personal and collegial enquiry?

Educational appraisal and professional development

Support for reflection and theorizing includes fanning the sparks that ignite enquiry, and creating the professional and collegial environments which sustain it. For teachers to focus on practice, to 'observe more widely and more minutely', to be connoisseurs and critics of teaching, it is necessary to take a long-term developmental perspective. Teachers' feelings of adequacy and worth, their public image, the conditions of work, and the concept of time, must be conducive to development.

Images of teaching and teachers

Teachers as a group suffer from low self-esteem (Lortie, 1975) and their attitudes and behaviour are influenced by this (Combs and Snygg, 1959). Successful and available role models and 'mentors' for teachers during their professional socialization have not been common; 'sink or swim' still characterizes many a teacher's first year in the classroom. After that, reference groups and colleagial transactions frequently take place in spite of institutional conditions and often outside of the institutions themselves (Nias, 1983). Teacher evaluation by others occurs rarely and is more often viewed as a threat rather than as an aid to professional development. And, while teachers are frequently criticized publicly, praise is unusual.

Conditions of work

Teachers, for the most part, practise alone (Lortie, 1975). They are isolated spatially, temporally, and often psychologically (Holly, 1983). According to Schön (1983, p. 333):

> The teacher's isolation in her classroom works against reflection–in–action. She needs to communicate her private puzzles and insights, to test them against the views of her peers.

Most teachers are women; most administrators are men. Few women are in leadership roles where they influence policies which effect practice (Spender, 1982). Institutional efforts in professional and staff development are rarely integrated by a conceptual framework and long-term district plans (Edelfelt and Lawrence, 1975). Professional development, like teacher evaluation, has been largely a do-it-yourself proposition with 'in-services', workshops and institutes, college courses, and teachers' centres available. Unfortunately, time for participation is not always possible. Many teachers with family responsibilities are unable to attend after school and weekend activities.

Time

Time to reflect and gain insight into practice, to plan, and integrate short-term goals with long-term aims, seems to be in short supply in schools today. Teachers reflect and plan, but with little time and support for the systematic and sustained self-critical enquiry necessary to improve practice. As teachers spend more time with bureaucratic tasks and standardized materials and procedures, there seems to be less time for their own enquiry. As one teacher recently said:

> Now the big push is on critical thinking skills. We had an 'inservice' on it Friday afternoon. What I want to know is, how do they expect me to teach it when I don't have any time to do it myself?! There aren't any minutes left in the schoolday!

For many teachers, time for 'just thinking' and 'reflecting' is viewed as a luxury – separate from teaching and learning. Tom (1984, p. 207) points out a related problem with increasing standardization: 'externally imposed criteria . . .

magnify the sense in which we feel we must respond to our environment rather than create it'.

Jackson (1968) estimated that teachers engage in over 200 decisions every hour of teaching. Most of these decisions are 'new' and call for immediate judgement based on situational perceptions (Schön, 1983). Appraisal, the process by which teachers form 'qualitative judgements about an activity, a person, or an organization' (HMI, 1985) is at the heart of teaching. For, as one teacher put it, 'the twenty second holocausts' and 'the daily trivial, but sometimes earthshaking events' are those which define teaching and can 'melt a teaching day into a dizzy haze'.

When teachers dare to question themselves critically – 'Why am I doing this?' – cognitive dissonance is inevitable. As the above teacher found:

I began to look at things very differently. I had spent a good deal of time reflecting on the institutional and societal functions of schooling and the art of teaching, but always as an observer. Now I was looking at myself as participant. Seeing myself in the roles I had described in a detached manner.

Then things went straight to hell. No matter what, I could not resolve the question of what I was doing in a . . . [primary] classroom . . . I wanted out . . . (Holly, 1986)

The discrepancies between aims and behaviours, and between and among expectations and institutional environments, become apparent when teachers enquire into their practice. It is a discomforting process, for it demands stepping out of the march of events in one's surroundings. This is more likely to happen in an environment where helping others gain self-knowledge is something one does with them rather than to them (Jersild, 1955).

An environment conducive to reflective practice requires new images of administrators as well as teachers:

Accountability, evaluation, and supervision would acquire new meanings. There would be a shift from the search for centrally administered, objective measures . . . toward independent, qualitative judgments and narrative accounts of experience and performance in learning and teaching. Supervision would concern itself less with monitoring the teacher's coverage of curriculum content than with assessment and support of the teacher's reflection-in-action. (Schön, 1983, pp. 333–4)

Conceptualizing appraisal consistent with professional development

Support for teachers in strengthening their abilities to appraise teaching and learning takes many forms. It includes, but is not limited to, the following processes and forms of documentation:

- *evaluation* is a general term used to describe any activity by the institution or the LEA where the quality of provision is the subject of systematic study;

- *review* indicates a retrospective activity and implies the collection and examination of evidence and information;

- *assessment* implies the use of measurement and/or grading based on known criteria (HMI, 1985).

Recent attempts to make regular evaluations, reviews and assessments open to public critique indicate growing interest in schooling. Though intentions underlying such critiques are usually worthy, such forms are useful only to the extent that they contribute to and enable deeper and ongoing reflection on practice. While 'objective' measures provide important information for change, it is the 'subjective' questioning of practice that provides the rationale and context for interpreting and using such information.

Whether we are addressing teacher appraisal or pupil appraisal, it is the engagement of people that influences the extent to which the broader purposes of schooling can be achieved. For example, reading skills, though important in pupil appraisal, are of little consequence if pupils do not read. Being literate requires more than the ability to decipher the forms of representation that the culture affords, whether these forms be visual, literal, aural, numerical, temporal or spatial. It means interpreting, reconstructing and using these forms to gain insight and understanding of human beings, culture and the natural world.

In conceptualizing appraisal schemes which are consistent with principles of development and designed to enhance teachers' abilities to form professional judgements, there are at least five general and necessary elements to consider.

1 *Context specific.* Whether the scheme is for forming qualitative judgements of pupils or teachers, the context for defining and interpreting must be specific to the people and circumstances.
2 *Ongoing and formative.* This includes evaluation, review and assessment of what has been, and of what is to be – intentional and unintentional consequences and long-term aims.
3 *Flexible and evolutionary.* Like the perceptual field, an appraisal scheme must have stability, purpose, direction and fluidity for the continuing orchestration of planned change.
4 *Comprehensive and relational.* A holistic framework makes it more likely that figure–ground elements and relationships can be distinguished and understood.
5 *Personal and institutional relevance.* Communication, cooperation and collaboration in creating and defining educational purposes and philosophy provide bases for designing appraisal schemes that are relevant to persons and institutions.

Several assumptions about the benefits of appraisal underlie schemes which are consistent with principles of professional development:

1 Appraisal procedures and results enhance the educator's ability to make professional decisions and judgements.
2 Appraising is an educational process.
3 Appraisal promotes professional practice in several ways:

- through reflection;
- by bringing tacit knowledge to consciousness where it can be questioned;
- through removing isolation and enhancing communication and critical analysis;
- by promoting a professional culture and lexicon;
- through enabling educators to learn from practice;
- through encouraging interpretations from broader perspectives and contexts;
- by providing a sense of history and direction.

4 Appraisal supports enquiry and research which contributes to an evolving pedagogy.

Documentation and educational enquiry: keeping a personal, professional journal

An appraisal scheme with the aim of facilitating the quality of teaching and learning is designed to run on two tracks at once – the idiographic and personal, and the colleagial and professional. The two are interdependent, and each focusses on a different dimension of professional life: 'travelling outward and inward at the same time is less a matter of physical impossibility than a condition of mental health and moral well-being' (Mallon, 1984, p. 105).

A personal, professional journal can be a valuable aid in gaining perspective and insight into teaching. It is both a form of data collection and analysis, and a method for systematic self-critical enquiry. Writing enables the writer to gain new perspectives on practice. Reflecting on writing later provides other perspectives. Identifying themes, patterns, persistent questions and challenges can help educators put these into larger contexts. Issues, when clarified and defined through writing, can serve as a basis for discussion with others. Opening topics for professional dialogue can strengthen communication, belief in education, and confidence in one's colleagues. This leads teachers to invite dialogue and critical analysis – the very dialogue and critical analysis which enables continuing reflection: 'Why did I do that?', 'What am I doing?', 'How do I make decisions; on what do I base them?', 'Why am I doing this instead of this or this?'

There are three basic forms of documentation which can contribute to professional enquiry: logs, diaries and journals.

- *Logs* are factual descriptions of practice.
- *Diaries* are personal documents of experiences and observations over time; personal opinions and interpretations, as well as factual descriptions are included. Facts are usually tied to the writer's thoughts and feelings about daily events. Writing is often 'spontaneous' in nature.

- *Journals* contain factual and interpretative writing and more. They are documents for ongoing reflection, for personal, professional dialogue. The writer keeps a journal with the intent to return to it and learn from reflection on practice (Holly, 1984).

When teachers keep professional journals they write factually and interpretatively as well as reflectively and analytically. Teachers write for different purposes and in different ways. Descriptive writing (log) is useful for planning and recounting lessons, whereas therapeutic writing (diary) can relieve everyday pressures and provide contextual data for interpreting experiences and establishing patterns and themes in practice. Several other types of writing have been documented in teachers' journal writing: evaluative, ethnographic, reflective, introspective and creative (Holly, 1988). Each type provides documentation for systematic, self-critical enquiry and appraisal of practice – for both self-evaluation and student evaluation.

Teachers who keep journals carry on a dialogue with themselves over time. They note patterns in their teaching and student learning. They can also begin to confront their feelings of inadequacy, grow in self-acceptance, and learn to criticize their practice, as the following excerpts from a primary school teacher's journal illustrate. The first is from early writing, the second from after a few months of writing, and the third after 4 months:

Wed. 3/4

Very interesting – on way to school thought about things I needed to get done. There was nothing in those thoughts about the kids. It was all completing bulletin boards, grading papers & getting everything for averaging grades . . .

Thurs. 3/5

Well here it is. Lesson plan day. It seems everyday I have so much paperwork that must be completed. I'm seeing a pattern here. Paperwork vs child time . . .

That leads me to my own feelings of inadequacy. I feel like I'm out of my league. . . . This is something I'm going to have to deal with. It's known as an inferiority complex.

Writing makes me look at myself. I see two levels in this. One is sort of superficial while the other is really confronting myself. Many times this is painful, but I certainly feel better when I see areas that I know I can improve upon or admit to behavior patterns that I have.

I've seen my writing evolve. At first it was very difficult and sometimes it still is. I find that I have two levels of writing. A surface level – telling about the days' events, etc. On a second level – here my writing tends to get sloppy because I try to put down my inner thoughts and feelings before they escape . . . . I must confront myself with things that I normally would push out of my mind. Once things are down on paper they cannot be turned away from – they must be dealt with . . . writing about them has made me see some things that I don't think I would ever have. (Holly, 1988)

Idiographic and personal dimensions of appraisal

Teachers have pasts, presents and futures which interactively influence their teaching: 'Who am I as a teacher?', 'Why did I become a teacher?', 'Why do I remain a teacher?', 'What are my memories of schooling and teachers who were important to my development and learning?', 'What are the satisfactions, joys and challenges of teaching?', 'What aims and hopes do I have for the pupils I teach?' Responses to these and other fundamental questions about the environment and circumstances surrounding practice are not only interesting in unravelling the autobiographies and life histories of teachers, they are essential to the awareness and understanding of current practice (Abbs, 1974). 'In what ways', for example, 'do my experiences, education, temperament, and aspirations influence my teaching?'

Collegial and professional dimensions of appraisal

While autobiographical and introspective reflection helps teachers gain insight into themselves as professionals, the social and educational world within which their life histories unfold and are created provide the necessary contexts for interpretation of practice. Data gathering, which helps teachers to understand the circumstances of teaching, can be focussed at different levels and take many forms. Traditional forms, such as in-service education and professional reading, when combined with action-research with colleagues, with clinical supervision, dialogue with others on issues of current concern to educators, and when reacting to pertinent literature and research, can provide new perspectives through which to view teaching and schooling.

Reflection on interactions in the classroom, school, district and the profession, can bring broader dimensions of work into perspective where relationships, connections and further development are made possible. Each experience and engagement contributes to professional life and provides information for appraisal.

Gathering descriptive information for pupil appraisal also takes many forms, the most important of which might be providing an educational environment where pupils are challenged and invited to question, and then listening to them as they do so. The simultaneous keeping of anecdotal records over time can be valuable aids to appraisal.

Helping pupils to appraise themselves can be beneficial to pupil and teacher alike. Having pupils keep journals enables the teacher to document their development and learning, while it enables the pupils to see and feel their own progress, to become more aware, reflective and responsible for their work.

Central to journal keeping, as it is for all personal documents, is the fact that the writer is the owner of the journal. The journal helps its author make sense of experience; it is a means for reflecting on a professional life and practice, for building confidence, trust and judgement; and it is the source of documentation for critical analysis. For pupils and teachers alike, selecting and integrating information from the journal for others to analyse is an educative process. Reflective writing and collegial discussion make possible broader educational contexts within which the many forms used for appraisal can be heuristic aids to teaching.

Concluding comments

Teaching is a complex, dynamic, human process that taxes and challenges teachers from their first day of teaching to their fiftieth year. Teaching is reflection in action; it is enquiry, a continuing dialogue of theory and practice, of helping each child to acquire the attitudes, knowledge, skills and values that contribute to life and culture.

Professional teachers are sceptics who constantly theorize, hypothesize and test their knowledge and hunches in practice. While our understanding of teaching is undergoing change, so too are our images of teachers and professional development. Providing the support necessary for personal and collegial reflection and systematic, self-critical enquiry includes giving serious attention to the professional climate and conditions under which teachers practice. It means providing teachers the time, resources and psychological support to look critically, both individually and with others, at teaching.

Documentation of teaching is necessary for conscious reflection and ongoing evaluation. Keeping a professional journal for planning, describing and learning from practice provides an evolving database for making qualitative decisions about teaching and professional development. Dialogue and the critical analysis of issues and themes emerging from journal documentation contribute to educational connoisseurship and criticism. Professional dialogue and critical analysis also help to build a climate within which curiosity can be sustained long enough to withstand the discipline necessary to become research.

Though 'It is teachers who, in the end, will change the world of the school by understanding it' (Stenhouse, 1975), this will come about and be sustained only in an evolving ethos where 'sense making' and enquiry are sanctioned and orchestrated, where professional reflection and collaborative action govern practice.

References

Abbs, P. (1974). *Autobiography in Education: An Introduction to the Subjective Discipline of Autobiography and its Central Place in the Education of Teachers.* London: Heinemann Educational.
Broudy, H., Smith, B. and Burnett, J. (1964). *Democracy and Excellence in American Secondary Education.* Chicago: Rand McNally.

Bussis, A., Amarel, M. and Chittenden, E. (1975). *Beyond Surface Curriculum: An Interview Study of Teachers' Understandings.* Boulder, Col.: Westview Press.

Combs, A. (1965). *The Professional Education of Teachers.* Boston: Allyn and Bacon.

Combs, A. and Snygg, D. (1959). *Individual Behavior: A Perceptual Approach to Behavior.* New York: Harper and Row.

Clandinin, D. (1985). Terms of inquiry into teacher thinking: The place for practical knowledge and the Elbaz case. *The Journal of Curriculum Theorizing,* **6**, 2.

Devaney, K. and Thorn, L. (1975). *Exploring Teacher Centers.* San Francisco: The Far West Laboratory for Educational Research and Development.

Dewey, J. (1916). *Democracy and Education.* New York: Macmillan.

Dewey, J. (1934). *Art As Experience.* New York: Minton, Balch & Co.

Edelfelt, R. and Lawrence, G. (1975). In-service education: The state of the art. In R. Edelfelt and M. Johnson (eds), *Rethinking In-Service Education.* Washington, D.C.: The National Education Association.

Eisner, E. (1985). *The Educational Imagination: On the Design and Evaluation of School Programs.* New York: Macmillan.

Elbaz, F. (1983). *Teacher Thinking: A Study of Practical Knowledge.* London: Croom Helm.

Elkind, D. (1982). *The Hurried Child: Growing Up Too Fast Too Soon.* Reading, Mass.: Addison-Wesley.

Elliott, J. and Adelman, C. (1973). Reflecting where the action is: The design of the Ford Teaching Project. *Education for Teaching,* **92**, 8–20.

Eraut, M. (1985). *The Acquisition and Use of Educational Theory by Beginning Teachers'.* Sussex: Sussex University, Mimeo.

Erikson, E. (1950). *Childhood and Society.* New York: Norton.

Erikson, E. (1975). *Life History and the Historical Moment: Diverse Presentations.* New York: Norton.

Greene, M. (1982). A General Education Curriculum: Retrospect and Prospect – A Viewing. Paper presented at the American Educational Research Association Annual Conference, New York.

HMI (1985). *Quality in Schools: Evaluation and Appraisal.* London: HMSO.

Holly, M. (1983). Teacher reflections on classroom life: Collaboration and professional development. *Australian Administrator,* **4**(4), 1–4.

Holly, M. (1984). *Keeping a Personal–Professional Journal.* Geelong: Deakin University Press.

Holly, M. (1986). *Teacher Reflections on Classroom Life: An Empirical Base for Professional Development.* Final Report to the National Institute of Education, Research and Practice Unit, Knowledge Use and School Improvement, Washington, D.C.

Holly, M. 1988. *Reflective Writing and Teacher Inquiry: Keeping a Personal – Professional Journal.* London: Heinemann-Educational.

Jackson, P. (1968). *Life in Classrooms.* New York: Holt, Rinehart and Winston.

Jersild, A. (1955). *When Teachers Face Themselves.* New York: Teachers College Press, Columbia University.

Kuhn, T. (1962). *The Structure of Scientific Revolutions.* Chicago: University of Chicago Press.

Lortie, D. (1975). *Schoolteacher: A Sociological Study.* Chicago: University of Chicago Press.

Mallon, T. (1984). *A Book of One's Own: People and Their Diaries.* New York: Ticknor and Field.

Nias, J. (1983). Learning and Acting the Role: In-School Support for Primary Teachers.

Paper presented at the American Educational Research Association Annual Conference, Montreal.

Percy, W. (1980). *The Moviegoer*. New York: Avon Books.

Polanyi, M. (1967). *The Tacit Dimension*. New York: Doubleday.

Postman, N. and Weingartner, C. (1969). *Teaching as a Subversive Activity*. New York: Dell.

Richey, H. (1957). 'Growth in the modern conception of in-service education'. In Nelson B. Henry (ed.), *In-Service Education for Teachers, Supervisors, and Administrators, Fifty-Sixth Yearbook of the National Society for the Study of Education*, pp. 30–66. Chicago: The University of Chicago Press.

Rudduck, J. and Hopkins, D. (1985). *Research as a Basis for Teaching: Readings from the Work of Lawrence Stenhouse*. London: Heinemann Educational.

Runyan, W. (1984). *Life Histories and Psychobiographies: Explorations in Theory and Method*. Oxford: Oxford University Press.

Schön, D. (1983). *The Reflective Practitioner: How Professionals Think in Action*. New York: Basic Books.

Spender, D. (1982). *Invisible Women: The Schooling Scandal*. London: Writers and Readers Publishing Cooperative.

Stenhouse, L. (1975). *An Introduction to Curriculum Research and Development*. London: Heinemann Educational.

Stenhouse, L. (1981). What counts as research? *British Journal of Educational Studies*, **29**,2.

Tom, A. (1984). *Teaching as a Moral Craft*. New York: Longman.

Tripp, D. (1984). From Autopilot to Critical Consciousness: Problematising Successful Teaching. Paper presented at the Conference on Curriculum Theorizing, Dayton.

11
Pupil assessment from the perspective of naturalistic research

David Bridges

Recent developments in pupil assessment

Any overview of the developments in pupil assessment at this particular point has to recognize some divergent and indeed conflicting trends. In the United States, the pupil assessment industry, based on the prolific generation of 'objective' testing instruments, has never been more buoyant. Pupil scores on tests are being used as an instrument for holding individual teachers, school superintendents, school districts and even State Governors to account in what is already close to a witch hunt for educational laxity and a crusade for 'excellence' in educational achievement. Embedded in the test instruments, of course, are the attainments which pupils are expected to achieve and by fairly simple implication the curriculum which schools had better start providing if they do not wish their inadequacy to be paraded before their parental or political paymasters or mistresses.

In England and Wales the Secretary of State has assumed considerable detail of control over the curriculum and testing, first through the establishment of national criteria governing the General Certificate of Education examination and, then, though the national curriculum itself, the authority for which passed into the statute books in 1988. With the national curriculum has come an awesome structure of assessment, which provides both an instrument of detailed control over what is taught and a basis for judging and rendering schools accountable for the success of their teaching. Unconvincingly, perhaps, we are asked to believe that the same tests which serve these purposes will also assist in diagnosing pupil needs.

In the rhetoric of the General Certificate of Secondary Education (GCSE) was a commitment to a shift from norm-referenced to criterion-referenced testing. The GCSE examinations do include certain innovative features: they give more emphasis than the old 'O' level exams gave to the assessment of performances (e.g. oral and aural) other than written ones; they extend the previous use of course-based projects as the basis of assessment; and they attempt to provide an arrangement of alternative papers which is intended to ensure as far as possible that pupils will secure grades on the basis of a relatively successful completion of a graded task (typically by scoring at least 70%), rather than by marginal success and substantial failure (e.g. scoring 20%) on a more difficult one.

By extension, some of these same principles – in particular, the aspiration to criteria-related assessment and forms of assessment which permit successful performance – are contained in developments in the 'graded objectives' move-ment (notably in modern languages and mathematics), which has a special but not exclusive concern to recognize the achievements of pupils whose work does not extend to the level which will give them a useful GCSE award.

Alongside these developments are others clustered under such titles as records of pupil achievement and pupil profiling which highlight other dimensions of performance assessment. Some schemes claim to introduce, for example:

● a more holistic assessment which attempts to capture a wide range of dimensions of human personality;
● multifaceted assessment, bringing together in one record judgements derived from the child, teachers, supervisors responsible for work experience, etc.;
● the 'negotiation' of an agreed statement by pupil and teacher;
● the use of assessment over a period of time as a developmental tool supporting self-knowledge by the pupil; and hence
● the integration of the assessment process as part of the curriculum.

An agenda

The background to this paper then was a veritable turmoil of educational innovation led by developments in the refinement, sophistication and extension of traditional psychometric modes of assessment, and developments regarding the rhetoric and reality of new departures which could be construed as offering a critique of the old.

What insights did the Cambridge conference have to offer from the perspec-tive of naturalistic research on this scene? Running through the conference were certain key, organizing concepts, each of which was related to a contrast between some different approaches to assessment. Sometimes, we grouped these contrasts crudely under such headings as 'traditional' and 'reformist' but, although this was on occasions a useful shorthand, nobody was deceived into thinking that such a simple distinction could be maintained. In particular, a good deal of the discussion was concerned to offer a critique of 'reformist' practice which questioned whether the reality rather than the rhetoric con-stituted any significant change in assessment practice. To represent all this schematically is to run the risk of an agenda being mistaken for a conclusion, but it may help to make sense of the several strands of the discussion if these are set

Table 11.1 Pupil assessment: an agenda for discussion

Key concepts	Some contrasting assessment practices	
	Traditional (?)	*Reformist (?)* *Rhetoric or Reality (?)*
Holism	fragmentary and narrow in what they capture of personal achievement	holistic and broad
Individual uniqueness	comparative and standardizing	individualist and self-referenced
Contextualization	measures performances abstracted from context	describes performances in context
Motivation	allows only few to succeed	allows a wide range of 'success'
Multiple perspectives	single judgement sought	multiple perspectives valued
Dialogue/negotiation	assessment protected from pupil's questioning	assessment open to negotiation or dialogue
Truth	based on a correspondence theory	based on consensus theory (?)
Ownership	data owned by testers	data owned by pupils
Integration of curriculum and assessment	curriculum led assessment *or* assessment-led curriculum	integration of assessment with curriculum
Development	supports selection process	supports process of personal development

alongside each other at the beginning, with the warning that the account which follows will progressively untidy an apparently simple antithesis (Table 11.1).

Holism

One aspiration of some forms of pupil profiling and records of pupil achievement which are being developed is to offer a more holistic picture of the pupil than is represented by psychometric tests, which typically report on a very narrow range of performance, or traditional examinations like GCSE, which are open to the criticism that they offer a portrayal of personal achievement which is fragmented, partial and narrowly academic in orientation. These criticisms of traditional testing and examination procedures are commonly voiced, but do not the alternative aspirations of the reformist assessors have their own problems? Indeed they do. The question of what constitutes 'the whole child' cannot be answered as if it were a simple question of fact. Rather – if I may lump together something of an assortment of theoretical perspectives – it is 'an essentially contested concept'; it is problematic; it is a social construct which has to be interpreted in relation to a given social context; it is value laden; it is a prescriptive rather than a descriptive concept.

The consequence of all this is that any aspiration to report on 'the whole child' carries the implication of a prescription of what counts as, or what ought to constitute, that whole child. Any such prescription ought properly to be accompanied by some explanation and defence of the values and/or social context which it assumes.

Concern was also expressed that any attempt to record and report parts of a child's personality as an aggregate deconstructs the whole and then reconstructs it as merely the sum of its parts. It carries too the implication of a deficient model of the child, prompting the impulse to 'top up' or 'put in' the missing or deficient parts.

One response to this sort of critique of would-be holistic assessment is to suggest that the appraisal or report might become even more child-centred than it is, that the children might have a progressively increasing role in the definition and, indeed, in Heideggerean terms, the constitution or creation of their own versions of their whole 'selves'. Indeed, it might reasonably be represented as a central purpose of education to assist a person in that self-knowledge (self-assessment?) and those acts of self-determination which together constitute the unique individual. The aspiration to 'holistic' assessment of pupils – notwithstanding its prima facie appeal to naturalistic researchers who commonly apply the same notion to their own studies – is, then, not without its problems.

Uniqueness

The tension between the desire to reflect the uniqueness of a child and the function of many test instruments to compare children on the basis of a limited range of commonalities was recognized, similarly, as closely analogous with a central preoccupation of naturalistic research. Naturalistic researchers seek to preserve the uniqueness of the objects of their study by, among other things: (i) providing a detailed description in (ii) responsive and un-predetermined terms, along (iii) a wide variety of dimensions, (iv) generated by a variety of individual interests and perspectives, (v) with explicit reference to the situational contexts and (vi) without attempting to aggregate all this into a summative, still less a summary conclusion ('overall assessment – very good'!).

In terms of pupil assessment, much the same requirements have to be made if the individuality of the case – the child – is not to be lost, and hence, in language which may resonate more easily with traditional psychometrics if the assessment is to have real validity. If only a limited range of dimensions of performance is explored, then it is more likely that significant aspects of personality will be lost (cf. comments on 'the whole child') and more likely that the assessment procedures will offer us pictures of apparently identical people. The more carefully we predetermine the dimensions of personality and achievement we assess, the less alert and responsive we shall be to the unusual or idiosyncratic qualities of individual human beings. By extension, if we can call upon the interests and perspectives of a variety of 'assessors', we may open the talents of the child to recognition by an expanded range of imaginations driven by a diversity of values and interests. If we can resist the temptation to represent the complex picture of human personality as an aggregate grade or summary comment we can stay loyal to the unique individuality of the child and enable different audiences to the assessment to make different evaluations based on their own priorities, even if (in the terms all too familiar to teachers concerned with the development of pupil profiles) we frustrate the wishes of employers looking for a shorthand formula on the lines 'worth interviewing/not worth interviewing'.

Contextuality

The view that cases have to be understood (and thence described or assessed) in context has a number of applications to pupil assessment as well as to naturalistic research. It is a feature of many traditional psychometric tests that they attempt to test skills in a way which is context-free or, more accurately, seek to test them in the rather peculiar context provided by the test itself. The conviction that runs through many such tests is that skills or performances demonstrated in the test are generalizable to other contexts. Similarly, faith in the generalizability of artificially contextualized or supposedly decontextualized skills (listening skills, communication skills, interpersonal skills) appears to run through many of the would-be reformist profiles and the curriculum developments to which they are attached.

Discussion at the conference was consistently sceptical about the claim that any skill could be demonstrated free of context (tests provide contexts whose conventions and expectations are both very extensive and very distinct) and the claim that variety of context is insignificant either to a child's capacity to express a performance or the kind of performance which is called for (and hence the kind of learning which is required to generate that performance). The implication for pupil assessment was that if we wished to assess skills we had to be able to describe performances in context and, further, in a variety of contexts.

Motivation

One of the motives which underlies some teachers' and administrators' commitment to more holistic or multidimensional forms of assessment, to assessments derived from a variety of perspectives, to assessments designed, as it is commonly expressed, 'to enable pupils to demonstrate what they can do rather than what they cannot', and to assessments which are either self-referenced or perhaps criterion-referenced rather than norm-referenced, is a concern to enhance pupils' motivation. There is now ample documentation of the bitterness of the experience of many pupils and their understandable sense of grievance with the education system which submits students to 11 years of compulsory schooling and which culminates in assessment procedures *designed* to ensure that a whole section of their number leave school without any serious record or acknowledgement of their achievements. From an early age, norm-referenced tests provide them with a regular and humiliating sense of their own inadequacy and a demoralizing premonition that it is their destiny in schooling to fail.

Many of the more recent initiatives on assessment outlined in the introduction to this chapter arise out of a concern to challenge this downward spiral of motivation and to develop assessment procedures which will recognize, and help pupils to recognize, the achievements which they have secured. This programme is pursued through a readiness to assess and put on record modest achievements secured a little bit at a time (as recognized, for example, by step-by-step graded objectives) and also a wider variety of achievements (including, for example, those secured out of school) than had traditionally been encompassed in school records or reports.

The conference was understandably sympathetic to the aspirations expressed through these developments, but this was insufficient to blunt its sceptical spirit. One contributor spoke dubiously about 'unearned tokens of esteem'. More generally, the group was unpersuaded by the rhetoric of universal success and esteem in a social and economic context, which would all too soon confront young people with the reality of selection, or more probably non-selection, for shrinking and in some areas already negligible employment opportunities. Were teachers merely caught up in a process of 'gentling' pupils whose bitterness and frustration might otherwise be the stuff of revolt, if not of revolution?

The analogies between pupil assessment and naturalistic research in respect of this issue were not fully drawn at the conference, but they perhaps deserve exploration. Naturalistic researchers would no doubt want honesty to be one criterion against which their efforts should be judged. But honest opinion can be offered with kindness and support or with hostility and the intention to undermine (not to mention a range of dispositions between these extremes). To which of these two positions naturalistic researchers incline varies a good deal. Perhaps they reserve gentleness for those who are relatively powerless and full severity to those with the greatest power. (Thus perhaps the Robin Hood image that they like to have of themselves!) In this case, they may have a natural sympathy with those who seek to restore to the 'failures' of the educational system some sense of their own worth. In any case, the receptiveness of naturalistic researchers to an almost infinite diversity of values must predispose them to expect that somewhere in that universe of values there is at last one criterion that any individual can satisfy.

Multiple perspectives

A number of threads of this chapter so far, including this last, have led to the idea that multiple perspectives might have a proper and useful place in pupil assessment – and this, of course, readily accords with practice in naturalistic research. In most traditional forms of assessment, the provision of multiple or more typically dual perspectives (e.g. by the moderator of an exam) is simply a device for ensuring the reliability, comparability and fairness of a particular assessment. If the test or exam is well constructed and the criteria are clearly laid out, it should in general produce results which alternative testers can agree on without much difficulty. If they regularly fail to agree on an assessment of this kind, this will typically be taken to indicate that a particular test item or the whole test is poorly constructed. The same general picture holds with application to psychometric research.

In naturalistic research, however, as in some innovative patterns of assessment, the generation and availability of several, diverse and even conflicting evaluations of an object of enquiry, far from constituting a methodological problem, is precisely what is expected, sought and valued. The expectation is rooted primarily in the epistemology of naturalistic research (not that this is entirely of a piece). Social or interpersonal events have to be understood in terms of the perceptions or understandings of the intentional agents who play them out. These perceptions are at least in part determined by the interests, values, purposes, predispositions and past experiences of the perceiver, and these in turn can be expected to be diverse and individual. Hence, their perceptions of events and their evaluation of them will predictably diverge. The value of this divergence of opinion is that it can act educatively to alert any one individual to aspects of a case of which he or she had not previously been aware.

So also with pupil assessment, which must take into account the intentionality of the pupil in interpreting the significance of performances, which can be enriched and enlarged by allowing scope for a variety of perspectives on pupils' individual qualities and which should allow the possibility that alternative evaluations of a pupil may be made on the basis of the same data.

Negotiation and dialogue

Assessment practices that do generate multiple, or at least more than one, perspective on a pupil's achievement vary, however, in terms of how they handle the resulting divergence. Many of those in the pupil-profiling movement attach considerable importance to the process by which pupil and teacher 'negotiate' an agreed statement out of their divergent perspectives. The Cambridge conference gave considerable attention to the related notions of negotiation and dialogue and to the difference between them.

Our first response to the idea that pupils and teachers might negotiate an agreed assessment focussed on the inequality of power in the relationship. With some qualification it was reckoned that, in a one-to-one relationship with a teacher, a pupil would be in a weak position to insist that his or her perspective was fairly represented if it conflicted with that of the teacher. There were, however, a number of ways in which pupils' hands could be strengthened in this negotiation:

- Pupils could be given personal support in the form of, for example, a sympathetic friend or another teacher in the role of advocate committed to supporting the pupil's position in the negotiation.
- Structures could be devised which armed pupils with rewards or sanctions, e.g. pupil assessment by the teacher could be linked with teacher assessment by the pupil.
- Pupils could be given training designed to enable them courteously but firmly to stand their ground in negotiations – not unlike, perhaps, some of the training offered as part of a health education programme in how to say 'no' to friends persuading you to have a sniff or a cigarette.

However, this line of argument did not satisfy for very long. This picture of pupil and teacher haggling over a grade or a phrase seemed to present an inappropriate model of the relationship – reminiscent more of 'plea bargaining' in a court of law, in one opinion, 'borrowing too heavily from a capitalistic notion of exchange' in another. For reasons already indicated in the previous discussion of multiple perspectives, the reduction of two perspectives on the pupil to one seemed to represent an impoverishment of the assessment data rather than any qualitative improvement. Was the notion of negotiation really the appropriate one to apply to the transaction in which pupil and teacher sat down to respond to their individual and possibly divergent assessments?

Reference to some of the thinking which has gone into the development of the methodology of naturalistic research was helpful here. In case study, it was argued, you 'negotiate' with teachers about the release of a study but you have 'dialogue' with them about its validity. We must take care in naturalistic research and in pupil assessment to distinguish between negotiation about what people will allow and dialogue about what is true. When we are looking at pupil assessment we should be concerned with a better understanding of the pupil's achievements and person, with, in some sense, the truth or validity of statements made and not merely with what assessment can be arrived at on the basis of a process of exchange of gifts and concessions. It was thus a notion of an educative dialogue, centred around alternative assessments of a pupil and aimed at better mutual understanding of those assessments and that pupil, which emerged as the preferred conceptualization of this interaction.

Such a dialogue might, but need not necessarily, result in a 'synthesis' of opinion which brings together and expands into a new illumination the different opinions contained in initial assessments, but this should not be confused with a 'compromise'.

Theory of truth

In the process of its discussion of negotiation and dialogue the group considered what theory of truth underlay the idea of the negotiations of an assessment. The question was posed: 'Are we seeing the replacement of a correspondence theory of truth with a consensus theory?' However, the distinction drawn between negotiation and dialogue seemed to help us to escape the pitfalls of consensus theory. Negotiation was a political activity about what we could agree to do or to allow. Dialogue was an epistemological activity concerned with truth and understanding. Its objective was not agreement or consensus, but a clearer perception of the evidence, or grounds for belief, underlying assessments of pupils and a richer view of the valuation or interpretation which might be set on that evidence. This is not to defend a naive correspondence theory of truth but is to avoid some of the cruder relativism of a consensus theory.

Ownership

However, if it sought to redefine the political notion of negotiation as an epistemological notion of dialogue, the conference nevertheless recognized important areas in pupil assessment, as in naturalistic research, where questions were appropriately expressed in terms such as the ownership of data.

This concern for the proper location of ownership and for the protection of pupil assessment data was sharpened by the observation that 'we cannot help but be hurt by exposure', which was the focus of a small group discussion. One of the aspirations of some of the more recently developed forms of pupil profile and records of pupil achievement is explicitly to document and put on record a richer and more comprehensive picture of individual personality than has hitherto generally been the case. It includes material which has previously been treated as private (e.g. achievements arising out of school activities, and personal strengths and weaknesses), or as personally sensitive (e.g. judgements about the pupil's honesty). It is difficult to imagine that any record which is genuinely revealing in these ways might not also be seriously damaging when exposed. More particularly, what about the child who, not entirely exceptional in adolescence, is unhappy about many aspects of himself or herself? Does he or she have to have all this laid out on record? How can children be protected from these dangers or be helped to protect themselves? These were not questions which the conference tried to resolve, but two major alternative cases were, however, briefly explored.

The first was the presumption in favour of total pupil ownership of assessment, which could include agreement as to what is assessed, what and whose assessments are put on record, the physical possession of any such records and control over access to records. The onus in this case would be on other people to justify to the child or to some other overseeing judge their intervention or access as an exception to this general presupposition. Pupils who exercised their power very restrictively would, of course, have to be alert to and accept the consequences of this policy, including, for example, any reduction in how informed their teachers or prospective employers are, any loss of credibility of the assessments generated from their protected sources and, more insidiously, the growth of a black market in alternative forms of assessment unprotected by any form of accountability.

An alternative presumption which could be made would be in favour of public access to information. In this case, the presumption would be that, for example, any information gathered from any source about any pupil could be put on record and made publicly available. The onus in this case would be on the individual pupils, or someone claiming to act in their interests, to make a case for particular restrictions. It was suggested that this presumption might be associated with the idea that, given the compulsory and public nature of education, 'being a pupil' is itself a public role for which a pupil can legitimately be called to account.

These two rather stark alternatives leave out, of course, a range of more familiar and perhaps more plausible intermediate options in which, for example, a restricted range of people (e.g. teachers) have various forms of restricted access to pupil assessments or records under conditions which do not allow them to pass the information on without the pupils' consent. However, the presentation of the alternatives as a dichotomy in this case is perhaps helpful. In the end we have to settle disputes about intermediate cases by reference to some fundamental priority between the two presumptions offered here, and it may be helpful to confront this choice directly.

Rather differently, however, the presentation and recognition of a dichotomy presented in terms of the public and the private is perhaps revealing of the socio-economic context in which we are addressing these issues. For some (though perhaps not all) of the conference membership, the distinction between the public and the private is itself a function of, and has significance in, only a limited range of socio-economic orders, notably those associated with an advanced stage of capitalism. While we might recognize the significance of teachers and pupils operating in a given society at a given time, we should not perhaps assume that it will have the same significance in all other societies, real or hypothetical.

Assessment and curriculum

Little has been said explicitly yet about the relationship between assessment and curriculum, yet for some of those attending the conference this was a central issue. Many traditional forms of assessment purport at least to reflect or to be led by the curriculum. More commonly, perhaps, the taught curriculum is led by the received pattern of assessment. Indeed, new assessment schemes (e.g. GCSE) are introduced with the explicit intention of changing the curriculum. Even where this is not intended, individual teachers and schools will seek to protect their positions by 'teaching to the test', particularly in any conditions in which public comparison can be made of the assessment-related 'success' of their teaching. The assessment system can have substantial intended and unintended consequences for the curriculum: expanding it by legitimizing new topical coverage; narrowing it by encouraging teachers and pupils to ignore topics which are not tested for; complicating it by emphasizing higher mental processes; oversimplifying it by its over-focus on basic or core skills. Consequently, it may be expected that the curriculum will become progressively more standardized, more emphatic on matters easy to test and less esoteric. In the view of many of those attending the conference these possibilities demand much closer attention and research. Much may be guessed at but little is researched about the damage which assessment procedures can do to the curriculum.

This said, however, some of the new approaches to assessment challenge the separation of assessment and curriculum. Where assessment is based on dialogue between pupil and teacher and where that dialogue has as its focus the expansion of an individual's understanding of his or her own achievements and aspirations – perhaps, by extension, the setting of new educational goals – then the assessment itself becomes part of the curriculum. It is indeed recognized as such in many schools which build it into the curriculum quite explicitly as part of, for example, personal and social development. In the rhetoric and perhaps the reality of such developments, assessment and curriculum are part of an integrative whole and assessment serves fully the developmental purposes of the curriculum.

Development

This chapter has run almost to its end without directly addressing the question of the purpose(s) and function(s) of assessment, partly because this rarely emerged in the conference as an issue of explicit debate. Positions on the purpose of assessment – or in this case an unusually unified position – tended to emerge rather indirectly from a discussion of issues like the place of negotiation and dialogue in the assessment process.

The conference recognized as a matter of plain fact the *central social function* of pupil assessment as an instrument of social selection. At the time, however, its members sought to advance its *central purpose in an educational context* as that of personal development. It is always relevant or, more strongly, one ought always to be required, to ask of assessment procedures employed in the context of education how they advance the development of the pupil and whether the ones which are employed are chosen and administered so as to maximize their possible contribution to that development. This was perhaps the central single principle underlying the conference's response to a whole range of assessment-related issues. It was not always, however, an easy principle to apply. (What constitutes personal development is in itself deeply problematic in any case.) In particular, members found themselves torn in their response to, for example, developments such as we are seeing at the moment in the UK in the area of technical and vocational education. These are generating initiatives which look remarkably liberal and 'progressive' when viewed at the level of classroom pedagogy but, some would argue, predictably 'impositional' when viewed in their wider social context. Similarly, participants were often uncertain whether to respond to perceived deficiencies in both traditional and reformist approaches to assessment by strategies which restricted themselves to 'damage limitation' or strategies which addressed themselves to weaknesses in the assessment system structurally embedded in the wider political economy. Two distinctly different chapters might have been written from the standpoint of these two major perspectives. This chapter has merely attempted to represent some of the ways in which these intertwining threads ran through the conference discussion.

12
Assessing the whole child[1]

Louis M. Smith and Carol S. Klass

Introductory perspective

Most lay people seem to have a conception of the whole child which they use when thinking about education and schooling. Most educational theorists, whether they be as radical as A.S. Neill (1960) or as conservative as Ron Edmonds (1979), explicitly or implicitly have a conception of the whole child. This whole-child construct creates multiple problems for the educational or psychological assessor. This chapter attempts to discuss how we have wrestled with the issues in our current research.

We are not initially overly optimistic about the search for the 'whole child'. Our first concern lies in using the construct personality as the broadest term in which to phrase our thought, for some texts in child development (Bee, 1981) use the term more restrictively, i.e. as social emotional development. Most personality theorists (Mischel, 1976; Hall and Lindzey, 1978) use the label as the broadest construal of the individual person. In addition to the linguistic and definitional disparities, we have long been enamoured with a tongue-in-cheek view of this construct:

Consider for a moment what a psychologist ought to know before he ventures to speak with any authority about personality. To begin with, he must be thoroughly grounded in the basic principles of psychology, in learning theory, for instance, where he should be able to deduce a theorem from Hull's postulates, draw one of Tolman's 'balloons' properly, master the facts on conditioning and learning, and so forth. He should know the tremendous literature on psychological paper-and-pencil tests from the

[1] The ideas in this paper do not represent official policy of either Washington University or Illinois DCFS.

Bernreuter Personality Inventory to the Minnesota Multiphasic Test. Ultimately this should lead him into the intricacies of factor analysis so that he can understand the contributions of men like Cattell and Guilford. After he has spent a year or so on this he ought to take up anthropology, and travel, mentally at least, throughout the South Seas with Margaret Mead and Malinowski, to Alor with DuBois, the Southwest with Kluckhohn and Leighton. After studying culture and personality in books, he should· of course spend a year or two in the field, after which he will be ready for psychoanalysis. For who can understand the Old Masters like Freud without three to seven years of 'didactic' therapy? Perhaps by choosing one's analyst carefully, some of the views of the neo-Freudians like Horney, Fromm, and Alexander can be learned in the process. To save a little time, our hypothetical well-educated student of personality could take a summer off to attend a Rorschach Institute so that he can make a stab at understanding the some eight hundred studies of personality made with this instrument. But even this is only a beginning. What about the Thematic Apperception Test and its intricate interpretations? How about some of the ancient techniques, like hypnosis, or some more modern ones like nondirective interviewing? Surely he should know these. And if he is to be really educated he should have read the 'great books' and should be familiar with the history of culture of Western civilization. How else will he be able to understand the depth and complexities, the richness and variety of human personality? (McClelland, 1951, pp. xi–xii)

More recent surveys of the field (Mischel, 1976, Hall and Lindzey, 1978) show that the literature is immensely larger, but the problems remain.

Of the multiple ways in which a conceptual analysis of the construct might be undertaken (e.g. historical, clinical, or in terms of a major theory and its operational measuring devices), we have elected a more situational and pragmatic alternative. We will pose the 'personality' of the 'whole child' issue in terms of a research project that is currently underway. As we work our way through the particulars of this problem we will try to confront situationally specific as well as the more general and abstract issues latent in the construct itself.

The research problem

In our 'Research and evaluation of a therapeutic program for abused and neglected children and their parents' (Klass and Smith, 1985), we stated the overall problem and design for the inquiry this way:

The goal of this proposed project is to *research* and *evaluate*, through a quasi-experimental design, the effectiveness of the Illinois DCFS Therapeutic Family Day Care Program, a prevention/treatment program for young children at risk of maltreatment and these children's parents. First, this proposed project will evaluate the improvement in the children's developmental status; and second, will evaluate changes in the quality of the mothers' caregiving skills. The primary research design will utilize pre and post testing of both children's developmental status and their mothers' caregiving skill, before and after their 12–15 month involvement in the DCFS Therapeutic Family Day Care Project. These quantitative results will be integrated with a qualitative field study used to describe and analyze the day to day happenings and the situational context within the project.

Several comments might be made on the implicit and explicit aspects of the study. The term 'developmental status' is a synonym, we think, for 'personality' and 'whole child'. The quasi-experimental design requires measuring instruments for assessing the changing status of the child. Selecting these requires some idea of the conceptual domain being observed, an obvious, but we think underestimated, set of problems. Creatively integrating an ongoing qualitative, ethnographic study and the more quantitative study of the quasi-experimental design is not easy.

Initial field note accounts

In the DCFS programme, the 'providers' are women who care for children in their homes 7 hours a day, 5 days a week. Once each week the mothers of the children spend half a day with the providers learning parenting skills and attitudes. The providers keep 'field notes' on the children and their mothers, stated in commonsense terms. We present three brief sets of such notes in Examples 1, 2 and 3, which are typical of one strand of the programme documents. The first is an early summary account of twin boys dictated to the project director; the second is a brief set of provider's observations of a child's entry behaviour; and the third is a summary report written by the provider after 1½ years in the programme.

Example 1   Provider's report at support/training session

Twins Ronnie and Dick, entering project at 27 months: After first week of child care

The children are so dirty that their skin is very dry; especially their knees, hands and elbows are cracked as if the children were very old. Dirt is encrusted in their skin, and their hands and feet are so filthy that a bath doesn't get them completely clean. The boys have either shirts or blouses on their bottoms as diapers, and sometimes, no underwear at all.

They are not very playful at all. They just don't seem to know how to play but just sit. They pick up a car and merely hold it. I tell them: 'roll it', and they do nothing until I first show them. They don't know what it means to run or race or crawl until I first show them. When they come into the room with the toys, they will pick up a toy, and merely hold it. They don't seem to be curious about anything. And they seem to neither cry nor laugh.

They don't know how to use a fork or spoon. But they are terribly hungry and just 'gobble' as if they couldn't get enough to eat. They don't seem to know what to do with a lot of common food, like hot dogs on a bun, or hamburgers on a bun. They just stare at the food like: 'What am I supposed to be doing with this?'

They don't know their body parts, so that when I tell them to 'get on your knees', they don't know what I mean, and I must show them. They both can say 'bye' and Dick says 'look'; however they have no other words.

Example 2   Observations from provider's field notes

Trina (June 1985): Third week of child care

Trina is the most passive child at 21 months I have ever seen! She sits, uninterested three fourths of the time unless I am directly relating to her. She watches the other children as they play. Perhaps she'll play with a toy after Nancy and Ricky quit playing with it and have moved on to something else. We played with play dough. Trina wouldn't touch it. (We played with it one other time at my home and I've seen a small can at Trina's home.) I had a plastic knife and a small cup in front of Trina. I cut some. She wouldn't try. I tore some off. She did this after I started helping Ricky and Nancy with something. Ricky and Nancy started patting their play dough flat. Dawn (Nancy's mother) and I joined in laughing and chanting softly. Trina wouldn't pat her dough or show much of a grin.

We took a wagon to the park. Trina hummed as we rode in the wagon. It was her only sound during the trip, even as we played there. She would have stood in the grass, as if lost, confused and scared if I hadn't helped her onto different toys. She showed no enjoyment of toys – only watched the other kids.

She cries too easily (not normal). I can ask her a question and she'll hang her head crying – for example, 'Can you help me with this puzzle? Would you like to get down (from the stool)? Are you ready to get out of the car?' She cries as I change her poopie diapers. I ask her to stop crying, but she'll keep gasping and definitely isn't relaxed. She cries as we wash her hands before and after we eat. She's uncoordinated, walks unordinarily slow, drools constantly, and no jabbering. In summary – NEEDS HELP, and I don't know if I'm doing any good.

Example 3   Provider's summary observations and interpretations

November 1985: After 1½ years of child care with Nancy

One child I care for is almost 3 years old, and I've cared for her about one and a half years. When Nancy started coming to my home, she was practically speechless, had very little jabbering, and had a vocabulary of maybe four or five words. She was unable to feed herself and couldn't go up or down stairs. She had had little or no experience with other children and few play experiences with adults. But most surprising to me was the fact that she was almost totally expressionless. How many fifteen month old children do you see not smiling, laughing, giggling, whining, or even crying at some time during the day? Nancy did none of these. She was extremely passive and uninvolved all the time. The most likely reasons for these characteristics of Nancy are that her mom, Dawn, kept her in a playpen at home all the time.

When I started caring for Nancy at fifteen months, her mother told me that Nancy ate only thinly sliced lunch meats and a limited variety of baby food fruits and vegetables; she didn't drink milk from a cup and still used a bottle. When Nancy came to my home I found her able to eat anything offered to her, drink milk from a cup fairly well, but was very passive. She would let my son, Ricky, who is two months younger than she, take toys from her and just watch him quietly as he played. After caring for her for one month, I started the half day mother assistance in my home. I could then see the extent of Dawn's limitations and why Nancy behaved as she did. Physically, there was still no holding or touching, or cuddling occurring between them. Verbally Dawn only gave directives to Nancy such as 'Don't do that!', 'You can't have that', or 'Stay out of there.' There was *very* little talking, commenting on behaviors or pleasant conversation directed toward Nancy.

Let us look briefly at what these lay people are saying. In Example 1 the provider is first of all concerned with the physical condition of the children, especially the lack of cleanliness. In the second paragraph a number of issues around playfulness, curiosity and emotional passivity appear. In the third paragraph the provider comments on the knowledge and skills of simple self-help activities regarding eating. In the final paragraph the focus is on self-knowledge of body parts, following simple directions and language development. In Example 2, concerns of emotional passivity and playfulness reappear along with a focus on motor coordination and interactive/communication skills. In Example 3, a provider gives a further portrayal focussing on playfulness, emotional and social passivity, self-care skills and language development, and adds a focus on the caregiving skills of the child's mother.

Although stated in 'lay language' terms and in the form of simple paragraphs with clusters of illustrations, the providers' observations present a powerful set of images. Translating these images and illustrations into theoretical language and into measurable formats (dimensions or ratings) seems necessary for the kind of research we want to do. But these translations seem open to question regarding their power for meaningfulness and, consequently, present a haunting uneasiness lurking in the background of our effort. That is, do we lose more than we gain by such efforts at translation and objectivity?

Problems and issues

In the context of the overall theme of this volume, we see several major issues. First, the research approach can draw upon contextualized descriptions or upon

Table 12.1 Domains of development (after Bee, 1981)

Physical	Thinking	Social
Physical growth	Language	Personality
Perception	Thinking	Social
	Intelligence	Sex concept/gender
		Moral

a context-free profile of dimensions. We have a strong commitment to anchor our theoretical work in the commonsense understanding and situational context of practitioners, regardless of the level of 'theoretical sophistication' of these practitioners. In our instance, the providers, who work on a day-to-day basis with the children, are the individuals who will make any difference to be made in our programme. The programme has multiple built-in efforts to increase both provider understanding and their skill in caregiving. The project staff's observations in providers' homes, the providers' field notes, providers' talking about their daily work and observations with each other and the project director, and doing various reading and listening exercises, are part of the continuing training of these surrogate caregivers. But our point here is that we believe in a dialectic between the project researchers and the project caregivers. Neither runs ahead of the other.

A second issue, central to both contextualized descriptions and the more measurement-oriented profile of the dimensions approach, is the choice of language system used to discuss the 'whole child'. Contextualized descriptions such as our providers' observations often rely on commonsense, 'lay' language. In contrast, an array of language systems is embedded in available theories of personality. Mischel (1976) clusters several dozen of these into a typology of four 'approaches': trait, psychodynamic, behaviourist and phenomenological. In scanning the array of language systems used in researching personality, we think the choice comes back to 'it depends' upon one's problem and one's purpose.

If the researcher chooses to break down the 'whole child' into a profile of dimensions as most measurement-oriented researchers prefer, then a third issue emerges: the differentiation of dimensions, i.e. how many dimensions does one need to capture the personality of the 'whole child'? And what labels do you use to name these dimensions? The contemporary literature is not very satisfactory regarding these issues. Bee's (1981) organization of her book, *The Developing Child*, divides the 'whole child' into three realms: physical, thinking and social (see Table 12.1 for a portrayal of the suptopics within these realms). One might ask, is perception more a part of the physical or the intellectual, and is the moral more a part of the social or of thinking and reasoning? Our view of all this takes us back one step into the very nature of social scientific theory. We are 'constructivists' in the Berger and Luckman (1966) sense and believe that one can slice into the domain at one or another level of specificity and one or another categorical system. In terms of the old image of 'slicing nature at its joints', we

Table 12.2 The Vineland Taxonomy of Adaptive Behaviour (from Sparrow *et al.*, 1984)

Communication	Receptive	What your child understands
	Expressive	What your child says
	Written	What your child reads and writes
Daily living skills	Personal	How your child eats, dresses, and practises personal hygiene
	Domestic	What household tasks your child performs
	Community	How does your child use time, money, the telephone, and job skills
Socialization	Interpersonal relationships	How your child interacts with others
	Play and leisure time	How your child plays and uses leisure time
	Coping skills	How your child demonstrates responsibility and sensitivity to others
Motor skills	Gross	How your child uses arms and legs for movement and coordination
	Fine	How your child uses hands and fingers to manipulate objects

do not believe that such joints exist, although for some purposes there are more strategic 'cuts' than others.

If one is choosing to depict a profile of dimensions, a fourth issue involves the degree of differentiation, the degree of which often depends both upon the nature of the problem and the purpose of the endeavour. The Vineland Adaptive Behaviour Scales illustrate both this issue of differentiation and returns us to the issue of different language systems. For many years, we have been enamoured with the Vineland Social Maturity Scale (Doll, 1935, 1965), now called the Vineland Adaptive Behaviour Scales (Sparrow *et al.*, 1984). The very change in the title illustrates the change in language systems accompanying the historical changes within the social sciences. Social maturity has evolved into adaptive behaviour. Synonyms for the same 'reality'? The Vineland Scales now give 'scores' on one dimension, i.e. adaptive behaviour composite. And it will give scores on four domains: communication, daily living skills, socialization and motor skills. And if one wants a more analytic or differentiated view, the Vineland Scales will break each of these four domains down into several more 'subdomains'. Thus, one can reduce the 'whole child' to 11 slices, as shown in Table 12.2. Too many? Or too few? Perhaps the most extreme case of this general differentiation issue is the controversy over intelligence. The Stanford Binet test gives a single 'g' IQ score, Sternberg argues for three, and Guilford's 'structure of the intellect' presents a 120-dimension model.

Finally, we would raise briefly the possibilities of developing, in common-sense and/or theoretically sophisticated language, both contextualized descriptions and profiles of dimensions of the 'whole child'. One of the more powerful exponents of this tradition is Lois Murphy (Murphy and Moriarty, 1976). Murphy's work is replete with poignant descriptions and vignettes portraying her understanding of the 'whole child'. Yet she also has developed the concept of coping which has great similarity to Sparrow's conception of social maturity and adaptive behaviour, although neither cites the other. Murphy splits coping into two kinds: coping I, 'with the environment'; and coping II, 'ways of keeping comfortable, or maintaining internal integration' (p. 335). Vulnerability and resilience are added to her overall conception. She seems to play back and forth between the two approaches – the qualitative, contextualized descriptions and the more quantitative context-free dimensions. Such is one more resolution of the dilemma. And that may be the more powerful stance. Rather than trying to squeeze the total world of the whole child into a single format, we feel our problem and purpose in research may demand a blending of the contextualized descriptions with the more quantitatively measured profiles of dimensions.

Conclusions and implications

The first conclusion is that the label, the whole child, is an unattainable goal in research. The multiple choices in available theories, in settings in which one works and in practical problems focussed upon, is too diverse. The general theory of personality, in spite of 100 years of psychological effort (4000 in Western civilization) and some magnificent attempts (e.g. Freud, Piaget and Murray), is not available.

As idealists, with a touch of true belief, the idea remains important because it sensitizes one to the need to remain flexible in any one research or practical problem, to the possibilities of alternative construals of personality and development. For us it demands a more open-ended stance, even while getting on with the task as well as one can.

Thirdly, we are struck with the idea of trade-offs in this part of our work; the benefits and costs for taking one alternative versus another are never simple. Each problem must always be considered in terms of the specific alternatives under investigation, its very phrasing, the audience to whom one is directing the research proposal or the final report, where the research fits into one's personal agenda, and where it fits into the knowledge in the field. The latter even breaks down into subfields and communities of researchers and practitioners, each of which has its own norms, both procedurally and substantively, as to what is important and what is legitimate.

For our own specific piece of research, we note that we have a series of qualitative and descriptive perspectives on the problems of child abuse and neglect, a programme for remediating those problems, and a descriptive, analytical and synthetic conception of the child relevant to such a programme. Earlier work highlighted descriptive portrayals of the children, each portrayal accenting a central or dominant pattern of traits. That seemed an important step. Now, as we are trying to isolate components of the programme that seem to be most helpful in the child's development, we are moving to quasi-experimental designs which require the measurement of changes in the children. This is pushing us to develop scoring schemes and content analysis procedures for the overall views of patterns and for specific dimensions within those patterns. In turn, this approach has taken us into the more traditional test and measurements literature for instruments that are most related to our evolving conceptions.

The closest we come to a general conclusion is a pragmatic one: keep one eye clearly on the problems one wants to solve, keep a second eye on the evolution of those problems in one's own personal serial or agenda, and keep the 'third' eye on the broader available literature and ideas that historically run back in time and that contemporaneously run wider than one's local professional community or immediate reference group. And then begin making the necessary decisions regarding the 'whole child'.

References

Bee, H. (1981). *The Developing Child,* 3rd edn. New York: Harper and Row.

Berger, P.L. and Luckman, T. (1962). *The Social Construction of Reality: A Treatise in the Sociology of Knowledge.* New York: Anchor Books.

Doll, E.A. (1935). A genetic scale of social maturity. *American Journal of Orthopsychiatry,* **5**, 180–8.

Doll, E.A. (1965). *Vineland Social Maturity Scale: Condensed Manual of Directions.* Circle Pines. MN: American Guidance Service.

Edmonds, R. (1979). Some schools work and more can. *Social Policy,* **9**(5), 28–33.

Hall, C. and Lindzey, G. (1978). *Theories of Personality.* New York: John Wiley.

Klass, C.K. and Smith, L.M. (1985). *Research and Evaluation of a Therapeutic Program for Emotionally Maltreated Children and Their Parents.* NCCAN Proposal. East St. Louis, Ill: DCFS.

McClelland, D. (1851). *Personality.* New York: Dryden Press.

Mischel, W. (1976). *Introduction to Personality,* 2nd edn. New York: Holt, Rinehart and Winston.

Murphy, L.B. and Moriarty, A.E. (1976). *Vulnerability, Coping, and Growth, from Infancy to Adolescence.* New Haven: Yale University Press.

Neill, A.S. (1960). *Summerhill: A Radical Approach to Child Rearing.* New York: Hart.

Sparrow, S., Balla, D. and Cicchetti, D. (1984). *Vineland Adaptive Behavior Scales, Manual.* Circle Pines, MN: American Guidance Service.

13
Psychometric test theory and educational assessment

Harvey Goldstein

Types of assessment

A basic distinction underlies what I shall have to say between assessment connected to learning and assessment separated from learning. In the former case, which I call *connected assessment*, there is a further distinction between assessment as part of learning and assessment as terminal evaluation of learning – a distinction roughly the same as summative and formative assessment. In the case of what I call *separate assessment*, its defining principle is its deliberate attempt to avoid connection with particular learning environments (e.g. curricula); perhaps the most celebrated example is the IQ test.

It is not my purpose to argue the merits or demerits of separated assessment, but rather to explore how the assumptions which historically have underpinned it have conditioned also our approaches to connected assessment. At one level my argument is about the details of the doing of assessment, and at another level it is about the role of a technological discourse in persuading people to accept a notion of objectivity based upon mathematical theory.

While my main concern is to explore the historical role of a particular kind of separated assessment, namely that emanating from psychometrics, other kinds are clearly possible, if not actually thriving. It is simply that because the psychometric model provides the most potent influence on our thinking it has become very difficult to separate that model from our whole understanding of what assessment is or can be. In supporting that statement I shall attempt to show why it is important to extend our view of assessment beyond this historically constrained framework. Much of what I have to say can be regarded as developing further Wood's (1986) lucid discussion on the theme of educational versus psychological assessment.

The psychometric tradition

The development of so-called 'test score theory' as a branch of psychometrics has been concerned with proposing ever more sophisticated mathematical models for the behaviour of exam or test questions or items. This much is clear, though we still lack a complete historical account of this development (for useful contributions, see Gould, 1981; Sutherland, 1980; Mackenzie, 1981). Having its roots in cognitive psychology, test score theory is inevitably concerned with making inferences about mental processes and has chosen to do this by hypothesizing mental 'attributes' which are possessed by individuals, either in continuous or discrete form. Common examples are concepts of 'verbal reasoning ability' or 'IQ' itself. Moreover, it is clear that these labels are not mere conveniences attached to collections of items which are assembled to form a test, although we *could* regard them as such if we so wished. The mathematical models of test score theory in fact assume that such attributes really exist. Indeed, in a strong sense, these attributes *only* exist via the mathematical models, since they cannot be directly observed nor defined in other ways. In this sense, the term 'theory' is applied correctly, being understood to mean 'mathematical theory'.

In the next section, I shall outline the assumptions of test score theory and follow this by exploring how they have come to influence our basic understanding of assessment.

Assumptions of test score theory

The 'classical' treatise on mental test score theory is still the book by Lord and Novick (1968), even though it is now 20 years old. In this book the authors give a detailed account of methods for constructing and analysing tests, and set out the mathematical and statistical assumptions of such procedures. They make an interesting distinction between 'weak' and 'strong' test score theory. The former is applied to the collection of so called 'item analysis' techniques which have been used by most test constructors for choosing items, calculating test reliabilities, etc. The term 'strong' is reserved for what has now become known as Item Response Theory (IRT; Lord, 1980), and which has been an area of considerable development in the last 20 years. It has been applied both to attributes which are supposed to have a continuous distribution and to those which assume only a small number of discrete 'states'. An example of the latter are so-called 'mastery' models, and the best known example of the former is the 'Rasch' model.

The older item analysis procedures (see, e.g. Anastasi, 1968) consist of a collection of indices designed to measure concepts such as reliability, discrimination, difficulty, etc. One virtue of IRT is that, unlike the older item analysis procedures, it is fully explicit about its mathematical assumptions. I will therefore address most of my remarks towards IRT. Nevertheless, what I have to say concerning IRT can be read as applying to all statistically based test score theories. Thus, item analysis procedures are also based on an implicit mathematical model which shares all the basic features of IRT, and one of the most serious weaknesses of Lord and Novick is their failure to point out that the *essential* difference between the weak and strong models lies in the particular form of mathematical relationship which is assumed to exist between the observed responses to the test items and the underlying attribute values. Thus, depending on which mathematical relationship one decides to choose (e.g. arithmetic or logarithmic scale), one is led to somewhat different statistical procedures for estimating individual attribute scores or for judging the adequacy of a particular item. Such differences, however, are matters of technical detail and should not be allowed to obscure the fundamental unity of all test score theory. (A technical account of the differences which arise from choosing different forms of mathematical relationship can be found in Goldstein, 1980.)

Dimensionality

The debate about the number of 'dimensions' of mental ability goes back to at least the 1920s involving Burt, Spearman and others in arguments about the uses of factor analysis. In simple terms, the number of dimensions of a test is equal to the number of distinct quantities belonging to each individual subject which are necessary in order to describe the observed relationships among the test item responses. (The original debate, it should be noted, concerned the number of dimensions underlying a set of test scores rather than item responses, but the ideas are the same.) Thus, a test is one-dimensional if the set of item responses (typically correct/incorrect) can be described in terms of a single ability value or, for example, mastery state for each individual, together with a set of 'parameter' values for each item (difficulties, discriminations, etc.), plus a random residual component representing unexplained variation.

Because they have underpinned virtually all of IRT to date, I will concentrate my discussion on unidimensional (continuous) models. More recent developments of multidimensional test theory models, often under the name of 'binary factor analysis' (Bartholomew, 1980; Bock and Aitkin, 1981), certainly extend the range of IRT but have had little empirical exposure to date. Nor do they represent a different *kind* of conceptual model, rather they provide a more realistic explication of the notion of mental attributes by allowing the possibility of several, rather than a single, dimensions.

If we study closely the idea of dimensionality, we immediately face a difficulty. In much of the mental test literature an (one-dimensional) attribute is assumed to be a property of an individual with respect to her responses to a set of items. Thus, a 'verbal ability' test might be regarded as such a set of items. Yet nothing in the mathematical theory actually allows us to make such an inference. The theory is concerned solely with the dimensionality of the test with respect to a particular 'population' of individuals. The specification of the population in fact is crucial. At one extreme it might consist of all possible individuals, but the choice of population must be made somehow. It is perfectly possible for a test to be unidimensional in one population and two-dimensional in another. Thus, one can imagine a case where a unidimensional test existed for each of several distinct populations, but where the average item responses differed among populations, i.e. the item difficulties changed. The population formed by combining these populations would then in general contain at least two apparent dimensions. For example, if we had one population where the order of difficulty of just two of the items in a test was the reverse of the order in a second population for all values of the underlying attribute, then the test could not be unidimensional in the combined population.

If we wished to infer something about attributes which could be regarded as something like mental characteristics possessed by individuals, then we should have to demonstrate, at the very least, that these attributes could be identified in every subpopulation of the population of interest, which is no mean task. In reality, therefore, the notion of dimensionality, and hence of mental attributes inferred from sets of item or question responses, is inextricably linked to a choice of population, and inferences about an individual's underlying attributes are very much concerned with the company she is expected to keep. This is not to deny that the explanation of dimensionality in particular populations is without interest, since it may well indicate the existence of relationships and perhaps provide insights into the reasons for such relationships. Whether such analyses tell us anything about the nature of mental processes is quite another matter.

In short, I am suggesting that mental test score theory is simply just a statistical device for summarizing (providing one or more weighted averages) a set of observed test item responses. It operates by making substantively arbitrary assumptions about the form of underlying mathematical relationships, a choice made typically on grounds of statistical convenience or mathematical elegance, with claims concerning dimensionality being relative rather than absolute ones. This point is important since the notion of individual attributes coinciding with measurable dimensions is a key one underlying common notions of 'standards', especially in connection with 'absolute' assessments. The widespread assumption that there really are attributes whose values remain only to be estimated has often seemed to be legitimated by the existence of a large body of mathematical theory predicated on this same assumption. Certainly, if these mental attributes really did exist then we should want something rather like IRT in order to describe them. It seems, however, that so close is the connection between test theory and assumptions about mental attributes, that our thinking has been conditioned to regard the existence of the former as requiring the existence of the latter rather than the reverse. Such legitimation may perhaps best be described in terms of shared cultural values. Given the dominant status of mathematical knowledge in Western culture, we need not be too surprised at the influence which psychometric ideas continue to have.

There is a further consequence of these views, which has echoes in much of the current assessment debate. The idea of mental attributes possessed by individuals implies that these attributes in a real sense exist independently of the context in which they are observed. Thus, although the context may modify the expression of an attribute, this is essentially a practical problem for the test constructor. So, for example, a test or exam constructor might 'sample' a 'domain' by selecting items relating to a number of contexts and then carry out a suitable IRT or item-averaging procedure to predict the score on the underlying attribute. This view of context-free assessment is examined in more detail below.

Standards

The topic of 'standards' in education is complex and I shall deal only briefly with one aspect; the attempt to relate different assessments, based on different instruments at different times, to a common measurement scale. The assessment might be a formal examination or one made by a teacher, but that will not affect my argument.

Clearly, if standards are to have any meaning then a common scale for expressing them is necessary, and for every relevant assessment it must be possible to convert it unambiguously on to this scale. Thus, for example, if standards in the new GCSE exam are to be compared over time, then the 'meaning' attached to each grade must remain the same. This implies that if a group of individuals (from a well-specified population) took two exams, we would expect on average that they should get the same grades on each exam. This, however, will only be possible if the two exams either both share a single dimension in the sense I have already described, or share the same proportionate mixture of several dimensions. Furthermore, in practice we require standards to be applicable across *different* groups of individuals (different exam boards or different years), and hence that all the relevant populations are essentially equivalent. If we add to this the diversity of methods of assessment and actual syllabuses, then such a requirement seems unlikely to be met. It needs hardly to be said that there is precious little existing evidence which bears upon this issue, nor is there any serious attempt on the part of those responsible for the GCSE to examine the issue. Similar comments apply to other current discussions of assessment, such as graded tests. This lack of awareness is surprising, given the extensive discussions in relation to GCE and CSE exams during the 1970s in England and Wales, and also an airing in some of the discussions during the formative years of the Assessment of Performance Unit (APU; Gipps and Goldstein, 1983).

The idea of test or exam 'equivalence' relies upon similar notions concerning one-dimensional attributes as does traditional test score theory, albeit without the same explicit models. Moreover, to judge by the experiences of the GCE boards in attempting to equivalence O-level exams, there is little empirical support for the theoretical possibililty. The idea that it is both desirable and possible to achieve equivalence – or maintain marking standards – nevertheless persists, just as it persists among those who continue to advocate IRT as a theoretical basis for assessment. Undoubtedly this persistence has considerable practical convenience, and it would be interesting to study the reasons for it in more depth, but that lies beyond the scope of this chapter.

To the obvious question of how one might replace the IRT notion there are several responses. One, of course, is to reduce the importance of examinations and tests as selection instruments, so that the demand for equivalencing and standardizing is less urgent. Another response is to recognize the unreasonableness of the demand for equivalencing and adopt a different procedure. Thus, in the context of public exams in the UK, suppose that an exam is viewed as an index of achievement, a summary measure whose derivation is a matter for judgement and negotiation and where grading is with reference only to those who take that particular exam, with no attempt to equate grades across time or across exam boards. Then at least the implications can be made clear. While it may not be 'fair', in the sense that an achieved grade will depend upon which other candidates take the exam, it does at least share that property with most other aspects of social existence. As I have argued elsewhere (Goldstein, 1986), the openness of a well-understood procedure is both valuable and acceptable.

This discussion about standards in public exams lies within the theoretical framework of separated assessment rather than connected assessment, even though exams would appear to be connected in their intention through the medium of a syllabus. The reason is that in order to achieve equivalence between assessments which are linked to different learning environments (curricula), it has to be possible to separate an assessment from a *particular* environment, and this can only be done either by postulating effectively equivalent environments or environment-free assessments. Such a context-free view of assessment is precisely the inheritance which the standards debate has acquired from psychometrics. One may see this inheritance again in current debates about school records of achievement and profiles in the way in which terms like 'skills' and 'competencies' are proposed as context-free.

Connected assessment

In contrast to the idea of, and the mathematical edifice concerned with, separated assessment, we have little of any kind of theory for a discussion of connected assessment. In fact, a very great deal of such measurement is carried out, much of it by teachers and students in the normal course of learning, some by the application of formal (e.g. diagnostic) tests, and some by researchers using more ethnographic type techniques. Its feature is its commitment to providing a specific evaluation of learning in a fairly well defined context, with little concern for external equivalence. Nevertheless, connected assessments may still be used to make particular comparisons across contexts where the contexts share 'common' features, which implies a judgement and hence a debate about the commonality of different features.

Connected assessment is a more general notion than that of 'formative' assessment though most of this is certainly connected; it can also include 'summative' assessment which is not necessarily intended to feed back to learning. Because of its concern with a specific environment, however, it is generally unsuitable for selection purposes. To be suitable for selection, different measurements must be commonly scalable, and apart from particular common features, connected assessments are not designed to do this. It follows that any attempt to use connected assessments as selection instruments either leads to negotiated compromises which may contain political as well as theoretical justification, or in fact may destroy the connectedness of an assessment by forcing it to assume a separated form.

If this argument is accepted, then it raises serious questions about the role of teachers in separated assessment. It would be possible to encourage teachers to try to make separated assessments of their students on the basis of projects, etc., rather than by using external exams or tests, and certainly current GCSE proposals seem to make the assumption that this is feasible. If that is the case, and if teachers are still expected to make connected assessments in their teaching, then there arises some doubt about whether it is possible for teachers to carry out both types of assessment on the same students, and, further, whether the role of teachers may change if they are to shoulder much of the responsibility for separated assessment. Thus, for example, teachers may come to view student achievement more closely in accord with test theory tradition than formerly, so that notions of traits and underlying equivalences may come strongly to influence connected ways of evaluating learning.

Conclusions

I have argued that there are two distinct kinds of assessment with different aims and procedures. Furthermore, they are so different that attempts to use one kind in circumstances that demand the other are inappropriate. I have suggested that public examinations in particular are an example of a basically connected assessment which has had the demands of a separated assessment imposed upon it, and most recently in a severe form. To remain connected, exams would in practice have to satisfy a number of requirements. First, there would have to be a single exam board, as in Scotland, and only one syllabus per subject would have to exist, so that explicit or implied equivalencing becomes unnecessary. Secondly, equivalencing across subjects and across time would have to be abandoned. The notion of fairness, which I suggest is the one which predominates in public exam assessment, would therefore be dependent on the content of the assessments and relative to the population of examinees. As such, it would become a matter for open debate, as I have suggested, where negotiated agreement rather than mathematical theory would be the prime mover. In this sense it is hardly different from most other forms of competition, and it is only curious why there should be any expectation that it should be otherwise. Of course, there will still be a need for interpreting exam results, but such interpretations can differ according to purpose and context, which actually suggests a more useful system than one which provides a single all-purpose assessment.

It is also clear that other forms of assessment such as graded tests and profiles face a similar dilemma to exams. If they are to be connected then their use in selection is open to some doubt, given typical current demands for selection devices, and if they are to be separated then this may undermine much of the reason for the current support which these developments are receiving from government and other funding sources. Above all, whether my thesis is accepted or not, there remains a real need for some serious thought about the directions in which assessment systems are being driven. We seem to be witnessing a great deal of activity developing new assessment instruments, but very little activity concerned with reflecting on where these developments are leading.

Finally, I do not argue here either for or against one or other kind of assessment in general. Rather, I am concerned to put each in its place and to understand when and where each may be used, and what assumptions underpin them. I am persuaded that existing psychometric test score theory is largely inappropriate for that part of educational assessment which claims to be separated, and is irrelevant to the large amount of educational assessment which is of the connected type. If we are to have theoretical bases for educational measurement, then alternatives to existing psychometric theory are needed.

Acknowledgements

I am grateful to Patricia Broadfoot, Caroline Gipps, Alison Wolf and Bob Wood for their helpful comments on a draft on this article.

References

Anastasi, A. (1968). *Psychological Testing*, 3rd edn. New York: Macmillan.

Bartholomew, D. (1980). Factor analysis for categorical data. *Journal of the Royal Statistical Society*, **B42**, 293–321.

Bock, R.D. and Aitkin, M. (1981). Marginal maximum likelihood estimation of item parameters: Application of an EM algorithm. *Psychometrika*, **46**, 443–58.

Gipps, C. and Goldstein, H. (1983). *Monitoring Children*. London: Heinemann.

Goldstein, H. (1980). Dimensionality, bias, independence and measurement scale problems in latent trait test score models. *British Journal of Mathematical and Statistical Psychology*, **33**, 234–46.

Goldstein, H. (1986). Models for equating test scores and for studying the comparability of public exams. In D.N. Nuttall (ed.), *Assessing Educational Achievement*, pp. 168–84. Lewes: Falmer Press.

Gould, S.J. (1981). *The Mismeasure of Man*. New York: Norton.

Lord, F.M. (1980). *Applications of Item Response Theory to Practical Testing Problems*. Hillsdale, N.J.: Lawrence Erlbaum Associates.

Lord, F.M. and Novick, M. (1968). *Statistical Theories of Mental Test Scores*. Reading, Mass.: Addison Wesley.

Mackenzie, D.A. (1981). *Statistics in Britain 1865–1930*. Edinburgh: Edinburgh University Press.

Sutherland, G. (1980). Measuring intelligence: English LEAs and mental testing, 1919–1939. In J.V. Smith and D. Hamilton (eds), *The Meritocratic Intellect: Studies in the History of Educational Research*, pp. 79–95. Aberdeen: Aberdeen University Press.

Wood, R. (1986). The agenda for educational measurement. In D.N. Nuttall (ed.), *Assessing Educational Achievement*, pp. 185–203. Lewes: Falmer Press.

14
Negotiation and dialogue in student assessment and teacher appraisal

Mary James[1]

Introduction

The literature of naturalistic inquiry in general, and democratic evaluation in particular, explores many of the methodological and ethical issues surrounding the case study researcher's interest in gaining access to data of a personal, and therefore sensitive, nature. Similarly, it addresses many of the problems associated with the need to make reports, especially evaluations, publicly available without exposing the most vulnerable to invidious social control (e.g. Simons, 1979; Kemmis and Robottom, 1981). In both contexts, 'negotiation' has emerged as an important concept and has assumed considerable prominence in social contracts which provide a basis for working relationships among researchers, sponsors and research subjects.[2]

The fact that the term 'negotiation' also features prominently in some new student assessment and teacher appraisal schemes may be entirely fortuitous, but there are distinct parallels with forms of naturalistic inquiry. In most cases, a teacher or senior colleague is interested in eliciting information of a personal nature from those who are likely to have less power. The purpose of this is partly diagnostic or developmental but there is usually also an intention to make an agreed statement about the individual, available to others. How access to, and release of, information is negotiated is therefore as crucial in assessment and appraisal of individuals as it is in naturalistic inquiry and evaluation at institutional or programme level. It would be reasonable to suppose that theory and practice in the latter might have something to contribute to the former. Such a possibility provides the focus for this chapter. First, however, it is necessary to look in more detail at the role that negotiation is assumed to have in the context of assessment and appraisal.

For convenience I have chosen to take student profile assessment as my example, although there is plenty to indicate that what can be said also applies to teacher appraisal. The basis for many appraisal schemes is the one-to-one 'developmental' interview involving teachers and their superiors or peers, who usually make some kind of semi-permanent record (see Turner and Cliff, 1985, for a review of teacher appraisal schemes). Thus the activity has both formative and summative aspects and is analogous to many student profiling or records of achievement schemes. The fact that teachers are adults obviously makes a difference but, because they may be relatively powerless compared to their interviewers, issues concerning the nature of negotiation are still relevant. So also are the points that will be made later about dialogue in relation to understanding, since an important stated purpose of many appraisal schemes is the deepening of mutual understanding of the performance of teachers in context.

Negotiation and dialogue in new forms of student assessment

Student profile assessment and records of achievement schemes have developed with such rapidity that they seem to bear the stamp of an evangelical movement. As with many such movements, emphasis on development and action often outweighs critical reflections (see Broadfoot, 1986, for a critique of some of the issues arising). Even a cursory examination of profiling practice reveals a confusion of purposes, processes, concepts and principles. On the one hand, processes aspire to be formative, developmental and confidential; on the other hand, they have a summative element and claim public currency. One can argue that this dichotomy represents a fundamental division of purposes that is not easily reconciled.[3]

Similar tension is manifest in the almost arbitrary use of the terms negotiation and dialogue as labels for what goes on in the process of reviewing the experience and achievement of individual students. The following definition of negotiation, for instance, makes passing reference to aspects of social control but, by treating them as unproblematic, implicitly denies the need for negotiation in the sense in which the term is commonly understood, i.e. with an assumption that the parties involved have different interests and values:

Negotiation

A process of discussion between pupil and teacher, either to draw out and nourish a view of significant experience and achievement in the past or to plan some future action, course or curriculum. A progress [*sic*] whereby aims, objectives, goal and content of a training programme are agreed jointly by tutor/trainee/student.

Negotiation presupposes open relationships between students and staff where discussion of issues can come to mutually agreed acceptable conclusions without undue pressure or prejudice by one party or the other and where due allowance is made for inexperience, lack of maturity or inarticulateness. (National Profiling Network, 1985)[4]

Elsewhere, as in the illustration given below, even this minimal recognition that negotiation has something to do with power relations is absent. 'Negotiation' and 'dialogue' are therefore often used interchangeably.

I will begin by examining a recorded and publicly available example of negotiation/dialogue between a teacher and two of her students, then I will comment on some of the issues raised. In subsequent sections I will develop the idea that negotiation and dialogue are logically distinct processes which assume different contexts, have different purposes and need to be governed by different sets of principles and procedures. This is where I perceive the methodology of naturalistic inquiry to be potentially very helpful.

The critical question that emerges is whether negotiation, as more appropriately applied to summative assessment, and dialogue, as appropriate to formative assessment, should be considered as two entirely separate and polarized activities or whether they can both be accommodated in a unified profiling assessment or appraisal scheme. My feeling is that the latter is possible provided that the worth of formative and summative aspects or stages is judged according to different, though not conflicting, criteria. In other words, formative dialogue could be expected to contribute to understanding and development, while summatively oriented negotiation should aim to promote credibility, accountability and justice. My argument is mainly for greater clarity and an end to some of the muddle that threatens the baby as well as the bath-water.

An instance

The following is a transcription of an excerpt from an Open University television programme.[5] A teacher of French is conducting one-to-one review sessions with students. She talks first with Michelle, then Kelly, about their achievements. Before each interview the teacher prepared an assessment sheet and the student wrote a self-assessment. Teacher and student sit side by side and the teacher refers to the two assessment sheets during the interview.

> **Voice** One of the main objectives of this kind of assessment is to make students and teachers more equal partners in the learning process. So, instead of the teacher merely completing her side of the form by herself, she discusses her judgements with each student. There's a process of negotiation.
>
> **Teacher** Let's have a look. [Reads] 'Have you enjoyed your work in this subject?' 'Yes, I have enjoyed this subject very much, especially the oral work.' Why especially the oral work?
>
> **Michelle** I just like speaking it. Y'know, it's good.
>
> **Teacher** You like the language? You like the sound of it?
>
> **Michelle** Yeah.
>
> **Teacher** Yeah. Well, you've got a *wonderful* accent, as I've always told you, and you really sound very good indeed. What do you think you would deserve for your grading and for your attitude?

Michelle	Um, . . . One?
Teacher	Well, I agree with you. Yes, very good. [Reads] 'Presentation of your work.' What would you say about that?
Michelle	It's O.K. Say about Two.
Teacher	Mm, absolutely agreed. Yes, Two. Different pieces of work are different, aren't they? . . . in the neatness, and so on. But generally it's fine; it's lovely. [Reads] 'Your general ability in the subject: strengths and weaknesses'. You can 'speak it O.K.'; yes, I agree. But you are 'not very good at writing it down'. But you are not that bad, Michelle; you are really very good, aren't you?
Michelle	I suppose I am. I don't know.
Teacher	Well, I've given you a One.
Michelle	A One!
Teacher	Mm.
Michelle	Oh.
Teacher	Do you agree with that, or do you want me to put it down?
Michelle	O.K.
Teacher	I'd like to keep it as One because I believe that. And how good do you think you are at writing? [Reads] 'Not that good. I have trouble with my verbs.' Um . . . I would say Two, because I think you're good. You're not excellent, and you're not sort of just fair. You're just in the middle. So a Grade Two for that, and you agree?
Michelle	Yeah, I agree, yeah.
Teacher	Good, lovely. That's it then Michelle. I'll hang on to this.
Michelle	O.K.
Teacher	Thanks very much. (Michelle leaves.)
Voice	As with Michelle, so with Kelly.
Teacher	I think we'll try and do this fairly quickly because if I look at my own gradings I'm fairly certain of the good gradings that I have given you, all right? So I don't think really we need to discuss it that much. I feel that you enjoy this subject generally very much, yeah?
Kelly	Yeah.
Teacher	You do? Good. And you're fairly good at speaking it so I am going to leave out the first few questions and then just . . . We can come back to it another time. How good are you at speaking? [Reads] 'There are some words that I find difficult to understand, but most of them are O.K.' Well, I think you are very good at speaking and I've given you a Grade One for that. Would you agree?
Kelly	I don't think I'm that good.
Teacher	You don't think you're that good! Do you want me to change it to a Two, or a One/Two?

Kelly	I don't mind.
Teacher	You'd prefer I kept it at a One, I'm sure. Well, I'll just pencil in a One/Two, all right? Then I'll have another think about it later on. How good are you at understanding? [Reads] 'If the teacher talks to me using all French words there would be quite a few I wouldn't understand.' Well, of course, yes, but do you generally get the gist of what I'm saying?
Kelly	Yeah, I do really.
Teacher	Yeah, you won't understand every single word but, I mean, if you understand the basic ...
Kelly	Yeah, some words I know what it means, but then the little words I don't.
Teacher	Yeah, O.K. What would you give yourself for that then?
Kelly	. . . Three.
Teacher	A Three! I wouldn't. I've given you One/Two again. Well, I'm sticking to that because I believe in it anyway. And your home-work? How have you got on with the homework? [Reads] 'Sometimes I think we get a bit too much.' Ha, ha! I don't! ... Um, regularity: do you always do it?
Kelly	I do do homework. Sometimes it's hard.
Teacher	Yes, even if it's hard, but you always do it, and it's always given in when you should do?
Kelly	Yes.
Teacher	Yes. And the quality of it? . . . What do you think? And do you always try to do your very best, even though you find it difficult?
Kelly	Yeah. Some of them are hard and I don't understand 'em, so I try as much as I can and if I can't do the rest I just sort of leave it.
Teacher	Mm.
Kelly	I would always do most of it.
Teacher	Yes, O.K. Well, I agree. I have been fairly pleased with that and I have, in fact, given you a One for each of these. Right. And you would like to take it next year? [Reads] '. . . think I would because I enjoy most of the work.' I would like you to take it next year as well . . . [Fade out]
Voice	Surely a useful conversation.

Commentary

This example of a reviewing process invites a number of comments, and poses several questions regarding the nature of the process itself and the validity of the assessments made.

Issues of power and authority

The teacher sets the pace and tone of these interviews, especially the second: 'I think we'll try to do this fairly quickly because if I look at my own gradings I'm fairly certain of the good gradings that I have given you, all right?' This has the effect of giving priority to the teacher's assessments but it also means that she has no time to explore the learning difficulties that the student is signalling to her. Thus, she passes up the opportunity for diagnosis and planning of future action on both her part and the student's.

Eight grades are assigned in the course of these two interviews. On three occasions the teacher invites the student to state her self-assessed ranking before offering her own judgement, and on three occasions the teacher offers her grading first but asks whether the student agrees. Yet on two occasions the teacher assigns a grade without discussion. If a teacher gives her assessment first, will it inevitably be established as 'authoritative' and invite acquiescence on the part of the student?

On three occasions the assessments of students and teacher are clearly at variance (regarding Michelle's 'general ability in the subject' and Kelly's 'speaking' and 'understanding'). In each case the teacher disagrees, sometimes quite forcefully, with the student's judgement and substitutes her own assessment, twice without change and once with only minor modification (from Grade One to One/Two, with the option of changing it back later, possibly without the student's explicit agreement). On all three occasions the student's 'agreement' looks like capitulation. Is this an inevitable consequence of the value traditionally ascribed to the professional judgement of teachers, and claimed by them? Would this be undermined if they 'compromised' their judgement in areas of special expertise, e.g. subject areas? Can they 'afford' to concede to the judgements of students?

In each case of disagreement, the students assessed their achievement less favourably than did the teacher. Are these students deliberately underselling themselves to avoid risking any loss of self-esteem, which might be occasioned by downgrading by the teacher? Is this one way of ensuring that they retain some power in a situation that is weighted against them? Or, do they deliberately undervalue their own worth in order to encourage a favourable assessment by the teacher, who will probably approve of their modesty? (Such an interpretation may appear to ascribe a high level of conceptualization to students' analyses of the situation but it is quite possible that they act on intuitive understandings.) Alternatively, in interviews such as these, is there a tendency for teachers to 'upgrade' students, either because they do not wish to do anything to destroy motivation, or because they find it too difficult to be totally honest when face-to-face with the person they are assessing? Whatever the reason, is downgrading of self by students, or corresponding upgrading of students by teachers, a common phenomenon, and is it particularly characteristic of the profile assessment process experienced by girls?[6]

Issues of validity

The teacher enthusiastically reinforces occasions when the student's self-assessment agrees with her own. There is no further discussion. Are we to assume that agreement or consensus is equivalent to a valid assessment, or should the evidence for both 'agreed' and disputed assessments be examined more fully in the light of tangible evidence? Is the main purpose of the review session to agree assessments that can be made public, or should it aim to deepen mutual understanding? Can these two goals be pursued simultaneously, or will one inevitably pre-empt the other?

Is anything of value, therefore, being learnt in these exchanges, apart from the interpersonal skill of predicting the kind of things the other wants to hear? Are they merely ritual exercises in how to keep everyone happy?

Discussion

The terms 'negotiation', 'conversation' and 'dialogue' are all used in the Open University programme to refer to the face-to-face interaction that is part of this assessment process. Although profiling or records of achievement schemes vary in many respects, most regard a formative process of one-to-one review as essential. Indeed, although sponsors, for example, DES, MSC, examination boards, and some 'consumers' (e.g. parents and employers), may still conceptualize profiles and records primarily as summative documents, there is some evidence that they are taking on board the fact that many developers attach much importance to the formative process. Thus, for instance, the DES Policy Statement (1984, p. 4) made the point that: 'Regular dialogue between teacher and pupil will be important.' Moreover:

> Such discussions should be of direct benefit to pupils. They should also help schools to improve their organisation, curriculum and teaching and the range of opportunities open to pupils. (DES, 1984, p. 5)[7]

Interestingly, the DES favours 'dialogue' and 'discussion' over 'negotiation'. I have no doubt that this was a deliberately neutral choice, for 'negotiation' has political overtones which makes its use controversial. Whereas, according to the *Oxford English Dictionary,* 'conversation' simply means talk, and 'dialogue' means conversation between two parties, 'negotiation' has the sense of 'conferring with another with a view to compromise or agreement'. Therefore, although agreement does not necessarily assume compromise, the term 'negotiation' implies differences of perception, interests and values. Certainly, in any encounter between teachers and students there are likely to be differences in these respects. Moreover, the distribution of power is manifestly unequal.[8] Given this reality the major issue seems to be whether to recognize these differences and try to develop structures for making mutually acceptable agreements/compromises, or whether to relinquish any claim to do more than raise students' self-esteem and motivation by spending some time talking with them individually. To choose the first option risks disturbing the status quo by countenancing radical change in relationships between teachers and students and therefore in the nature and control of schooling. The second option is easily dismissed as merely cosmetic, although it may have considerable intrinsic value, as evidence from the national evaluation of pilot schemes indicates (see PRAISE, 1987, p. 30).

The majority of profiling and records of achievement schemes have a liberal/progressive aspiration to improve pupil self-esteem and motivation without appearing to have anything very much more radical in mind. Some, for instance, refer to 'counselling', 'guidance' and 'tutoring' rather than 'negotiation' or even 'dialogue'. However, one suspects that those profile developers who emphasize negotiation feel this does not go far enough. They would indeed like to change the nature of the relationship between teachers and students in a radical direction. The trouble is that few are prepared to take the radical argument to its logical conclusion, so it tends to fall between two stools. Even the eminently reasonable definition quoted above is too bland. It conveys no sense of the difficulties associated with the resolution of differences that we are familiar with in industrial relations. If 'negotiation' is to be more than a pleasant social encounter, but with the less powerful ultimately acquiescing to the views of the more powerful, it must be more hard-nosed. It must acknowledge that there will be stated or unstated disagreements, and if students are to be given real power their judgements should not be explicitly or implicitly overridden by teachers.[9] Without the exercise of judgement in real situations it is unlikely that students will learn to have the autonomy that is so frequently stated as an educational goal. Moreover, if they begin to perceive the process as a hollow exercise, it may turn out to be not only a waste of time but educationally counterproductive. So what are the possibilities for developing situations conducive to genuine negotiation?

If the problem is unequal distribution of power, with students being relatively powerless, then it can be argued that the need is for structures or procedures that will create a better balance. Three possibilities present themselves. First, the student's hand could be strengthened by a third party who takes the role of an advocate committed to supporting the student's position. Such a person might be a school counsellor, another teacher or tutor, a parent or another, perhaps older, student. Secondly, students could operate systems of rewards and sanctions that would give them more power. The most obvious device, given current trends in the UK, would be to link student assessment with teacher appraisal. In this way it would become a reciprocal, and symmetrical, activity. Thirdly, various kinds of 'assertiveness training', which find a place in life skills courses, could be developed for application in teacher–student negotiations. In the last analysis, however, all these 'solutions' appear negative and profoundly depressing. With the exception, perhaps, of the second, they rest on a conflict model of interaction, invoking notions of 'trade-off', having little to do with education. Is it possible to find a more positive and educational conception of what negotiation might be?

A way forward

This is where the literature of naturalistic inquiry is pertinent, especially the methodology of 'responsive' and 'democratic' evaluation which pays particular attention to political and ethical dimensions. Since the mid-1970s, when Mac-Donald (1977) developed his political classification of evaluation studies,[10] evaluators working within a 'democratic' mode have acknowledged multiple perspectives and value-pluralism in the framing and exchange of information. Thus, they have sought principles and procedures to safeguard those who are least able to protect themselves from the effects of exposure. According to MacDonald: 'The key concepts of democratic evaluation are "confidentiality", "negotiation" and "accessibility".' These concepts or principles are not entirely discrete since they all relate to a superordinate concept of ownership.[11] The assumption is that participants in an evaluation study have a right to control the dissemination of *personal* information about themselves and, therefore, privacy must be respected and access and use of such data should be negotiated. To meet these requirements evaluators have derived practical procedures from these principles and advocate 'negotiation of access' to data sources and 'negotiation of clearance and release' of reports (see Simons, 1979; Kemmis and Robottom, 1981). With this I have no problem. However, they also suggest that evaluators should 'negotiate the boundaries' of studies in terms of what should be included or excluded, and likewise 'negotiate accounts' in terms of accuracy and relevance. In both cases validity is the issue, which raises a question about whether it is appropriate to 'negotiate' truth and relevance.

If one adheres strictly to MacDonald's position that evaluators should act as 'brokers' in exchanges of information and judgements, then the task is to ensure that they have accurate accounts of the truth *as participants perceive it*. If, on the other hand, evaluators give any interpretations of their own, and I personally think this is unavoidable since some interpretation is implicit even in the organization of accounts, then validity is crucially important. However, to talk of negotiating the validity or truth of accounts with participants implies a consensus theory of truth that is naive and relativistic. As I suggested in relation to the transcribed teacher – student review session, the fact that two people agree a judgement does not guarantee its truth.[12] The grounds for an interpretation or judgement need to be scrutinized and this is not a matter for negotiation. It is an epistemological activity, concerned with meaning, understanding and the ascription of value. In this context the term 'dialogue', with all its Socratic associations, seems more appropriate.

It takes little imagination to see how closely the relationship of evaluator to participant corresponds to the relationship between teacher and student in the process of recording achievement. In both contexts, the individuals concerned are characteristically involved in both a formative and summative activity, i.e. deepening mutual understanding during face-to-face interaction and preparing accounts for possible public consumption. Since the second of these activities may place the student in a vulnerable position, it is appropriate to establish

Table 14.1   Negotiation and dialogue: purposes and processes

Purpose	Concepts	Process	Procedures
Formative (developing understanding of experience on the basis of evidence)	Validity, understanding	*Dialogue*	Discussion of relevances (i.e. boundaries); discussion of facts, interpretations and judgements
Summative (preparing mutually acceptable accounts possibly for public consumption)	Ownership, currency	*Negotiation*	Negotiation of access; negotiation for release

procedures for negotiation of access to information, including such things as personal diaries, and release of summary accounts, records or reports. However, when defining the bounds of relevant discussion (e.g. how far teachers should enquire into personal qualities or out-of-school achievements in making an *educational* record), and certainly when examining the evidential bases for assessments, then dialogue seems the better description of a process that is educational in intent. This distinction is presented in Table 14.1.

One major question remains. Is it possible for negotiation and dialogue to be associated with different sets of concepts, principles and procedures and yet continue to co-exist within one activity, e.g. profiling or recording activity?

There are those, like Don Stansbury (1985), who have for a long time been saying that the formative and summative elements of profiling are uneasy bedfellows. The pressure to produce an 'agreed' summative document, of use to employers and the like, could so easily come to dominate and therefore diminish the potential for genuine educational dialogue between teachers and students concerning, not only students' achievements, but curriculum content and processes in institutional and social contexts. Certainly, the rather inadequate and superficial attempt by the French teacher to 'negotiate' assessments with her students could be explained by reference to the conflicting pressures inherent in the situation. Somehow she had to juggle her roles as subject expert, assessor, diagnostician, facilitator of learning, authority figure, manager of time and resources – and television star! Even in the absence of a television crew, could any teacher be expected to do very much better? One feasible suggestion might be to develop further the distinctions made above and put them into practice as entirely separate but complementary activities. Together they could still be described as recording achievement but the process would be plural rather than singular.

Notes

1 The author was Deputy Director of the Pilot Records of Achievement in Schools Evaluation (PRAISE), based at the Open University School of Education and Bristol University School of Education from 1985 to 1988. Funding came from the Department of Education and Science and the Welsh Office. She gratefully acknowledges her colleagues' helpful comments on drafts of this chapter, also those of Dave Ebbutt, Helen Simons and Ian Stronach. The opinions expressed represent a personal view, however. At the time when this chapter was first written, field-work in relation to the DES-funded pilot schemes was still in its early stages, so the data used were drawn from other sources. By the time of publication PRAISE interim and final reports were available. However, since the contents of these reports supported many of the issues raised in this chapter, there seemed to be no need to substitute PRAISE data simply to make the same points.

2 PRAISE conducted 23 case studies of schools as one strand of its evaluation strategy. Access to all schools was negotiated on the basis of a 'site brief' and a set of ethical guidelines concerning access, storage and reporting of data (see Murphy and Torrance, 1987, pp. 291–3).

3 This parallels the tension in school self-evaluation schemes between demands for accountability and aims of educational improvement. The question of whether a single activity can serve both purposes is also similar.

4 National Profiling Network (1985). A glossary of terms used in profiling: First draft. *Newsletter, 2*. Available from David Garforth or George Pearson, Advisory Service, Education Department, County Hall, Dorchester, Dorset DT1 1XJ, England. By January 1986, the NPN held a register of 79 profiling schemes generated at national, regional, county or school level.

5 Open University (1978). *Course E206, Personality, Development and Learning,* TV 10 *'Measures of Success',* Milton Keynes, OU/BBC Productions. The school and teachers involved in making this programme have pointed out that they have now moved on in their thinking and practice. This should be taken into account, as should the obvious constraints placed on students and teachers by the presence of a television crew.

6 This observation is confirmed by evidence from the national evaluation of DES-funded pilot records of achievement schemes (PRAISE), although underestimation of achievement by students appears to be characteristic of both boys and girls.

7 See DES (1984). The point about the importance of planned discussion between teachers and pupils was reinforced in DES (1987), and is likely to be included in national guidelines which are expected around the time this book is published.

8 Andy Hargreaves (1986) examines the ideological implications of records of achievement schemes, as does Ian Stronach in this volume.

9 Some profiling schemes place the teacher's and student's assessment side by side, instead of presenting an agreed statement. It is likely that many adults, though not all, would automatically give greater credence to the teacher's assessments.

10 Earlier versions of this paper were published in MacDonald and Walker (1974) and Tawney (1976).

11 In Chapter 15, Ian Stronach criticizes the commodity and exchange metaphor that dominates much thinking in this context. The concept of ownership must be considered part of that same metaphor and, therefore, subject to the same criticism.

12 It can be argued that people can reach agreement without reaching consensus. However, this is a fine distinction that the users of profiles or records of achievement are not likely to make.

References

Broadfoot, P. (ed.) (1986). *Profiles and Records of Achievement: A Review of Issues and Practice.* London: Holt Educational.

Department of Education and Science (1984). *Records of Achievement: A Statement of Policy.* London: HMSO.

Department of Education and Science (1987). *Records of Achievement: An Interim Report.* London: HMSO.

Kemmis, S. and Robottom, I. (1981). Principles of procedure in curriculum evaluation. *Journal of Curriculum Studies,* **13**(2), 151–5.

MacDonald, B. (1974). Evaluation and the control of education. In B. Macdonald and R. Walker (eds), *SAFARI I: Innovation, Evaluation, Research and the Problem of Control,* pp. 9–22.

MacDonald, B. (1976). In D. Tawney (ed.), *Curriculum Evaluation Today: Trends and Implications,* pp. 125–36. Schools Council Research Studies. London: Macmillan Educational.

MacDonald, B. (1977). A political classification of evaluation studies. In D. Hamilton, D. Jenkins, C. King, B. MacDonald and M. Parlett (eds), *Beyond the Numbers Game,* pp. 224–7. London: Macmillan.

Murphy, R. and Torrance, H. (1987). *Evaluating Education: Issues and Methods.* London: Harper and Row.

PRAISE (1987). *Interim Evaluation Report, 1987.* Milton Keynes and Bristol: Open University School of Education and Bristol University School of Education.

Simons, H. (1979). Suggestions for a school self-evaluation based on democratic principles. *CARN Bulletin 3.* Cambridge: Cambridge Institute of Education.

Stansbury, D. (1985). *Programme to Develop Records of Experience as an Element in the Documentation of School Leavers: Report on the Preliminary Phase, March 1984–July 1985.* Totnes: Springline Trust.

Turner, G. and Clift, P. (1985). *A First Review and Register of School and College Based Teacher Appraisal Schemes.* Milton Keynes: Open University School of Education, mimeo.

15
A critique of the 'new assessment': from currency to carnival?

Ian Stronach

A novice may be given a long basket and told to go and fill it with mushrooms, which are in any case non-existent during the cold, dry weather. (White, quoted in Turner, 1967, p. 250)

I'm holding the Brynmawr Profile. I can't quite believe it because it's a brown, stiff-boarded folder in mock leatherette, with gold embossing. It looks exactly like a handbag, neat flap and no catches. Why does it look like that? At first I think 'presentation', 'look good for employers'. Then I remember the shock of reading an advertisement in the *Glasgow Herald* (Jan. 1982) – a girl wanted a job and took a 3″ column to say who she was – and around that time the Personal Columns began to offer professional CVs. So it's marketing, that's what the leatherette extravaganza is all about. Packaging. Gift-wrapped surplus youth. Stop me and buy one, it says to the employer – and inside are over 230 'can dos' and 'have dones' so you know what you're getting and you can't say that schools don't do a lot. Mac-Donald's phrase comes to mind, about schools wanting the gift-wrapping but not the merchandise of innovation (MacDonald, 1973, p. 87). But is this something new – the gift-wrapping *is* the merchandise? (Fieldnote)

So ran some of my prejudices about pupil profiling, or what I intend to call the 'new assessment' in this chapter. Does the view that profiling is a form of marketing survive scrutiny? Should we look at the pupil profile and the school brochure as components of a single strategy? And if not (or not only), what *is* new about profiles? What educational value do profiles have, and how well does the sociology of assessment cope with their novelty? These are the principal questions that this chapter will address.

The need to address such questions is clear. Profiles, or records of achievement, with their associated notions of 'ipsative'[1] reference, negotiation, ownership and participation, form a loose, untested and sometimes contradictory constellation of innovative projects that are held to offer the new 3 Rs – Reinforcement, Respect and Relevance 'for potential consumers of such records' (Broadfoot, 1986, p. 6). That phrase reintroduces the marketing hypothesis that profiles are a form of sales presentation for pupils, especially for those pupils who lack the currency of formal qualifications, but also for schools in the wake of accountabililty debates. Some proponents go further and represent profiles as emancipatory, a liberation from the authoritarian relationships of schooling (cf. Broadfoot, 1986; FEU, 1982). Others have promoted the recording rather than the profiling process of the 'new assessment', arguing that they introduce a dialogue between teacher and learner which acknowledges the learner's voice and encourages an unfettered expression of interests, attitudes and ambitions.[2] Just about everyone has stressed the holism of this 'new assessment', a consideration and development of the whole student, of the affective as well as the cognitive, the extra- as well as the intra-curricular, the social competencies of young workers as well as their technical skills. The consensus of approval seems to have rested on four major claims: that the 'new assessment' is ipsative rather than normative; motivational rather than judgemental; that it encourages an educational dialogue between teacher and learner; and that it is holistic in nature. Together these claims constitute the basic feature of the new assessment – its centredness on pupil, student or trainee.

Occasional doubts about profiling and recording have been expressed. When I first evaluated profiles in 1980–81, I concluded that they acted as a 'one-way mirror' offering 'increasingly detailed pictures of pupils to increasingly anonymous administrators. It is a bureaucratic knowing as opposed to a personal knowing.' Politically, I saw the implications of a holistic appraisal of the child, of an assessment reach that exceeded the curriculum span, as being totalitarian – a malevolent surveillance of marginal youth (Stronach, 1981). But my political reach exceeded my empirical span and I now feel that interpretation was extravagant, and that the key Foucauldian notion underlying profiles is not *surveillance* (although it is relevant) but *utopian duplication*, a notion to which we will return.

More recently, Andy Hargreaves has offered an ambivalent but representative critique. On the one hand, he casts doubts, invoking Habermas (motivation crisis of late capitalism), and Foucault (surveillance). On the other hand, he declares that the 'positive potential is very real' (Hargreaves 1986, p. 219), and spans these polarities with two continua:

> What is at stake is a fundamental choice between a system which will define, declare and strengthen young people's identities and independence on the one hand, or a system which will train and tailor these identities to the requirements of efficient employer selection and systematic social control on the other. (Hargreaves, 1986, p. 205)

That critique is typical in that it affirms the positive values of the 'new assessment', the promotion of identity and independence. It implies that ipsative, holistic, dialogic and student-centred techniques are to be approved, and that any slippage of the rhetoric towards 'employer needs' or the values of subordinacy are to be resisted. My argument will be that these continua contain no fundamemtal choice, and that it is the apparently benign features of the 'new assessment' that demand critique.

The 'student-centred' profile

If student-centredness is central to the 'new assessment', what does it mean and how did it evolve? Certainly, it was no new theme in vocational preparation. Self-concept theories dominated vocational counselling in the 1960s (Hopson and Hayes, 1968). Self-evaluation was a key technique. Individual adjustive orientations, such as motor, intellectual, supportive, conforming, etc., were determined via interest inventories. Polar scales sorted the abstract from the concrete dispositions, the active from the reflective, and even the oral from the anal (Holland, 1959, pp. 35–43). As Super (1953, pp. 185–90) put it at the time: 'The process of vocational development is essentially that of developing and implementing a self-concept.' Thus, personal qualities, expressed in dichotomized scales, were familiar explanations of vocational success and failure. The raw materials for profiling were available for counselling rather than curriculum, but in a *more* rather than less student-centred form, since 'self-concept' dominated occupational choice – 'the job must have some element in harmony with his self-concept or he would not consider it' (Starishevsky and Matlin, 1968, p. 27).[3]

This vocational discourse was increasingly challenged by economic crises in the late 1970s (no choice without jobs), and by more instrumental work-centred versions of personal qualities derived from 'employer needs', rather than life-stage theories. A political discourse on youth and its vocational deficiencies came to dominate educational debate in the 1970s and 1980s. This discourse rested on an all-party theory of the 'unreadiness' of youth for social and vocational maturity, and related both to social disorders and to economic uncompetitiveness. The metaphor behind these deficiencies shifted from the poor 'match' to the inadequate bridge between school and work, and so policy came to centre on the inadequacies of education and training, rather than on 'matching' or, indeed, on a broader social or economic critique. In 1986 the dominant feature of the debate was again its highly ideological nature. While the Minister of State for Education in England and Wales warned against the 'yob society' and pointed to the social role schools must play in preventing this, a YTS advertisement read:

> Watch out Japan, here comes Tracey Logan.
> Tracey Logan is a typical British sixteen year old, leaving school this year. But to Japan, and our other international competitors, she's a big threat. That's because she'll be starting 2 years paid skill training on the new YTS .... But from now on they're going to have to watch out. (*The Guardian*, 28 January 1986)

Inevitably, profiles encapsulate some of this ideological pressure in their categories – enterprise was a topical attribute highlighted by the original SCRE profile (Broadfoot and Dockrell, 1977). Adaptability, responsibility and self-reliance remain popular Thatcherite categories with sufficient vagueness to appeal to those standing outside a Samuel Smiles vision of economic redemption. Although these categories have remained fairly constant over the 10 years of profiling development, there are signs that the education system has domesticated some of the more punitive categories and assumptions (see, for example, the subsequent reforms to the FEU pre-employment profile of 1979, and the evolution of the Humberside and Helston profiles), and has translated vocational notions like self-reliance into similar-sounding but actually rather different ideas, such as autonomy. There are also signs that growing unemployment helped to shift the major ideological themes from work preparation to a more personal and developmental agenda and then on to more economically regenerative themes, with notions like self-reliance and initiative giving condensed expression to small business start-up themes.

Nevertheless, most profile category lists still reflect a straightforward 'work ethic index', in Bucholz's terminology, stressing the qualities of hard work, independence, self-reliance and responsibility (Cook *et al.*, 1981, p. 137). The figures that stand behind the profiling debate, therefore, are not individual. They are ideal-typical constructions, whether presented as pathologies or utopias:

- self reliant
- quick and accurate at complex calculations
- adept at most kinds of verbal encounter
- can independently derive, implement and evaluate solutions
- copes sensibly with moral dilemmas
- sensitive to others' perceptions, etc. (FEU, 1982)
- with guidance can understand consequences of actions
- has to be given simple instructions
- speed well below industrial requirements
- makes little effort
- ordinarily obedient complying by habit
- is aware of own personality and situation (Humberside Vocational Preparation MK 1)

Thus, the history of student-centredness in vocational discourse looks something like this. 'Self-concept' theories dominated the 1960s debate. They centred on a profiling of the individual, and on the notions of choice and matching. They were expressed in counselling. This kind of centredness gave way to ethical formulae based on 'employer needs' in the 1970s and 1980s. The major themes were much more overtly political, a metonymic expression of political diagnoses based on eligibilty rather than choice, and employer-centred rather than student-centred. They became a curricular device.

A second major source of profile categories, or discussion issues for tutor and tutee in the reviewing process, has had an empirical base. Research into employer needs and basic job skills has yielded an agenda of categories and criteria for profiling. For example, Freshwater's (1981) basic skills analysis gave rise to the category 'can pull, push and lift things', and this category now appears with slight variations in several school and training profiles (e.g. Humberside MK2 CGLI). Occasionally, the entire profile is research-based, such as the Condensed Freshwater Profile used in some Strathclyde YOP schemes, or the 'Can-do' cards, but such lists of employer needs either tend to be too broad to be helpful (e.g. IPM, 1984), or so detailed that they produce trivial lists of job-related skills (e.g. Freshwater, 1981; Townshend *et al.*, 1982). They beg questions about their validity and usefulness (Do employers know their training needs? Are such skills really skills? Are they generalizable? Are they transferable?).

Nor are such lists even worker-centred in any unproblematic way. Kazamas' (1978) study of affective work competencies in the USA suggested that employers expressed improved efficiency in terms of human qualities (punctuality, honesty, reliability, dependability, initiative and helpfulness were the top ratings), whereas workers expressed it in terms of the quality of work (e.g. variety of role, ordering of tasks). It is interesting that the employers' needs formulation reduces a management problem to a problem of worker attitudes and that the profiling movement unwittingly takes the side of the employer in this respect. Employer needs turns out to be something of an ideological condensation, and hardly more sophisticated than the work ethic formulation of the politicians. Perhaps Oxenham (1984, p. 82) sums up the position best of all: 'a theory composed of unexamined assumptions, rules-of-thumb, inertia and narrowly considered responses to changing circumstances'.

Thus, attempts to research employer needs are problematic in a number of ways. They produce dubious lists of worker characteristics, loosely based on surveys of the generalized wants of employers, and detailed analyses of job skills that ignore the social and generic competencies of job performance (McLelland and Klemp, 1979).[4] They are employer-centred rather than worker-centred. They are neither student-centred, nor holistic. Finally, it is doubtful if they even have much utility in strictly vocational terms. They represent not so much a prescription of needs, as a retrospective of blame.

So far we have sketched out developments in vocational discourse that came to be reflected in profiling rationales. The underlying movement seems to have been from individualized 'self-concept' theories to personalized 'work ethic' formulations – a retreat from self to workplace conducted under the rubric of student-centredness. An interesting dilemma remains. Profiling rests on the assumption of a gap between what employers need, and what individuals (and schools) provide. How did that gap come to be thinkable and how did profiling and reviewing come to span that gap with the prospect (however implicit) of a successful transition?

Once, when youth labour markets still existed, vocational theorists argued about whether transitions were 'rough' or 'smooth'. The supporters of the latter interpretation tended to employ sociological analysis and local labour market studies to show that most young people found work a relief after school, and that notions of choice and self-development were redundant. A social or cultural reproduction theory underlay their analyses (one of the last of these was Sawdon *et al.*, 1979). The supporters of the 'rough transition' argued in a more psychological fashion that the transition was stressful, and a developmental theory informed their interpretation. They asked: 'How can we help young people to choose?' A thumb-nail resolution of that dispute might argue that, in so far as the transition potentially involved choice, opportunity and social or occupational mobility, the psychologists were right. To the extent that it did not, the sociologists were right. But by the late 1970s, a strange thing was happening. The more that events in the economy restricted choice and opportunity and seemed to indicate a socio-economic version of the problem, the more the developmental and psychologistic version of the transition process came to be emphasized. The problem of 'matching' became a problem of induction (1978), then of preparation (1979), of 1-year training (1982), and then of 2-year training (1986); the self-concept became Social and Life Skills, Personal and Social Development and Personal Effectiveness; occupational choice expanded into a training curriculum, and profiling and reviewing came to motivate and record progress through these burgeoning stages of preparation.

How did this happen? Normative and psychometric approaches to the transition manipulated a calculus of variables, including class, gender, ability, personality characteristics, school and family circumstances. Where relatively constant variables were held to be causative (like class or gender) there were few educational or training remedies to be suggested – confronting gender stereotypes was barely an issue until the late 1970s; confronting class divisions was notoriously difficult. Correlational studies, therefore, tended to take a greater interest in variations within gender or class populations, and so began to psychologize the 'problems of youth'. In so doing, they began to build a metaphysical bridge from school to work, and to lay the foundations for a pre-vocational curriculum and for the framework, categories and assumptions of profiling and reviewing. For example, Lindsay, writing in 1969, explained delinquency thus: 'a reflection of fecklessness or other psychological factors rather than simple poverty' and, in a similar way, Maizels (1970) identified stress as a transition problem. The developmental and psychological interpretation was expressed most articulately in the work of Super, and of Law and Watts. The patterns of variables tended to indicate attitudinal and educational explanations for 'rough' and 'smooth' transitions, to offer implicit profiles of successful and unsuccessful transitions, and to identify possible remedial strategies; in essence, to moralize economic conditions. The prescriptions and attitudinal profiles were 'triangulated' through employer interviews concerning the desirable attributes of young workers (e.g. Mathews, 1977), and also mediated through more general ideological debates about the extent to which economic decline could be attributed to deficiencies in youth, and hence in schools.

Thus, the notion of avoidable deficiencies, of *personal* transitions, of successful and unsuccessful transition qualities, was constructed and legitimated, and served to confirm more intuitive analyses of 'the problem'. Profiles, then, brought together eclectic elements from the vocational discourses of the 1960s and 1970s. From the self-concept and developmental theorists, the importance of personal qualities was asserted, of individual responsibility for successful or unsuccessful transitions. These qualities were rewritten in the late 1970s and looked forward more insistently to employer and adult 'needs'. But the profiles' content was also nostalgic, invoking a work ethic that was felt to be dissipated and in urgent need of revival. Thus, the profile came to face both forwards and backwards, while also seeking to accommodate the present – both in asserting the identity of its subject and in denying the predictive validity of its judgements within a rationale that could only make sense as an education or training *for* the future. (It is not surprising that profiles found it difficult to address simultaneously all the audiences they had in mind – teacher, employer, pupil.)

We have seen that profiles stand within a particular version of vocational explanation, one which is normative, and which sought to explain transition problems in psychological or personalized ways. What are the implications for profiles, and especially for their student-centred nature?

The first implication is that we should doubt the ipsative nature of profiles, and distrust the nature of the holism they display. The construction of their categories and content is based on a series of abstract typifications, rooted in polemic, in employer needs and normative vocational debates. The learner is invited to match himself or herself against these typifications, to accept a particular definition of needs, to measure progress against these constructs and criteria, and to call such matching dialogue.

The kind of negotiation is illustrated in the following passage from a narrative report:

My character, personal qualities
I am usually a quiet person, both at home and at school, but if I say something which I think is right I will argue my point. I am quite active when the weather is nice to be out in, in the way of sports. I am careful both in what I do and what I say so that I do not upset anybody. I try not to take large, unnecessary risks which put either me or anybody else into danger. I am not a good leader and I do not really like being a leader in social circles, but I think many people follow (or try to follow) my example in academic subjects such as maths. I try to be cooperative to everybody if they ask me to do something which I think it is possible for me to do but I do not really like joining in large groups. I always persist in finishing everything it is possible for me to do. I attach quite a lot of importance to appearance and try always to be clean and neat, though not always fashionable. I always try to be reliable and never late unless I can help it. I always keep my word, especially where I am asked to keep a promise. (Broadfoot, 1986, p. 10).

The narrative covers, but cannot obscure, the underlying and *a priori* categories (quietness, activity, risk-taking, leadership, example to others, cooperative-ness). It is a piece of directed writing. Nor can it disguise its normative rather than ipsative nature (usually, quite, good, always, quite a lot, never). Any such negotiation or culmination of negotiations invites a self-scaling by the learner and reduces educational dialogue to a discussion of these implicit gradings. It also focusses on the child/student/trainee, and comprises a *social* assessment. An educational dialogue, on the other hand, would have to include the tutor, the course, the institution, the economic context, the categories and criteria of assessment and a reflexivity on the part of the student about his or her learning in relation to all these things, and that is not a usual feature of the new assessment. The profile is channelled towards a particular version of the self, not towards the learning process. What such statements imply is a pupil-focussed confession rather than a learner-centred dialogue. They also imply a kind of assessment based on a consensus theory of truth, but where the grounds for agreement are largely predetermined.

A second aspect of the ipsative and holistic nature of profiling rests on the notion of underlying personal constructs identified by the normative vocational tradition. These are psychologizations, and carry within them a blaming strategy. 'Employability', they seem to say, depends on personal qualities and learnable skills – confidence not neuroticism, 'fight' not apathy [cf. Bazalgette's (1975) concept of 'fight'],[5] independence not dependence, and so on. So the holistic portrait is not just a detached ideal construct; it also carries a personal accusation, a presumptive unreadiness for work that is enshrined in the term 'employability'. That accusation is carried within a contradiction in profiles: they offer both positive assessment and polar scales. It is for this reason that the lower end of the positive scale sounds so punitive: 'can make suitable responses when spoken to' (confidential draft of Birmingham school), 'can write a single letter of the alphabet' (Freshwater, 1981), 'can make sensible replies when spoken to' (Essex TVEI/CGLI). The marriage of dichotomizing scales and positive assessment is not a happy one.

A third aspect of the false student-centredness of profiling is expressed in its narrative form. That narrative offers an apparently commonsense account of personal values and interests that carries what Eagleton (1976, p. 124) – in a different context – has called 'an essentially *metonymic* resolution of such issues (personal values, visions and relations as the solution to social ills)'. In this way, the profile offers a personal description of the student that is also a social explanation – a covert translation of social and economic problems into personal ones. At the level of *form*, therefore, profiles have an unbounded sense of personal responsibility. The narrative is also principally *about* rather than *by* him or her. Recurring phrases in profile and recording systems indicate this: 'justifiably self-confident', 'people who will speak for me', 'fuller picture of X', 'to get our picture of you as accurate as possible'. Indeed, there is a Catch 22 to some of the labelling: one school profile offers a poor assessment to any person who 'relies on others' assessment' (examples from, respectively: Barnsley Student Record 1982, Norton Priory Achievement Certificate 1984, Sir Leo

Schulz HS profile – last quote made anonymously).

There is a further point to be made about the structure of the profile. Bernstein distinguishes clearly between normative assessment and the dossier. The dossier involves multiple procedures, different codes, a focus on the person not the group, a holistic approach to the individual, and the absence of an 'objective' grid for assessment:

> In the case of invisible pedagogies, these highly condensed, unexplicated but public judgments are likely to be replaced by something resembling a dossier which will range across a wide variety of the child's internal processes and his external acts. (Bernstein, 1977, p. 525)

But, as we have seen, the vocational dossier in its categories and dichotomizing structures inherits a deep normative legacy from the visible code. The dossier, then, is an overlay: its place within vocational discourse reflects what Ranson (1984) refers to as 'deep closure'. Whether and how it classifies and frames is of limited interest, because it represents not a shift from the normative to the idiographic, but a re-expression of the normative as a personalized construction of the social. It stands within the normative paradigm; it belongs to the same epistemological tradition. It only appears to counterpoise idiographic for normative, and leaves student-centredness as the fundamental illusion of its project. It is also for this reason that we should not see the profile, or record of achievement, or reviewing process, primarily as an act of surveillance, ominously different from previous traditions. (After all, employers are as unwilling to read so much 'intelligence' as teachers are to write it for each pupil.) Indeed, profiles resemble Burt's (1925, p. 292) 'psychographic schemes' quite closely, and much else besides. Instead, it is a reform that is isomorphic, despite its 'idealism' within the disciplinary functioning – it is a case, therefore, of 'utopian duplication' (Foucault, 1977, p. 271), offering pupil-focussed but not pupil-centred assessment.

There is a final and central objection to vocational profiling and reviewing to be made. What the covertly normative and falsely ipsative process does is to treat qualities, such as honesty, carefulness and punctuality, as if they were properties, ignoring the problem that it is only in real decisions and contexts that we choose to be honest, punctual or whatever. In so doing, it becomes the opposite of student-centred profiles and instigates a subtle basis for self-alienation into the process of education. Its self-assessment is a flight from the self:

> The analysis of the human subject, therefore, which bases itself on the analysis of the independently existing object, not only distorts the truth about how a human being actually is, but serves to justify the flight from self. (Waterhouse, 1981, p. 142)

The 'new assessment', then, has hijacked the notion of centredness in education. Invoking some of its associated concepts – such as holism, self-activation, readiness, relevance and individuality – the 'new assessment' has inverted both their individual meanings and the project which originally informed child-centredness: 'a protest . . . against education conceived merely as a preparation for the future' (Entwistle, 1970, p. 17).

At the heart of the pupil-centredness of profiling and reviewing lies an educational paradox: by constructing the student-centred, holistic and person-alized profile, we de-individualize the learners by asking each of them at the same time to conform to a stereotype, and to be themselves. In that sense, perhaps, there is no alienation more subtle than self-assessment.

Interpreting the new assessment

Thus far, it has been argued that the terminology of the new assessment contains its own contradiction, that the ipsative is an instance of the normative, that the holistic is a very particular construct, and that the centredness of profiling is the opposite of child-centredness as education since Rousseau has understood it. Hence, an anti-educational and subtly alienating set of procedures has emerged. We might also note in passing that, to the extent that false needs are represented, it is equally anti-vocational in nature. The question arises: how do we explain these disjunctions and redefinitions? What do they imply for the sociology of assessment? The argument here will be that the sociology of assessment requires a new metaphor to understand the new assessment, and that the notions of currency, capital and correspondence which have dominated sociological ex-planation do not take into account the new contexts of vocational discourse and profiling.

Profiling and reviewing are part of a vocational discourse which is both a result of and a response to economic crises. Such crises and responses were in the past cyclical, but in the last 10 years seem to have become endemic. The relationship of that vocational discourse to the economic context is crucial to a rethinking of the sociology of assessment.

In 1976 utilitarianism lay behind the SCRE profile. The profile would help bridge a gap between school and work by promoting relevant skills and attitudes, as indeed would the plethora of school-to-work projects and the remedial courses funded by the MSC. By 1977 worries about youth unemploy-ment were growing, but transition was still a problem for a minority. The 'need' to retrain a large proportion of youth was inconceivable, as the Holland Report of the MSC insisted: 'We must not lose sight of the fact that the ideal situation is one in which a young person gets a satisfactory job and does not enter the programme at all.' (Holland Report, 1977, p. 43).

Up to this point in vocational history, Broadfoot's interpretation seems defensible:

The change in England from the Plowden era to the prevailing climate of utilitarianism and work accountability may be seen . . . as equivalent to the shift in emphasis from expressive to instrumental goals, from an egalitarian, integrative ideology to an elitist competitive ideology. (Broadfoot, 1983, p. 319)

But to continue to apply this utilitarian explanation to events after 1978 is to miss a fundamental switch in the role of vocationalism, and to assume wrongly that the surface preoccupations of assessment express its functionality, as Ranson (1984, pp. 239–40) tends to do:

> The means of achieving the limitation of opportunities for young people is being determined through more sharply differentiated curricular experience . . . in order to fit young people more directly into the developing needs of the economy and of employment.

The misinterpretation involves taking the utilitarianism expressed in training at face value, and failing to note the symbolic and *expressive* role of the instrumental themes. That such training reflects more than a desire to fit people for economic roles is easily illustrated. Vocational deficiency expanded in parallel with youth unemployment between 1978 and 1986. The 13-week remediation of 1978 (e.g. WIC, STC) for a minority of the less able became the 6-month Work Experience scheme under YOP. Then the need was recognized for a 1-year preparation for a large proportion of the cohort, YTS was introduced, and now a 2-year training programme is necessary. These training needs continue to be held in place by the bridging rationality, although lengthening of the bridge has led to the invention of a whole new conceptual structure of stages of pre-vocational development, involving occupational training families, generic skills and notions of transferability. Indeed, the original vocational curriculum of YOP has now been largely displaced back into the schools, in various TVEI, CGLI, RSA or CPVE guises, as the following Humberside table[6] neatly illustrates:

Elements of YTS	Elements of vocational preparation
Induction	Negotiation
Assessment	Counselling, guidance and assessment
Off the job training	Basic skills
Planned work experience	Experience and relevance
Guidance and support	Counselling, guidance and assessment
Core skills	Basic skills
Record and review of progress	Counselling, guidance and assessment
Occupational-based training	Work experience/work simulation

It would be hard to argue that this bizarre expansion of training simply expresses an ever-tightening instrumental connection of education to the world of work. I have argued elsewhere that such an expansion reflects a need to administer a surplus youth population, rather than to provide necessary pre-vocational training (Stronach, 1984). It is this socially incorporative goal that assessment embodied, in contrast to its traditional allocative role.

Thus the image of instrumentality, of connectedness to the economic order, came to express a disconnection of youth from economic life, but a disconnection that was expressed in socially incorporative terms. Occasionally, this is openly acknowledged in the profiling debate:

> Many a holder of CSE middle or low grades results (and not a few GCE 'O' level candidates) will be utterly dejected on realising that the credentials are given scant respect. If that dejection turns to alienation, society can pay a high penalty. (De Groot, 1981, p. 1)

Profiling expressed that incorporation in terms of the student-centredness of ipsative, holistic and negotiated accounts, designed above all to 'motivate' – for that is the term used before all others – an ever-increasing proportion of 15- to 18-year-olds.

Given such a socially incorporative rather than economically allocative project for assessment, what are the implications for our understanding of the 'new assessment'?

1. The surfaces of the 'new assessment' are vocational, preparatory, practical and instrumental. The first audience is the employer. But the insistence on the vocational is hollow. The needs are poorly established; British employers have little traditional regard for training; de-skilling is an important facet of contemporary industrial organization; and the coincidence of mass youth unemployment and the flourishing training industry is obvious. Thus, the indistinct figure that stands behind the profile and the vocational discourse is not the perfect worker, nor even the ideal citizen. It is the outline of the tractable client (Habermas, 1984), well-motivated, adaptable, indefinitely prepared for an uncertain future. This clienthood is far from being the sophisticated response of the State – it is the *ad hoc* and vulnerable construction of a curricular space that the collapse of work and its attendant socializations began to open up in the late 1970s, the result of an economic crisis whose effects were consciously channelled on to youth.

It is through the juxtaposition of economic context and vocational discourse that the incorporative nature of the 'new assessment' becomes apparent, and the expressiveness of the new instrumentality becomes evident. These paradoxes in the vocational discourse imply that we need a theory that will not be restricted to the surface themes of profiling, and will not seek to draw direct correspondences of category or frame between schooling and work. They also imply a modification of Bernstein's unit of analysis, 'the structure of social relationships which produces these specialized competencies' (Bernstein, 1977, p. 527), since it is the relations between matrices, rather than within them, that offers the best insight into the nature of the assessment project.

2. In such a context, the traditional sociology of examinations cannot apply. There is no zeal to capture and preserve status – that scarce, elusive and highly prized commodity of the education system (Eggleston, 1984, p. 31). Profiles are not like qualifications.

3. Hargreaves suggested two continua with which to profile profiles. They ran from employer needs and social control (negative) to the identity and independence of the student (positive). As we have seen, the notion of independence is represented in the new assessment by negotiation, participation, by ideal-typical constructions of self-reliance, and so on. Similarly, the notion of identity is carried by the holistic, student-centred and ipsative nature of the profile. These features express the incorporative and manipulative nature of the new assessment. The continua, therefore, separate different mechanisms of control, not different values or goals. The kind of motivation and the versions of identity that are on offer do not amount to an educational approach to profiling. In terms of Hargreaves' own Foucauldian argument, both ends of the continua stand within the power/knowledge configuration that he is opposing. Nor would any juggling of personal qualities (say, in the direction of autonomy) meet the objection that the process of profiling invites conformity with predetermined and highly ideological images. However enlightened the list of qualities, the process would remain alienating.

4. It follows from these peculiar novelties of the new assessment that the traditional metaphors of the sociology of assessment do not apply. Commodity becomes an unsuitable metaphor for an incorporative, as opposed to an allocative, assessment. The point is central to a rethinking of the meaning of the new assessment, and is worth examining closely.

The first metaphor of assessment is money. Collins' cultural money theory of the credential society is only the most vivid of numerous monetarist explanations of how assessment and certification work in an advanced capitalist economy. He argues that certificates are:

> formal summary announcements of the quantity of cultural goods an individual has acquired . . . In other words, the more formalized the culture-producing organisation, the more its culture tends to resemble a currency, and the more the cultural economy becomes subject to specifically monetary effects. (Collins, 1979, p. 62)

The monetarists of the Left include Bourdieu and Passeron (1977; cultural capital), Holly (1977; allocative capital), and Hextall and Sarup (1977; commodity production), their formulations resting usually on Durkheim or Marx. But the monetarists of the Right are just as unenthusiastic about the credential, seeing in it a violation of the 'minimal state' (Nozick, 1974, p. ix) or an absurd growth in occupational licensure (Friedman, 1962, p. 138). So Collins' (1979, p. 200) radical call to break down 'current forms of positional property' – abolitionism as his typology has it – makes a general appeal.

Thus theorizing about assessment tends to take place within the metaphor of money, and parallels the etymology of the *Shorter Oxford English Dictionary:* 'assessment' to fix the amount – (taxation, fine, etc.) – to be paid by a person or community; to determine the amount of and impose upon, etc. The *Oxford English Dictionary* (1933) lists no educational definition of assessment, nor does

Webster's (1961), and nor does educational sociology, with its concern for exchange value. Within this interpretative tradition, assessment is seen as restrictive, allocative and monetarist in the sense that money is made into a working metaphor whose associated concepts (e.g. inflation, exchange, currency) are also brought into play as explanation rather than merely illumination.

Nietzsche has argued that such a conflating of assessment with exchange values points to the ontology of thinking itself, and so to the nature of human beings:

> Making prices, assessing values, thinking out equivalents, exchanging – all this preoccupied the primal thoughts of man to such an extent that in a certain sense it constituted thinking itself. (Nietzsche, 1910, pp. 79–80)

This would suggest that some form of 'capital' theory of assessment is inevitable. If 'assessing values' is thinking, then the thinking of that thinking (= sociology of assessment) can hardly avoid the metaphor.

But it is wrong to think that the metaphor is a necessary rather than a historically contingent one. For example, Clastres (1978) has analysed the assessments that characterized stateless societies. The rituals of torture (criterion–referenced, affective assessment, centring on values such as endurance and courage) represented the socially incorporative rather than the allocative assessment that we have been discussing. The purpose of assessment in such societies was to establish an 'assertive pedagogy' so intense, so memorable, that the state was unnecessary. We should beware, therefore, of anachronistic metaphor, for that is the weakness of Nietzsche's interpretation and of the traditional sociologists of assessment. Mauss argued, in his study of potlatch exchanges, that potlatch was a total phenomenon containing religious and mythological as well as economic elements. In such contexts, it would be wholly inappropriate to define assessment in utilitarian terms, since 'The victory of rationalism and mercantilism was required before the notions of profit and the individual were given currency and raised to the level of principles' (Mauss, 1966, p. 74).

A similar point can be made for the 'new assessment'. If the project (I use the term 'project' with some circumspection)[7] of the new assessment is radically different from the allocative mobilizations of value in the past, then we must research a new metaphor on which to found an appropriate theory of that kind of assessment. In this case, we need a metaphor to replace currency to do justice to the project of social incorporation: 'Our feasts are the movement of the needle which sews together the parts of our reed roofs, making of them a single roof, one single word' (Mauss, 1966, p. 19). But what is the new word?

5. A researched and heuristic metaphor for the 'new assessment' is the final theme of this critique. What does that mean and how can it be achieved?

If a metaphor is to inform a theory it must not be divorced from the nature of its subject, either because it is an arbitrary choice, or because it is anachronistic

Table 15.1 The juxtaposition of the context of assessment with its content

	Content (profiling discourses) Warm	Context[8] (economic and social position of youth) Cold
Focus	*Centredness* • participation • ownership (of skills, of learning process) • consultation • need-based (vocational, personal)	*Alienation* • marginality; powerlessness • collapse of apprenticeship • substitutability of labour skill • isolation of young unemployed • unemployment; deskilling
Process	• ipsative and real • holistic • negotiated	• ideal-typical and abstract • vocationalist • imposed (non-involvement in waged labour, loss of benefit for non-participation in training schemes)
Outcome	• regeneration • inclusion, motivation • eligibility • maturity	• management of decline • exclusion of cohort; estrangement • deferred entry to adulthood • prolonged adolescence

(as Mauss indicated). Nor should it be inseparable from its subject, or it becomes tautologous. Normative and psychometric accounts of vocational choice and maturity tended to offer such interpretations. They explained coins with banknotes. They really amounted to a reinsertion of a metonymic instance (e.g. the delinquent) within the over-arching explanation to which it already belonged. Instead, a metaphor must be found which will connect with what is implicit in profiling. According to the previous analysis, the metaphor should span not just profiling, or profiling within a vocational discourse, but profiling in a broad social and economic context. In so doing, the metaphor should give some account of the anomalies between the themes of inclusion and exclusion that seem to be involved. That points to some notion of ritual: 'the symbol which is characteristic of ritual represents a conjunction of opposite tendencies' (Turner, 1969, p. 276). Such a claim involves a cost. Each metaphor has its blind spot, like any optic nerve, and cannot claim an exclusive or exhaustive purchase on meaning. But choice is inevitable – just as we deconstruct the metonymic nature of profiling, so too must we reconstruct its meaning round a metaphor that may offer rather more insight than mystification.

A first step, then, might be to juxtapose the context of assessment with its content (see Table 15.1). In terms of the analysis so far, there is a striking discrepancy between them, between warmth and coldness. The warmth suggests an inclusion and engagement – to share, recognize, name, induct and baptize (in the name of a vocational destiny). The coldness suggests exclusion and estrangement – to cut off, reject, veil. On the one hand, apparently liberal processes; on the other, impositional structures similar to Blauner's definition of alienation. In interpreting the new assessment some have chosen to write warm accounts; others, cold accounts. The logic of the metaphor is that the paradox must be accepted, rather than reduced to an *either/or* of repression or enlightenment. It is the insertion of the warm within the cold that marks the new transition ritual of which profiling is a central part. That insertion accepts the marginality of youth, and creates the way in which they will know it. It indicates, therefore, a ritual whose pedagogy involves a manipulative rather than an assertive or allocative assessment. That ritual promises warmth and a fantasy of superiority or at least equality; but it delivers a permanent liminality for an age group, a deferment of adult status until they are trained, developed, made employable. In a sense, the hierarchical division of labour, fed by normative and allocative assessment, gives way to a hierarchical division of life, wherein cohorts of the young are denied adult status (i.e. juvenalized) via an ipsative and incorporative assessment. The young are invited to celebrate their marginality and powerlessness, and to call it training. Within that training they are offered – ideologically rather than actually – power (in the form of negotiation and ownership), purpose and preparation. Outside of that training the world looks very different to them. What is such a 'fantasy of structural superiority' (Turner, 1969, p. 168), if it is not a carnival? Perhaps that is a metaphor with which to explore the paradoxes of profiling within vocationalism. The project of profiling, then, is to warm a generation, not to cool them out to make the happiness of content fill the sadness of form:

> The sadness meant: we are at the last station. The happiness meant: we are together. The sadness was form, the happiness content. Happiness filled the space of sadness. (Kundera, 1985, p. 314)

Notes

1 'Ipsative' assessment refers to individual progress, rather than group norms or external criteria of performance. The word seems to have gained currency in the profiling and recording debates.
2 Especially in the RPA, RPE tradition of Don Stansbury and its PPR development. See the *Springline Trust Newsletter,* November 1983. There are significant differences in the Stansbury approach. They are not the subject of this chapter.
3 The recurrent and cyclical nature of these concerns prior to 1976 is often neglected. See, for example, the 'relevance' debate in RSLA, the Scottish Brunton Report (1963) and Newsom (1964). Nor is such recurrence a UK phenomenon. US preoccupations in the late nineteenth and early twentieth centuries were similar. See Parsons (1909)

for both familiar themes and categories and a novel 'picture method of the presenting of the case' (p. 220), that anticipated both profile and 'social and life skills' curricular.

4 See, for example, McLelland and Kemp's approach in contrast to the atomistic approaches of job analyses. Most of the early profiles were guilty of crudely assessing attitudes or qualities such as punctuality, respect for authority, bearing, appearance.

5 This kind of criticism is also made by Willis (1977, p. 69): 'An additional focus', he writes, 'should always warn us of a mystificatory transmution of a basic exchange relationship into illusory, ideal ones.'

6 Humberside diary logbook (n.d.).

7 Discursive analyses tend to invest the discourse with 'purposes', 'intentions' and 'effects' that are quite illusory. The term 'project' includes the reactive *ad hoc* extemporizations and *post hoc* rationalizations that have contributed to the constructions of the vocational discourse. It indicates 'direction' as a resultant, but acknowledges the power of resistance (say by pupils, trainers, teachers) and subversion.

8 These are left as assertions in this account. See, however, Bates *et al.* (1984).

References

Bates, I., Clarke, J., Cohen, P., Finn, D., Moore, R. and Willis, P. (1984). *Schooling for the Dole: the New Vocationalism*. London: Macmillan.

Bazalgette, J. (1975). *School Life Work Life: A Study of Transition in the Inner City*. London: Hutchins.

Bernstein, B. (1977). Class and pedagogies: Visible and invisible. In J. Karabel and A.H. Halsey (eds), *Power and Ideology in Education*, pp. 525–7. New York: Oxford University Press.

Bourdieu, P. and Passeron, J.C. (1977). *Reproduction in Education, Society and Culture* (translated by R. Nice). California, Sage.

Broadfoot, P. (1983). Evaluation and the social order in advanced industrial societies: The educational dilemma. *International Review of Applied Psychology*, **32**, 307–25.

Broadfoot, P. (ed.) (1984). *Selection, Certification and Control: Social Issues in Educational Assessment*. Lewes: Falmer Press.

Broadfoot, P. (1986). Records of achievement: Achieving a record? In P. Broadfoot (ed.), *Profiles and Records of Achievement. A Review of Issues and Practice*. London: Holt, Rinehart and Winston.

Broadfoot, P. and Dockrell, D. (1977). *Pupils in Profile: Making the Most of Teachers' Knowledge of Pupils*. London: Hodder and Stoughton.

Burt, C. (1925). *The Sub-normal School-child: 1. The Young Delinquent*. London: University of London Press.

Clastres, P. (1978). *Society Against the State* (translated by R. Hurley and A. Stein). Oxford: Blackwell.

Collins, R. (1979). *The Credential Society. An Historical Sociology of Educational Stratification*. New York: Academy Press.

Cook, J.D., Hepworth, S.J., Wall, T.D. and Warr, P.B. (1981). *The Experience of Work. A Compendium and Review of 249 Measures and Their Use*. London: Academic Press.

De Groot, R. (1981). *Pupils' Personal Records*.

Eagleton, T. (1976). *Criticism and Ideology: A Study in Marxist Literary Theory*. London: Verso.

Eggleston, J. (1984). School examinations – some sociological issues. In P. Broadfoot (ed.), *Selection, Certification and Control: Social Issues in Educational Assessment*. Lewes: Falmer Press.

Entwistle, H. (1970). *Child-centred Education*. London: Methuen.

FEU (1982). *Profiles*. London: DES.

Foucault, M. (1977). *Discipline and Punish. The Birth of the Prison* (first published 1975) (translated by A. Sheridan). Harmondsworth: Penguin.

Freshwater, M. (1981). *The Basic Skills Analysis. How a Checklist can Help Make the Most of Training Opportunities*. London: TSD/MSC.

Friedman, M. (1962). *Capitalism and Freedom*. Chicago: Chicago University Press.

Habermas, J. (1984). *The Theory of Communicative Action* (translated by T. McCarthy). London: Heinemann.

Hargreaves, A. (1986). Record breakers? In P. Broadfoot (ed.), *Profiles and Records of Achievement. A Review of Issues and Practice*. London: Holt, Rinehart and Winston.

Hextall, I. and Sarup, M. (1977). School knowledge, evaluation and alienation. In M. Young and G. Whitty (eds), *Society, State and Schooling: Readings on the Possibilities for Radical Education*. Lewes: Falmer Press.

Holland, J. (1959). A theory of vocational choice. *Journal of Counselling Psychology*, **6**(1), 35–43.

Holland Report (1977). *Young People and Work: Report on the Feasibility of a New Programme of Opportunities for Unemployed Young People*. London: MSC.

Holly, D. (1977). Education and the social relations of a capitalist society. In M. Young and G. Whitty (eds), *Society, State and Schooling: Readings on the Possibilities for Radical Education*. Lewes: Falmer Press.

Hopson, B. and Hayes, J. (1968). *The Theory and Practice of Vocational Guidance: A Selection of Readings*. Oxford: Pergamon.

IPM (1984). *Schools and the World of Work: What do Employers Look for in School leavers?* London: Institute of Personnel Management.

Kazamas, H.C. (1978). *Affective Work Competencies for Vocational Education*. Ohio: NCRVE.

Kundera, M. (1985). *The Unbearable Lightness of Being* (translated by M. Heim). London: Faber and Faber.

Lindsay, C. (1969). *School and Community*. Oxford: Pergamon/EIS.

MacDonald, B. (1973). Humanities curriculum project. In *Evaluation in Curriculum Development: 12 Case-studies*. Papers from the Schools Council project evaluators on aspects of their work. London: Macmillan.

Maizels, J. (1970). *Adolescent Needs and the Transition from School to Work*. London: Athlone Press.

Mathews, D. (1977). *The Relevance of School Leaving Experience to Performance in Industry*. Watford: EITB.

Mauss, M. (1966). *The Gift. Forms and Functions of Exchange in Archaic Societies* (first published 1950) (translated by I. Cunnison). London: Cohen and West.

McLelland, D. and Klemp, G. (1979). In D.G. Winter (ed.), *An Introduction to LMET Theory and Research*. Boston: McBer and Co.

Nietzsche, F. (1910). The genealogy of morals. In O. Lery (ed.), *The Complete Works of Freidrich Nietzsche*, Vol 13 (translated by H. Samuel). Edinburgh: Foulis.

Nozick, R. (1974). *Anarchy, State and Utopia*. Oxford: Blackwell.

Parsons, F. (1909). *Choosing a Vocation.* Boston: Houghton Mifflin.

Oxenham, J. (1984). Employers, jobs and qualifications. In J. Oxenham (ed.), *Education versus Qualifications? A Study in the Relationships between Education, Selection for Employment and the Productivity of Labour.* London: Allen and Unwin.

Ranson, S. (1984). Towards a tertiary tripartism: New codes of social control and the 17+. In P. Broadfoot (ed.), *Selection, certification and Control. Social Issues in Educational Assessment.* Lewes: Falmer Press.

Sawdon, A., Tucker, J. and Pelican, J. (1979). *Study of transition from School to Working Life.* London: Youthaid.

Starishevsky, R. and Matlin, N. (1968). A model for the translation of self-concepts into vocational terms. In B. Hopson and J. Hayes (eds), *The Theory and Practice of Vocational Guidance: A Selection of Readings.* Oxford: Pergamon.

Stronach, I. (1981). Pictures of performance. *Clydebank EC Project Annual Report.* Jordanhill College of Education.

Stronach, I. (1984). Work experience: The sacred anvil. In C. Varlaam (ed.), *Rethinking Transition: Educational Innovation and the Transition to Adult Life.* Lewes: Falmer Press.

Super, D. (1953). A theory of vocational development. *American Psychology,* **4**(8), 185–90.

Townshend, C., Page, T. and Seedat, M. (1982). *Skills Needed for Young Peoples' Jobs,* Vols 1–5. Institute of Manpower Studies, University of Sussex.

Turner, V.W. (1967). *The Forest of Symbols: Aspects of Ndembu Ritual.* Ithaca, N.Y.: Cornell University Press.

Turner, V.W. (1969). *The Ritual Process: Structure and Anti-structure.* London: Routledge and Kegan Paul.

Waterhouse, R. (1981). *A Heidegger Critique. A Critical Examination of the Existential Phenomenology of Martin Heidegger.* Sussex: Harvester.

Willis, P. (1977). *Learning to Labour: How Working Class Kids Get Working Class Jobs.* Farnborough: Saxon House.

16
Conclusion: rethinking appraisal

John Elliott

Introduction

To what extent do the contributions in this book help us to rethink the process of assessment in the context of performance appraisal? Can a methodology of naturalistic inquiry, developed by educational researchers and evaluators in the 1970s to study curriculum change, provide a basis for such rethinking? And to what extent can attempts to rethink assessment as a form of naturalistic inquiry contribute to the further development of the methodology more generally? These are the questions I will attempt to address in this final chapter.

Before undertaking to do so, I want to clarify the way I shall use the terms 'assessment', 'appraisal' and 'evaluation'. These terms are often used interchangeably but conventions have developed for separating out their use. In education, 'assessment' tends to be used when the focus is on student learning. 'Appraisal' tends to be used in relation to performances of individual teachers. 'Evaluation' has often been used when the focus is broader than the individual, e.g. the curriculum, the institution, a policy or programme.

In this chapter I shall primarily use the term 'appraisal'. It appears to be generally used with respect to judgements of performance in their natural settings. How one goes about making such judgements in relation to either teaching or learning tasks is what this book is about. In discussing the issues raised in this book, it therefore seems reasonable to minimize possible confusion by referring to 'performance appraisal' rather than 'performance assessment' or 'performance evaluation'.

Many of the chapters contain critiques of either emerging appraisal policies in the UK or of established ones in the USA (see, for example, Chapters 2, 3, 4, 9 and 15). A range of principles are implicit in these critiques, many of them shared by the contributors. Other chapters simply aspire to map out conceptual issues and to formulate principles for handling them. So can we distil an internally consistent and coherent set of principles? I think we can. In this chapter I will attempt to highlight some of the major principles and discuss their implications for a naturalistic methodology of appraisal for both teacher and student performance.

Contextualizing appraisals

Appraisal of teachers or pupils needs to be considered in the context of other kinds of evaluation, e.g. of the curriculum, organizational functioning, educational management, and of the social environment of educational institutions.

Stake (Chapter 1) claims that the evaluation of teaching is an inseparable part of the evaluation of the school. But we know that teacher appraisal schemes are often implemented in isolation from any evaluation of how contextual factors influence performance. Stake is really making a point about what counts as a valid appraisal process. He asserts that teaching can be judged only in the context of these other factors, and if no effort is made to study them, the evaluation of teaching will be invalid. McIntyre (Chapter 7) makes a similar point when he discusses the problem 'of applying criteria of *competence* to evidence about *performance*'. The fact that the latter provides no manifestation of a particular competence does not necessarily imply that the performer lacks this competence. The context may simply have not provided opportunities for its display. McIntyre argues that the assessor 'must have an extremely sensitive understanding of the social and material context, as experienced by the teacher, within which the teaching occurs'.

During their negotiations with central government over the nature and form of a national teacher appraisal system, teachers in the UK frequently articulated their fear of being scapegoated for deficiencies in performance which might best be explained in terms of contextual factors. Most of the appraisal schemes which have subsequently emerged genuflect to the importance of context. The appraisal interview is supposed to give teachers an opportunity to articulate their experience of constraining factors in the context of their performance so that educational managers can reflect about the effectiveness of organizational arrangements, etc. But to my knowledge, most appraisal schemes do not specify how such information is to be analysed and utilized within the wider process of institutional review and development. In other words, although teacher appraisal schemes render teachers accountable to managers, they do not generally indicate how managers are to be rendered accountable for their organizational policies and practices through some form of institutional evaluation.

One can make a similar point about the isolation of pupil appraisal procedures. Stronach (Chapter 15), for example, argues that the personal profile 'offers a personal description of the student that is also a social explanation – a covert translation of social and economic problems into personal ones'. Since the account is controlled by another and is therefore '*about* the student rather than *by* him or her', it will tend to impute responsibility for performance to the person rather than to factors in the teaching and institutional context. Even the self-assessment element in the production of profiles assumes, according to Stronach, 'the analysis of the independently existing object' (self). He argues that the profiling process ignores 'the problem that it is only in real decisions and contexts that we choose to be honest, punctual, whatever. Its self-assessment is a flight from the self.' It is a process which involves a pupil-focussed confession rather than a learner-centred dialogue. The latter 'would have to include the tutor, the course, the institution, the economic context, the categories and criteria of assessment, and a reflexivity on the part of the student about his or her learning in relation to all these things.'

Most appraisal schemes assume that a focus on a particular kind of performance implies an appraisal of the performer alone. What Stake, Stronach and others appear to be claiming is that such an assumption renders the appraisal invalid. Valid appraisals of the performer cannot be separated from the appraisal of other potential influences on performance. Since it is the performers' actions which are shaped by such factors, they are in a good position to assess their influence. Valid performance appraisals, therefore, depend on a holistic process in which a type of performance is appraised in relation to its total context.

What is required is a comprehensive monitoring system for evaluating a number of critical factors which can influence performance in educational institutions. A concentration on one particular aspect of schooling, such as teaching, already presupposes a bias in favour of distributing blame for deficiencies in that direction. It also presupposes, as Burgess (Chapter 3) points out, an inequitable distribution of power.

Context and agency

Naturalistic evaluators of curriculum reform programmes have tended to avoid judgements about the quality of the agency exercised by those responsible for implementing change. They have concentrated on describing the ways in which contextual factors shape and constrain performance, and reporting the judgements of those who are interested parties in the implementation process. Such evaluators have argued that judgement is not part of their role. Yet one can argue that judgements are tacitly expressed in their naturalistic portrayals of activities. By exclusively focussing on the effect of contextual factors which influence performance, naturalistic evaluators have tacitly exonerated the performers from blame, and redistributed it. Moreover, the effect of providing a contextual description alongside judgemental data which imputes blame to the performers is to undermine the credibility of that data.

No doubt the approach I have described was a necessary corrective in an evaluation context where people assumed that blame for any shortfalls between curricular goals and practices lay with teachers. The refusal to judge, at least in any explicit sense, may have been a useful pragmatic device for challenging this assumption. But should it be elevated as a methodological principle of naturalistic evaluation?

The naturalistic paradigm is grounded in the symbolic–interactionist account of social action developed by George Herbert Mead. Central to Mead's theory of social action is the distinction between the 'Me' and 'I'. The 'Me' is the socially situated self reproducing through social interaction the normative and ideological structures of the social order. It is the self as defined by others. The 'I' is the reflexive self which is aware of itself as 'me', and able to exercise a measure of freedom and choice over how it is socially constituted.

Commenting on this distinction, Anthony Giddens (1976) points out that even though Mead's account of social action was built around the idea of reflexivity, involving the reciprocity of the 'I' and the 'Me', 'the constituting activity of the "I" is not stressed'. He argues that Mead's followers became even more preoccupied with 'the social self'. The 'social self' became reinterpreted as the 'socially determined self'. The 'reflexive self' which is aware of itself as a socially constituted being and able to exercise a measure of control over how it is so constituted, gets increasingly lost in the writings of the symbolic-interactionist school which spawned the naturalistic paradigm of social inquiry. And with it, according to Giddens, went the theoretical possibilities contained in Mead's original distinction.

It could be argued with some justice that naturalistic evaluators of curriculum development followed the trend and emphasized the 'social self' to the exclusion of the 'reflexive self', with the result that performance was not only portrayed as socially situated but also as socially determined. The emergence of performance appraisal in educational settings challenges us to develop a naturalistic methodology which accommodates both the need to describe the way context shapes performance and the need to judge the quality of the human agency it manifests. To what extent do these papers suggest methodological principles which give space to the reflexive 'I'?

A number of chapters (see Chapters 1, 6, 8, 9 and 10) suggest that appraisal processes should evaluate performance in terms of the personal qualities manifested in performances rather than the measureable characteristics of those performances. But, as Stronach (Chapter 15) argues, such qualities can be viewed as individual attributes which assessment systems reproduce in a power-coercive manner. They are not necessarily the manifestations of the powers of self-determining agents. What is required is a methodology for assessing the quality of the personal agency exercised in performance.

House and Lapan (Chapter 6) argue that performance characteristics like 'eye contact' and 'amount of teacher talk' are at best only secondary and indirect indicators of competence even when they are statistically 'validated' correlates of effective teaching. One can, they claim, easily find excellent teachers who do not maintain eye contact in the classroom. Appraisals should refer to qualities or characteristics which can be 'necessarily and directly' related to good teaching. The 'ability to control a class' is more directly related to good teaching, according to House and Lapan, than maintaining 'eye contact'. I would agree 'Maintaining eye contact' is a particular manifestation of a teacher's competence to control the class. But such a competence may be exercised by other means.

This is why good teaching cannot be assessed by simply aggregating observations of the presence or absence of a finite set of performance characteristics. What House and Lapan appear to be saying is that competence is constituted by certain powers of personal agency and should not be confused with its particular behavioural manifestations.

House and Lapan, following Scriven, dismisses occasional classroom observation using checklists as a valid means of appraising teachers. This is because 'both the amount of content presented to the student and the amount of learning inspired by the teacher are invisible in the occasional visit'. At best such visits should be only part of a more global strategy.

Another implication of focussing on the qualities of human agency manifested in 'good teaching' is that appraisal will be concerned to identify excellence as well as incompetence. House and Lapan suggest that a reliance on observable indicators stems from accountability pressures which are primarily concerned with eliminating incompetence. 'Unfortunately', they write, 'schemes aimed at discerning minimum competence, and thus allaying the fears of an anxious public, are employed with all teachers.'

Underlying the objection to using performance standards as measures of competence is a particular view of the origins of competence. It is only in a very minimalist sense that competence can be explained as the social production of standardized behaviour. The development of competence beyond a minimum level of acceptability depends on active, self-determining beings. On this view, 'the self' in action cannot be fully explained as a socially determined 'me'.

The methodological principle implied by House and Lapan's argument is as follows:

> Appraisals of performance should focus on manifestations of those powers of self-determination which are generic to high-quality and effective performance in the execution of the task.

Such a principle leaves space for the reflexive 'I' as the source of competence. However, House and Lapan tend to derive the competencies which define the quality of personal agency exercised in performance from analysis of the task. But the same task has to be performed in different contexts. And different contexts may require the exercise of different powers in human beings, a point that is also brought out by Stake (Chapter 1).

Stake echoes House and Lapan's reservations about checklists of performance criteria. He argues that 'criteria cannot be found that adequately fit all teaching situations' and that 'high marks on all criteria do not indicate the most valuable teacher for all situations'. A competence will manifest itself behaviourally in different forms depending on the context. But Stake also seems to be suggesting that differing contexts require the exercise of different competencies. In evaluating teachers we therefore need 'information of diverse types, relating to diverse situations, and drawn from diverse sources'. This will limit the extent to which teachers can be validly compared using scaled performance indicators. What are required are judgements about the extent to which the personal qualities

required for effective agency in a variety of contexts are manifested in performance. Stake reminds us that the manifestations of the 'reflexive self' are always
socially situated: that competence is bound to particular contexts although not
determined by them.

Naturalistic methodology can therefore accommodate the principle I culled
from House and Lapan's argument with the following proviso:

> . . . that the personal competencies which human agents manifest in success-
> ful performances should be determined in relation to particular contexts of
> performance and not independently of them.

As I will indicate later, such determinations will inevitably be biased by
perceptions of the values which the performer ought to protect and foster in the
situation. Since these values are liable to be controversial, it follows that the
competencies which presuppose them will be similarly liable.

But this is to run ahead of the present argument. What the above principle
implies is that competencies are not attributed to an 'I' abstracted from space and
time. They are only attributed to an 'I' which manifests itself in a particular set of
circumstances. There is no assumption that in different circumstances the same
competencies would be manifested or that their manifestation would take the
same form. Naturalistic appraisals of persons are always relative to context
rather than total attributions. Appraisals which aspire to define the individual as
a total entity are not only pretentious but totalitarian. Stronach (Chapter 15)
warns us against interpreting holistic appraisal as a process of defining and
categorizing the total self. Such a process is intrinsically power-coercive because
it distorts the idea of persons as reflexive and self-determining agents.

Smith and Klass (Chapter 12) remind us that there is no unchallangeable
theoretical basis for linguistic appraisal:

> . . . the whole child, is an unattainable goal in research. The multiple choices
> in available theories, in settings in which one works, and in practical problems
> focussed upon is too large. General theory of personality, in spite of 100 years
> of psychological effort . . . is not available.

Different theories of personality are embedded in different structures of belief
and value concerning human nature and society. Smith and Klass argue that the
idea of 'the whole child' has value when 'it sensitizes one to the need to remain
flexible . . . to the possibilities of alternative constructs of personality and
development'.

However, this kind of account of holistic appraisal does not go far enough in
acknowledging that the sources of competence reside in the powers of human
agency. It merely implies that holistic appraisal should take both the context of
performance and a plurality of judgements about the performer into account. It
is certainly open to the possibility that self-appraisals should form part of the
judgemental data. But it tells us little about the significance of self-appraisal
within a holistic process. A naturalistic methodology of holistic appraisal
must indicate the extent to which the qualities manifested in performance are

generated by the self-monitoring activity of the performer if it is to fully accommodate the reflexive self. Such a methodology would place situated self-appraisal
at the centre of a holistic appraisal process. From this perspective the value of the
idea of 'the whole person' is to remind us of the manifold and unpredictable
forms in which the reflexive self manifests its powers of agency (competences)
in a variety of contexts.

Naturalistic appraisal, in focussing on the contexts of performance, does not
have to presume that performance is entirely determined by factors in the
context. For the self is only revealed within the context of performance, not as
an independently existing entity to which clusters of properties can be attributed, but as both a socially situated and reflexive agency of performance.
This suggests the following methodological principle: *Appraisal data should
include evidence of how context both shapes and is shaped by human agency*.

From this perspective the personal qualities, manifested in performance,
neither mirror ideological structures operating in the social context nor constitute attributes of a substantial self existing independently of that context.
They are the qualities of a reflexive and situated self capable of self-awareness
and self-mastery. The self posits itself as an object of awareness and mastery – as
a 'me' – and in so doing adopts the standpoint of the 'I'. The personal qualities
which characterize excellence in performance are those of a self-aware and self-
determining agent.

It follows, therefore, as I argue in Chapter 9, that an appraisal system which
aims to foster excellence must protect and develop reflexivity. This is not
protected and fostered by getting appraisees to assess themselves in the light of
standardized performance indicators. Such an appraisal process, as Stronach
(Chapter 15) shows, is simply a mechanism of social control aimed at determining identities. What is required is a genuine appraisal dialogue between the
performer and others about the qualitative requirements of the situation, and the
extent to which they are manifested in performance. The judgements of others
are not definitive, but a resource for enhancing the performer's capacities for
self-awareness and self-determination.

The final assessment, in any appraisal system which aims to develop a
person's capacity to make responsible judgments and decisions in particular
performance settings, must rest with the performer. This dialogue process is
concretely illustrated by Franz Kroath's (Chaper 8) account of the way in which
trainee teacher supervisors are appraised in Austria. For example, in any conflict
between the external appraisal of the facilitator and the self-appraisal of the
student supervisor, the resolution consists of 'taking students' accounts and
feedback data (to facilitator) as a criterion for final assessment'. Kroath justifies
this on the grounds that hierarchically determined judgements of competence
are distorted and biased by unequal power-relations.

My own critique (Chapter 9) of developments in the field of teacher appraisal
argues that the self-appraisal of the qualities of human agency manifested in
performance must be accommodated in any valid system of professional
appraisal for teachers. I attempt to outline a two-tier model of appraisal which is

grounded in a process of action-research engaged in collaboratively by the practitioners themselves. Action-research is a form of naturalistic enquiry which accommodates both the 'me' and the 'I' in a dynamic relationship. The self is constituted as both socially situated and free. Through reflection, the structures which constrain and shape performance are not only brought to conscious self-awareness (with 'Me' as the object of awareness), but the deliberating 'I' formulates and tests action-hypotheses designed to modify the operation of such structures on performance.

Winter (Chapter 5) is surely right to advocate the incorporation of action-research as a form of self-appraisal within formal appraisal systems. It challenges us to rethink both naturalistic enquiry and the appraisal of performance as the facilitation of reflective practice through the provision of a database capable of sustaining informed dialogue between practitioners and others.

Appraising with validity

An appraisal process conceived in such terms implies that:

- appraisals should be validated in free and open dialogue with the performer; and
- it should not pre-ordain what evidence is relevant to judgement.

It is impossible to validate appraisals when the power structures operating impose constraints on the range and variety of evidence gathered. An appraisal process based on a hierarchically determined and predefined agenda of questions and issues will inevitably circumscribe those questions and issues which can legitimately be raised about the external constraints on performance. Valid judgements are formed on the basis of free and open discussion between all interested parties, not only in relation to the information gathered, but also in relation to what information should be gathered.

Burgess (Chapter 3) argues that teacher appraisal schemes tend to 'screen out' the ideological and political assumptions the appraisers bring to the appraisal process. The aims, interests and values which guide the questions asked, the data collected, the conclusions drawn, and who is given access to them, are all concealed by the procedural recommendations. Focussing on the recommendations in the influential Suffolk Report, Burgess concludes that they serve an interest in reproducing the ideological perspective of the established power structures in the schools, which, he argues, is permeated by male categories and concepts. It is therefore unlikely that appraisal would reflect badly on the actions of the males who control access to, and distribution of, scarce resources within the institution.

In his search for an alternative system of appraisal, Burgess entertains a process which enables practitioners at different status levels:

- to adopt a reflexive stance towards their actions and the assumptions and interests which underpin them;

- to share data about their practices collegially and laterally across status positions;
- to involve 'outsiders' as collaborators in generating the database. Such a democratic system is aimed at detaching the appraisal process from the vested interests which distort it when it is organized and controlled hierarchically.

Does this mean that the validity of an appraisal is that which people come to agree about through free and open dialogue detached from power constraints? Such a view reflects the consensus theory of truth formulated by Jurgen Habermas (1971): namely, that truth is what people come to agree about in unconstrained dialogue rather than something which can be unambiguously determined on the basis of objective evidence. This view of validating appraisals certainly appears to be implicit in contemporary developments in profiling student performance.

Mary James (Chapter 14) claims, on the basis of her research, that terms like 'negotiation' and 'dialogue' tend to be used interchangeably within the profiling movement. Her own view is that quite distinct ideas are being conflated by such use. Neither party in a dialogue need assume that the continuing existence of differences in viewpoint is an obstacle to improving or developing their own views. Indeed, the existence of differences provides a necessary context for sharpening, clarifying and developing one's own position. Negotiation, as James argues, places limits on dialogue. There comes a point where the search for understanding has to be sacrificed for the sake of agreement. I have for some time disagreed with those educational theorists who have attempted, after Habermas, to argue that unconstrained dialogue will result in an agreement about the truth. Instead, I prefer Gadamer's (1975) account of dialogue as a process of deepening one's own partial and inevitably biased understanding of human acts by exploring them from different points of view. Dialogue is not a matter of being open to conversion to alternative points of view. It is a matter of deepening and extending one's own understanding of a situation by bringing it into a dialectic with alternative understandings.

James makes good use of her distinction and argues that the appropriate context of negotiated appraisals is one of summative appraisal, while formative appraisals constitute the appropriate context for dialogue. She argues that the summative context assumes that appraisal serves the purposes of accountability and public access, while the formative context assumes it serves the purposes of diagnosis and development. Negotiation is not so much concerned with reaching agreement about the truth as with agreeing about which sort of account of performance should be released for public consumption. Here, considerations other than 'truth' or 'validity' are relevant, such as the con-sequences of publicly releasing an account on the individual it is about. Negotiated appraisal assumes that the appraised have a right to exercise a measure of control over what is said about them to a public audience.

James reserves considerations of validity to dialogue in a formative context. Here, appraisees have a right to dialogue, not by virtue of the possible consequences of the release of appraisals, but because they are in a position to appraise their own performance. An appraisal which failed to consider the appraisee's views would simply be an invalid one.

James appears to be drawing a constrast between 'the ethics of release' and 'the ethics of truth'. The former ascribes rights to appraisees on the basis of the potential consequences to their lives resulting from public access to accounts of their performance. The latter ascribes rights to appraisees on the basis of their right to a dialogue about the validity of other people's accounts of their performance. I have argued (Elliott, 1984) that democratic naturalistic evaluators of curriculum programmes tended to conflate 'the ethics of release' with 'the ethics of truth' by failing to distinguish the process of negotiating the release of an evaluation report from the process of determining its validity in discussion with practitioners. James argues that the exponents of pupil profiling methods tend to do the same thing. She suggests that the two processes should be kept separate but made complementary. If one attempts to validate accounts in the context of negotiating release then one stifles reflective conversation and dialogue.

In his discussion of the proceedings of the Cambridge Conference, Bridges (Chapter 11) points out that in naturalistic research 'the generation and availabililty of several, diverse and even conflicting evaluations of an object of enquiry, far from constituting a methodological problem, is precisely what is expected, sought and valued'. He goes on to argue that 'the value of this divergence of opinion is that it can act educatively to alert any one individual to aspects of a case of which he or she had not previously been aware'. In other words, the consideration of diverse judgements in dialogue is necessary for the educative or formative function of appraisal.

How, then, can we claim that dialogue is the process by which judgements are validated? What we have to do is to detach the concept of validity from objectivist interpretations: namely, that a valid judgement is one which either corresponds with objective evidence or one which everyone can agree about. Judgements of performance are necessarily value-biased. Values, as Bridges argues, are not simply ascribed to evidence of performance but enter into what counts as relevant evidence. People's perceptions of events, as well as their judgements about them, will inevitably be coloured by their values. Thus Bridges claims they will predictably diverge. So is there any sense in which we can claim that divergent appraisals can be equally valid? I believe there is. A valid performance appraisal is one which, given the value-position which underpins it, is consistent with all the evidence that is relevant to that position, and which has taken alternative views of that performance into consideration.

Appraisal in the context of government initiatives

The contributions of James and Bridges on the issue of negotiated assessment have implications which are relevant to the Education Reform Act in England

and Wales, which prescribes a national curriculum and system of benchmark testing at 7, 11, 14 and 16 years of age.

The report of the Task Group on Assessment and Testing (TGAT), chaired by Professor Black (1988), addressed the Secretary of State's proposal to develop a system of assessment which can be used for both formative and summative purposes. The TGAT report concluded that assessment data can be used for both purposes but only if it is initially collected for primarily formative purposes. The report argued:

> It is possible to build up a comprehensive picture of the overall achievements of a pupil by aggregating, in a structured way, the separate results of a set of assessments designed to serve formative purposes. However, if assessments were designed only for summative purposes, then formative information could not be obtained, since the summative assessments occur at the end of a phase of learning and make no attempt at throwing light on the educational history of the pupil. (Black, 1988, para. 25)

The Report concluded that the national assessment system should have a formative focus up to 16, at which point 'it should incorporate assessment with summative functions' (para. 27).

However, the very idea of specifying attainment targets is to standardize learning outcomes so that performances of individuals and groups can be publicly compared. In other words, summative purposes underpin the enterprise of specifying attainment targets. An assessment system guided primarily by formative and diagnostic purposes would not be so concerned with standardizing learning outcomes because it would not be dominated by a need to make comparisons between the performances of individuals and groups. Divergent outcomes and differences of view as to their educational significance and merit can all be accommodated within a dialogue-based system of formative appraisal.

The TGAT Report argued convincingly against norm-referenced and age-related comparisons on the grounds that they cannot fairly depict the progress of individuals. But substituting the idea of criterion-referenced assessment does not entirely solve the problem of how to make formative assessment the basis of the system. The specification of levels of attainment across a cluster of target components assumes that a genuine consensus about the nature of those components can be achieved. The danger of an assessment system built around nationally pre-specified targets is that it is likely to mask genuine and important issues about the nature and worth of individuals' achievements. There will be a considerable tendency to manufacture consensus for the sake of producing summative information capable of being aggregated for purposes of comparison. Even a genuine consensus about certain target components may mask issues by simply excluding areas of achievement which are controversial. As the TGAT Report admitted, 'the need to standardise may narrow the range of attainments being assessed'.

The report suggested that only a limited proportion of pupils' work should feed into the national assessment system. But I would argue that this is unlikely to significantly prevent teachers from focussing on a narrow range of learning outcomes, or confining their assessment practices exclusively to what is demanded by the national assessment system. Given the status of that system, and its ultimate aim of serving the accountability function of enabling comparisons to be made across teachers and schools, it is unlikely that teachers will give equal weight to a dialogue-based system of formative assessment which is undistorted by summative concerns.

The TGAT Report constituted a creative compromise between two incompatible demands. But it did us a disservice by claiming that they are not incompatible after all: that criterion-referenced assessment provides the answer. As I have argued, the very idea of criterion levels assumes that standards of achievement can be unambiguously specified. What is worth achieving in relation to any significant human activity will always be intrinsically open to dispute, and any attempt to foreclose on such issues through the form of assessment will not only be invalid but also unfair to individual pupils.

Goldstein (Chapter 13) argues that the assumption of standards is taken from test score theory developed in the context of separated assessment, i.e. the assessment of mental attributes. He contrasts this form of assessment, which attempts to avoid any connection between the attribute and particular learning environments, with connected assessment where learning is assessed in relation to a 'fairly well defined context, with little concern for external equivalence of validity'.

Goldstein suggests that connected assessments can be either formative or summative, depending on whether they are intended to feedback into the teaching–learning process. Formative assessments, he argues, are mostly connected. The problems arise when a requirement of separated assessment – that every assessment can be converted unambiguously on to a common scale for expressing standards and thereby ensure equivalence – is imposed on connected assessment. Underpinning this requirement is the theoretical assumption that the abilities, manifested in performance, can be attributed to individuals' minds rather than to the groups they belong to. If an individual manifests the ability measured by the test, it is assumed that it exists as the property of that individual. Thus, in comparing test scores, one is able to compare the extent which individuals possess the attribute measured. But suppose, as Goldstein suggests, that inferences about an individual's mental attributes are 'very much concerned with the company he or she is expected to keep', then it would be quite unfair to assume that comparisons of test scores provided a valid basis for inferring comparative judgements about the mental capacities of individuals. As I argued in Chapter 9, following Harré (1983), knowledge abilities and skills are the cultural property of social groups; resources that individuals draw on and manifest in their performances. In making a case for appraising the personal qualities manifested in a teacher's performance, I also argued that it was important to study the extent to which the social context of that performance enabled or constrained the exercise of such qualities. I made no assumption that their absence implied any deficiency in the mental capacities of individuals.

The TGAT Report represents an attempt to define standards in ways which avoid attributing defective performances to individuals, and thereby sanctioning streaming as an outcome of assessment. But in the final analysis it cannot avoid taking on the theoretical assumption which underpins separated assessment. If assessments are to provide a basis for comparative judgements across teachers and schools then some form of standardized assessment is necessary. The report argued that:

> if reliable results were to be required about every single attainment target, an excessive amount of assessment would be needed in order to disentangle the effects of context from more fundamental individual differences in the sequence of achieving targets. But profile components based on *aggregations* of target achievements *can* be reported with acceptable degrees of confidence.

In other words, one can disconnect the effects of context from the assessment by aggregating judgements across a number of target components. This statement reflects more recent developments in test theory towards multidimensional, rather than unidimensional, models of mental abilities. It implies that, when broad dimensions of ability are compared, differences in performance can be more validly attributed to individual mental capacities and disconnected from context. Multidimensional comparisons are fairer to individuals. However, Goldstein argues that multidimensional models do not fundamentally shift the conceptual basis of standardized assessment. It is still assumed that what is assessed is essentially mental qualities possessed by individuals independently of context.

What TGAT ultimately imposed on its proposals are the assumptions, however sophisticated, of a separated form of assessment. Ultimately, the possibility of standardized assessment rests on the validity of a quite unverified belief in mental attributes which exist quite independently of the contexts in which they are acquired. Even if one can eliminate differences in curricula, programmes of study, and assessment methodology, as the National Curriculum proposals aspire to, one still has to contend with social and cultural differences among the pupil population.

Separated assessment has yet to discover a fair way of comparing individuals for purposes of selection. TGAT aspires to propose a fairer way and to minimize teachers' involvement in maintaining this politically expedient, but educationally dubious, form of assessment. It remains to be seen whether its practical effects will indeed avoid the danger Goldstein warns about, namely, that:

> . . . teachers may come to view student achievement more closely in accord with test theory tradition than formerly, and come to rely more heavily on separated as opposed to connected ways of evaluating learning.

Similar danger is being risked by educational managers and administrators in their search for a way of making reliable comparisons between teachers for purposes of selection, placement and promotion. It is already being suggested that performance targets, and criteria for specifying levels of achievement in relation to them, should form the basis of a national teacher appraisal system. It is a short step towards the formulation of standardized targets for different types of jobs across the whole teaching profession. This development will disconnect the assessment of teachers from the contexts in which they teach, and prove costly in terms of the use of time and resources. In spite of all the rhetoric, this form of appraisal will reduce the amount of time and support available for staff development in schools. Formative modes of connected assessment, involving action–research and self-evaluation processes which are central to any valid notion of teacher appraisal for professional development, will have a very subordinate and minimal place in the teacher appraisal system.

Michael Eraut (Chapter 2) supports, albeit tentatively, this gloomy scenario of the future of teacher appraisal. If separated forms of appraisal become dominant for both pupils and teachers then it will be a sad day for those of us who have struggled to develop connected appraisal methods which serve the educative function of enhancing learning, whether it be of pupils or teachers. My analysis of the ACAS negotiated agreement with teachers, employers and staff associations suggests that things are moving very much towards the kind of appraisal interview which Eraut believes is likely to lapse into an expensive piece of bureaucratic tokenism, to neglect addressing fundamental issues, to divorce the appraisal of teaching from evaluations of its curriculum context, and divert resources away from staff development.

In this context, the prospects for the development of the kinds of research-based forms of connected teacher appraisal advocated by contributors like Burgess, Adelman and myself look somewhat gloomy. We must heed Goldstein's challenge to urgently provide assessment theory with an alternative basis of theoretical support to that of traditional test score theory. Naturalistic methodology offers the prospect of providing connected assessment with a decent theoretical rationale.

References

Black, P.J. (1988). *Report of the Task Group on Assessment and Testing*. London: Department of Education and Science.

Elliott, J. (1984). Methodology and ethics. In C. Adelman (ed.), *The Politics and Ethics of Evaluation*, pp. 19–25. London: Croom Helm.

Gadamer, H.G. (1975). *Truth and Method*. London: Sheed and Ward.

Giddens, A. (1976). *New Rules of Sociological Method*. London: Hutchinson.

Habermas, J. (1971). *Knowledge and Human Interests* (translated by J.J. Shapiro). Boston: Beacon Press.

Harré, R. (1983). *Personal Being*. Oxford: Basil Blackwell.

Name index

Adelman, C., ix, 7, 37, 104, 193
Aitkin, M., 142, 147
Anastasi, M., 141, 147
Assessment of Performance Unit (APU), 144

Bartholomew, D., 142, 147
Bates, I., 177
Bazelgette, J., 168, 177
Becher, A., 21, 23
Bee, H., 136, 139
Bernstein, B., 169, 172, 177
Berger, P., 136, 139
Biddle, B., 37, 42
Black, P., 190, 193
Blackburn, K., 32, 34
Bobbitt, F., 36, 42
Bock, R. D., 142, 147
Borich, G., 34, 38, 42
Bourdieu, P., 173, 177
Boyce, A. C., 36, 42
Bridges, D., ix, 9, 95, 98, 119, 189
Broadfoot, P., 25, 27, 30, 32, 33, 150, 160, 162, 164, 167, 170, 177
Broudy, H., 108, 116
Bunnell, S., 32, 34
Burgess, R., ix, 7, 182, 187
Burt, C., 169, 177
Bussis, A., 107, 117

Callahan, R., 36, 42
Clandinin, D., 107, 117
Clastres, P., 174, 177
Cliff, P., 150, 160
Collins, R., 173, 177
Combs, A., 103, 107, 110, 117
Cope, E., 31, 34
Croll, P., 29, 33, 34
Cronbach, L.J., 14, 19

De Carlo, M., 11
De Groot, R., 172, 177
Delaney, P., 46, 48, 52, 53
Denzin, N., 33, 34
Department of Education and Science (DES), 24–31, 44–50, 54, 81, 84, 98, 155, 160

Devaney, K., 103, 117
Dewey, J., 101, 102, 105, 117
Dockrell, D., 164, 177
Doll, E.A., 137, 139
Doll, W.E., 81, 98
Dunkin, M., 37, 42

Eagleton, T., 168, 177
Ebbutt, D., 159
Edelfelt, R., 103, 110, 117
Edmonds, R., 131, 139
Egglestone, J., 172, 177
Eisner, E., 29, 32, 105, 117
Elbaz, F., 107, 117
Elkind, D., 105, 117
Elliott, J., x, 8, 37, 38, 80, 88, 93, 94, 97, 98, 104, 189, 193
Entwistle, H., 170, 178
Eraut, M., x, 6, 7, 107, 108, 117, 193
Erikson, E., 102, 107, 117
Eysenck, H., 82

Faber, H., 51, 54
Fay, H., 52, 54
Fielding, N., 17, 89, 98, 99
Foucault, M., 162, 169, 178
Freshwater, M., 165, 168, 178
Friedman, M., 173, 178
Further Education Unit (FEU), 162, 164, 178

Gadamer, H.G., 188, 193
Gage, N., 30, 42
Giaconia, R., 38, 42
Giddens, A., 183, 193
Gipps, C., 144, 147
Goldstein, H., x, 10, 109, 117, 140, 142, 144, 147, 191, 192–3
Gould, S.J., 141, 147
Gouldner, A., 28, 34
Grace, G., 25, 34
Graham, D., 1, 27, 28, 30, 31, 32–3, 37, 45, 46, 47
Greene, M., 109, 117
Gray, J., 31, 34

Habermas, J., 172, 178, 188, 193
Hall, C., 131, 139
Hamilton, D., 4, 12
Hancock, D., 44, 45, 52, 54
Hargreaves, A., 159, 162, 173, 178
Harré, R., 82, 84–6, 92, 99, 191, 193
Hartley, L., 25, 27, 30, 32, 33, 35
Hayes, J., 163, 178
Hepworth, S., 164, 177
Hextall, I., 173, 178
HMI, 3, 29, 111, 112, 117
Holland, J., 163, 178
Holly, D., 173, 178
Holly, M., x, 8, 9, 100, 111, 114, 115, 117
Hopkins, D., 104, 105, 118
Hopson, B., 163, 178
House, E., xi, 7, 8, 39, 183–5
Humes, W., 41, 43

IPM, 178

Jackson, P., 111, 117
James, M., xi, 10, 149, 188–9
Jersild, A., 111, 117
Joseph, Sir K., 25, 44, 45, 46, 50, 52, 54

Kay-Shuttleworth, Sir James, 25
Kazamas, M., 178
Kemmis, S., 149, 157, 160
Klass, C., xi, 9, 131, 132, 185
Klemp, G., 97, 98, 99, 165, 177, 178
Kroath, F., xi, 8, 186
Kuhn, T., 108, 117
Kundera, M., 176, 178

Labbett, B., 38, 42
Lampert, M., 37, 43
Lapan, S., xi, 7, 8, 183–5
Lawrence, G., 103, 110, 117
Lindsay, C., 166, 178
Lindzey, G., 131, 139
Lord, F. M., 141, 142, 147
Lortie, D., 26, 110, 117
Luckmann, T., 136, 139

McClelland, D., 139, 165, 178
MacDonald, B., 4, 157, 160, 178
McIntyre, D., xii, 7, 38, 177, 181
Mackenzie, D., 141, 147
Maizels, R., 166, 178
Manpower Services Commission (MSC), 170
Mathews, D., 166, 178
Matlin, N., 163, 179
Mauss, M., 174, 178
Mead, G.H., 183

Measor, L., 33, 35
Mischel, W., 130, 136, 139
Murphy, L., 138, 139
Murphy, R., 159, 160

National Union of Teachers, 37
Neill, A.S., 131, 139
Nias, J., 108, 110, 117
Nietzsche, F., 174, 178
Novick, M., 141, 142, 147
Nozick, R., 173, 178
Nuffield Foundation, vii, 4
Nuttall, D., 30

Open University, 159
Oxenham, J., 165, 178

Parlett, M., 4, 12
Parsons, F., 176, 178
Pelican, J., 166, 179
Percy, W., 109, 118
Piaget, J., 107
Poggi, G., 49, 54
Polyani, M., 106, 118
Postman, N., 103, 118
Powney, J., 33, 35

Ranson, S., 169, 171, 179
Richey, H., 103, 118
Robottom, I., 149, 157, 160
Rosenshine, B., 37, 43
Rudduck, J., 104–5. 118
Rumbold, A., 45, 54
Runyan, W., 102, 118

Sawdon, A., 166, 179
Schon, D., 107, 108, 109, 110, 111, 118
Scriven, M., 57, 58, 61, 63
Shadforth, R., 88, 97, 98
Shavelson, R.J., 62, 63
Simon, B., 36, 43
Simons, H., xii, 4, 149, 157, 159, 160
Smith, L., xii, 9, 131, 132, 185
Snygg, D., 110, 117
Sparrow, S., 137, 139
Spencer, L., 96, 97, 99
Spindler, G., 29, 35
Stake, R., xii, 6, 181, 184
Stansbury, D., 158, 160
Starishevsky, R., 163, 179
Stenhouse, L., 31, 33, 35, 36, 43, 104, 118
Stern, P., 62, 63
Stones, E., 30, 31, 32, 35
Stronach, I., xii, 9, 159, 161, 162, 171, 179, 181, 183
Super, D., 163, 179

Surkes, S., 52, 54
Sutherland, G., 36, 43, 141, 148

Tawney, D., 159
Taylor, F., 36, 43, 46, 52, 54
Taylor, W., 30, 35
Thorn, L., 103, 117
Threadgold, M., 29, 35
Tobias, S., 37, 43
Tom, A., 37, 38, 110, 118
Torrance, H., 159, 160
Townsend, C., 165, 179
Travers, R., 36, 37, 43
Tripp, D., 106, 118

Tucker, J., 166, 179
Turner, G., 150, 160
Turner, V., 175, 176, 179
Walker, R., 159
Wall, T., 164, 177
Warr, P., 164, 177
Waterhouse, R., 169, 179
Watts, M., 33, 35
Weingartner, C., 103, 118
Whyte, J., 48–9, 54
Willis, P., 177, 179
Wise *et al.*, 7, 56–8, 63, 81, 99
Wolcott, H., 39, 40, 43
Wood, R., 140, 148
Winter, R., xii, 7, 49, 54, 187

Subject index

ACAS Independent Panel, 45, 46, 48,
    93–5, 98
accountability, 7, 10, 20, 21
action-plan, 20, 22
action-research, 51–3, 186–7
analogies with industrial practice, 22, 30,
    36, 37
appraisal of teachers
    and action-research, 51–3, 186–7
    against set objectives, 46
    benefits of, 112–13
    and bureaucratic principle of, 48, 49–
        50
    collegial model of, 31
    contradictions in, 44–6, 50
    criteria of, 7, 15, 40–1, 47, 57–9, 64–7,
        88, 96–8, 184
    democratic mode of, 31
    DES documents on, 24–31, 44–50
    diagnostic model of, 7, 48
    elements of, 112
    and evaluation, review, 111, 112, 180
    evidence of, 16, 22, 40–1, 62
    functions of, 6, 8, 9, 13, 22, 51, 93–4,
        129–30

and hierarchical control, 27, 37, 38, 92
inadequacies in methodology, 27–30,
    32, 33, 37–9
and institutional support/
    development, 6, 13, 15, 18
interviews and, 6, 7, 8, 23, 28–30, 38,
    57, 74
linked to contracts and salary
    structures, 25, 41–2
and managerialism, 25–6, 38–40
and merit pay, 17
multiple-purposes of, 48–9, 88, 95
in the ninteenth century, 25, 36
opportunity costs of, 7, 46–7
opposition from teachers, 45
and peer appraisal, 40–2, 92–3
performance criteria model, 7, 47
and personal/professional
    development, 8, 9, 96, 109–13
process model of, 7, 50
product model of, 7, 48–9
and professional principles, 50
and pupil attainment targets, 46–7
schemes of, 39–40, 56–7, 187
social and political context of, 24–30, 187

state intervention in, 81
and system efficiency, 39
target–output model of, 7, 46–7
and teachers consortia, 36
training for, 32
two-tier model, 92–3, 95
assessment
competence at, 75
and context, 37, 123, 135–6, 181, 182, 191–3
criterion-referenced, 8, 190
and curriculum, 128–9
descriptive, 9
and dialogue, 150–6, 168, 188
and ethics, 189
formative, 145, 157–8, 190–1
holistic, 5, 9, 120, 121, 162, 167, 168
and learning, 6, 9, 10, 140, 145–6, 191
and metaphors, 173–6
and motivation, 123–4
new approaches, 6, 150–6, 161
of performance, 5, 182–7
and power relations, 66, 154–5, 163–70
and profiling/records of achievement, 9, 150
and psychometric tradition, 141, 147
of pupils, 6, 119, 150–6
as ritual, 176
social, 10, 170–6
sociology of, 170, 173
summative, 145, 157–8, 190–1
and teaching to the test, 36
of tutorial competencies, 76–7
types of, 140

Better Schools, 26, 35, 46, 47, 49, 54

Cambridge Conferences on Educational Evaluation, 4, 5, 11, 12, 95
categorical funding, 2
Centre-Periphery Curriculum Intervention, 2, 5
checklists, 15–16, 33, 47
comparability and contextuality, 14
competence, 8, 17, 47, 67, 72–4, 81–2, 96–8, 181, 184–5
contextualized descriptions, 10
CSE exams, 144, 172

democratic evaluation, 157
dynamic vs. passive qualities, 92

employers needs and profiles, 164, 165

evaluation
concept of, 14
use of data. 14

field note accounts, 133–5
Fish Report, 52, 54

GCE exams, 144, 172
GCSE exams, 144, 146
generic abilities/qualities, 88, 96–8

Hargreaves Report, 52, 54
Holland Report, 170, 178
hierarchy of credibility, 87

Initial Teacher Training, 8, 103
Inservice Education of Teachers, 8, 20, 22, 45, 72, 74, 102–3

James Committee, 22, 23
journal writing, 113–16

LEAs, 22, 23

management functions of appraisal, 95–6
mental ability
and context, 143–4
dimensions of, 142–3
multidimensional models, 142, 192
unidimensional models, 142
merit-dimensions of, 57–9
Michigan Appraisal Scheme, 39–40
minimum competency, 7, 58
monitoring, 6, 20
multiple perspectives, 124–5

National Achievement Tests, 3
National Curriculum, 3
National Profiling Network, 150, 159
naturalistic evaluation inquiry, 4, 6, 78–9, 120, 149, 157–8
negotiation of appraisals/assessments, 5, 9, 120, 125–6, 149, 150–5, 167–8, 188
'new assessment'
assumptions of, 162–3, 169
interpretations of, 170–6
Newson Report, 176, 178

Oregon Appraisal Scheme, 39–40
organizational development, 92
ownership of data, 127–8

pay dispute, teachers, 24
payment by results, 4, 36
peer appraisal, 37
performance evaluation, 61–2

personal and professional development, 82–9, 92, 109–13
personal qualities
appraisal/assessment of, 85–6, 88–90, 163–7, 173, 183
placement and selection, 14
police, appraisals of, 89–92
politics and profiling, 164
politics of school development, 2
positivist rationale, limits of, 52–3
PRAISE Project, 156, 159, 160
professional development of teachers, 6, 80–1
profile categories, 164–5, 167–8
profile systems
Barnsley, 168
Essex, 168
Humberside, 164, 165, 171
profiling and records of achievement, 150, 156, 158, 161–3, 182
psychometric theory, 9
public examinations, 3

qualitative research, 28, 30
Quality in Schools, 26, 32
quota-fulfilment model, 46

Rasch Model, 141
reflective teaching, 22, 41, 105–9
reflexivity, 82–3, 85, 168, 183–7
reviewing, 7, 18, 20, 21
Revised Code (1862), 36
Ruskin College Speech, 39

self-appraisal/assessment, 84, 86, 87, 113–16, 170
self-concept and profiling, 164, 165
self-generated criteria, 67
self-monitoring, 83
self-reflective practitioner, 31
student-centred profiles, 163–70, 172
staff development, 41
staff development interview, 6, 8, 20
standards in education, 144–5

Suffolk Education Dept. Reports, 7, 8, 27–30, 31, 32, 33, 37, 45, 46, 47, 49, 52, 80–2, 84, 88, 94, 95, 187
summative personnel evaluation, 57, 58
symbiosis, 84

tacit knowledge, 59, 60
Task Group on Assessment and Testing (TGAT) Report, 190–2
Taylor Committee, 21
teacher thinking, 62
teachers'
council, 7, 41–2
effectiveness, 36, 27
life histories, 9
as researchers, 103–5
sabbaticals, 22
theories, 106–7
teaching
personal qualities in, 82
summary accounts of, 70–1
theories of, 61–2, 80–2
Teaching Quality, 26
Technical Vocational Education Initiative (TVEI), 171
test score theory, 141–4, 147, 191
theory of truth, 126–7, 187–9
training
for classroom observation, 74
competency-based, 38
for lesson planning, 74
for self-appraisal, 32
for supervisions, 74–6
TRIST, 39

'utopian duplication' and profiling, 162, 169

validity, 182, 187–9
vocational discourse and profiling, 166–7, 170–2

Youth Opportunities Scheme (YOP), 165, 171
Youth Training Scheme, (YTS), 163, 171